GOD'S IMAGE IN MAN AND
ITS DEFACEMENT

WORKS BY THE SAME AUTHOR.

The Ritschlian Theology and the Evangelical Faith. *Fcap. 8vo, cloth, 2s. 6d.*

Ritschlianism: Expository and Critical Essays. *Crown 8vo, cloth, 6s.*

Neglected Factors in the Early History of Christianity. *Crown 8vo, cloth, 3s. 6d.*

The Progress of Dogma. *Crown 8vo, cloth, 7s. 6d.*

The Virgin Birth of Christ. *Crown 8vo, cloth, 6s.*

The Resurrection of Christ. *Crown 8vo, cloth, 6s.*

The Early Church: its History and Literature. *Cloth, 1s. net.*

LONDON: HODDER AND STOUGHTON

GOD'S IMAGE IN MAN

AND ITS DEFACEMENT

IN THE LIGHT OF MODERN DENIALS

BY

JAMES ORR, D.D.

PROFESSOR OF APOLOGETICS AND SYSTEMATIC THEOLOGY
UNITED FREE CHURCH COLLEGE, GLASGOW

FOURTH EDITION

Eugene, Oregon

Wipf and Stock Publishers
199 W 8th Ave, Suite 3
Eugene, OR 97401

God's Image in Man
And it's Defacement in Light of Modern Denials
By Orr, James
ISBN: 1-57910-043-0
Publication date 5/30/1997

PREFACE

THE lectures in this volume were delivered on the L. P. Stone Foundation before the professors and students of Princeton Theological Seminary, from September 28 to October 3, 1903. They are now published in accordance with the desire of the Faculty. Additional matter, with references to books and articles which have appeared since the delivery of the lectures, are put in footnotes and in the Notes at the end. I have to express my thanks to the Faculty and students of Princeton Seminary for the great courtesy with which they received the lectures.

The lines of doctrine followed in the lectures are the same as those laid down in my volume on *The Christian View of God and the World*, with parts of which this book may be compared. They run counter, I am well aware, to many currents of modern opinion, even in Christian circles. If any are stumbled on this account, I can only plead that I must speak as I believe. I confess that the newer tendency to wholesale surrender of vital aspects of Christian doctrine at the shrine of what is regarded as 'the modern view of the world' appears to me graver than it does to many. The modern view of the world—which is in reality not one view, but a congeries of conflicting and often mutually irreconcilable views—must, it is assumed, be accepted in the first place; the view we take of Christianity must adapt itself to this, and the doctrines of Christianity must take their chance, if they come into collision with its findings. But there is another standpoint possible. It seems to me to be truer to say that, in a multitude of respects, the Christian view of the world is *not* the so-called modern view; in principle, in fact, is irreconcilable with it; and we ought to have the courage to avow this, and take the consequences. I do not say that the Christian view is irreconcilable with true science or sound philosophy—that it is impossible for a believing man who is at the same time a thinking man to hold; but it is irreconcilable with many of the theories that profess to be based on science and philosophy, and is not capable of assimilation with these. We all acknowledge this in connection with the Materialisms, the Monisms, the Agnosticisms, the Pantheisms, that seek to supplant the Christian conception; but I would carry the principle a good deal further—into the region of the doctrines dealt with in these lectures. How far I have succeeded—and no one is more conscious of the imperfections of my treatment than myself—the reader must be left to form his own opinion. In the variety of views and reasonings that are presented, some food for reflection, at any rate, may be suggested.

My thanks are due to Ebenezer Russell, Esq., Glasgow, for valuable aid in the revision of the proofs.

JAMES ORR.

October 1905.

CONTENTS

I

THE CONFLICT OF BIBLICAL AND MODERN VIEWS OF MAN AND SIN—THE ISSUES STATED

Aversion to Doctrines of the Gospel founded on altered views of their Presuppositions. The Biblical Views of God, Man, and Sin, met by a Counter-theory of the World and Man. Scientific Monism (Haeckel, etc.). Change on Doctrine of God. On Doctrines of Man and Sin. Effect on Christianity. Lectures to discuss Relations of Doctrines of Man and Sin to Modern Anthropological Theories. Extent of the Antagonism. Evolutionary View of the Origin of Man (Haeckel, Fiske). Conflict with Biblical Doctrine in respect: 1. of the *Nature* of Man; 2. of the *Original Integrity* of Man; 3. of the Origin, Nature, and Effects of *Sin*. Idealistic Evolutionism. Incompatibility with Christian View. Reply that while Ecclesiastical 'Dogmas' fall, the real Essence of Christianity is untouched. Fallacy of this: 1. Not Ecclesiastical Christianity alone, but the Christianity of the New Testament (Apostolic Gospel) falls; 2. Christ's own Teaching is Subverted. Essence of Apostolic Christianity in Consciousness of Redemption through Jesus Christ. The Infinite Value of the Soul in Christianity. Humanity as Receptive of the Divine in Christianity. The Cross and Human Sin. The opposing Views Irreconcilable, ... 3-30

II

SCRIPTURE AND SCIENCE ON THE NATURE OF MAN—
THE IMAGE OF GOD IN MAN

Connection of Questions of Origin and Nature. Monistic View of Human Nature (Haeckel). Biblical Doctrine: Man Made in the Image of God. Creation Narrative in Gen. i. Agreement of Bible and Science on Man's Place in Creation. Man as Link between Natural and Spiritual Worlds. The Second Creation Narrative. Man as 'Living Soul.' Relation of terms: Soul, Spirit, Flesh. Man a Compound Being: Body and Soul. Bearing on Doctrine of Death. Image of God in Man. Not in Bodily Form. Essentially a Mental and Moral Image. Rationality of Man. Moral Nature and Freedom of Man. Religious Capacity of Man. Sovereignty over the Creatures. Opposition of Modern Theories. Denial of Man's Distinction in Nature from the Animals. This Distinction *Qualitative*, not simply in *Degree*. Attack on Man's Nature of the older Materialism. Change of Standpoint in Monism. The 'Parallel Series' Theory. Haeckel's Denial of the Soul, Freedom and Immortality. Theory practically Materialistic. Absurdity of Haeckel's Eternal 'Substance.' Stronghold of Monistic Theory: Dependence of Mind on Brain. Fallacies in this: 1. 'Parallel Series' untenable. 2. Erroneous to reason from Brain Conditions in Disease to Brain Conditions in Health. 3. Ignoring of Counter-class of Facts: the Influence of Mind on Brain and Body. The Biblical View unharmed, 33-78

III

SCRIPTURE AND SCIENCE ON THE ORIGIN OF MAN—
THE IMAGE AS A CREATION

Biblical View of Man's Origin. Counter-theory of Monistic Evolution (Haeckel). Present-Day Influence of the Doctrine of

Evolution. Extensions and Ambiguities of the Doctrine.
Evolution and Creation. Evolution not necessarily Darwinism.
Sketch and Criticism of Darwinian Theory. Fortuity invoked
to do the work of Mind. Change of Attitude of Evolutionists.
Inadequacy of Natural Selection to explain Evolution. Principal
Objections. Revised Evolutionary Theories. Evolution and
Involution. Evolution and Teleology; Directive Intelligence.
Evolution not necessarily by Insensible Gradations. Creative
Cause involved in Founding of New Kingdoms. 'Enigmas' of
Science (Origin of Life, of Consciousness, of Man). Bearing on
the Doctrine of the Origin of Man. Failure of Evolution to
account for the mental and moral *Differentiæ* of Man. Unbridged
Gulf between Man and the Lower Animals in a physical respect.
The Missing Links yet Undiscovered. *Pithecanthropus Erectus*.
Result: Higher Cause implied in Man's Origin, .   . 81-136

IV

SCRIPTURE AND SCIENCE ON THE PRIMITIVE CONDITION OF MAN—THE IMAGE AS ACTUAL MORAL RESEMBLANCE

Evolution in its Bearing on Man's Mental and Moral Nature.
Alleged gradual Development of Man's Mind from Animal
Intelligence (Darwin, Romanes, Fiske). Failure to explain true
Rationality in Man. Potentiality of Progress (Language, Education, Science, etc.) in Man. Free-Will and Morality in Man
(Haeckel, Fiske, Huxley). Bearing on Origin of Body in Man.
Mind and Body necessarily rise together. Creative Cause accordingly implied in both. Creation of Man 'male and female.' Unity
of Race. Question of Man's Primitive Moral Condition Does
Creation in the Divine Image imply actual Moral Resemblance?
Biblical View, and Contradiction of Evolutionary Philosophy.

Darwinian Picture of Primitive Man. Support sought in Facts of Anthropology. 1. Argument from Existing Savage Races; fallacy of this. 2. Argument from Remote Antiquity of Man. Ussher's Chronology Untenable. Former Exaggerated Estimates of Man's Antiquity. Revised Views. Post-Glacial Man. Physical Science on Age of Earth (Kelvin, Tait, etc.). Recent Beginnings of History (Babylonia, Egypt, etc.). Evolution does not establish this View of Man. 1. Evolution is not necessarily by slow Gradations. 2. Palæontological Evidence: Cave Men, etc. High Character of Oldest Skulls. 3. High Character of Early Civilisation. 4. No Proof that Civilisation has Originated from Barbarism. Subject Viewed in light of true Idea of Man. The Primitive Man of Evolution not simply in a Non-Moral, but in an Immoral and Wrong State. Contradiction of Divine Fatherhood. Destiny of Man to Divine Sonship and to Immortality. These Ideas Contradictory of Evolutionary Hypothesis,. 139-193

V

SCRIPTURE AND SCIENCE ON THE ORIGIN AND NATURE OF SIN—THE DEFACEMENT OF GOD'S IMAGE

Defacement of God's Image Matter of Experience. If Man Created pure, a 'Fall' is presupposed. Idea of Sin as Apostacy from God underlies all Scripture. Counter-theory that Man has not *Fallen* but *Risen*. Objections to this View. On Evolutionary Theory Sin loses its 'Catastrophic' Character. Alleged necessity of Sin (Fiske, Sabatier, etc.). Evolutionary theory robs Sin of its Gravity. Effect on Idea of Guilt. Insufficient to speak of Realisation of Moral Ideal. Moral Law demands an Upright Nature and Pure Affections from the first. Biblical Doctrine of Sin: that which absolutely Ought not to be. Contrast of Religious and Philosophical Ethics. Sin as violation of Duty to God. Religion recognises Duties to God as well as to Man. Inmost Principle of Sin: Self-Will, Egoism. Sins graded on this Principle. Narrative of Fall. Connection with Superhuman Evil. Effects of Sin. 1. The *Spiritual* consequence of Sin in Depravation. Bond cut with God. Ascendency of Lower Impulses. Sin as Anarchy and Bondage. 2. The *Racial* Consequences of Sin. Organic Constitution of Race. Relation to Doctrine of Heredity. 'Ape and Tiger' Theory of Original Sin. Objection to Doctrine from Non-transmissibility of Acquired Characters (Weismann). Effects of Ethical Volition on Mind and Body *are* transmissible. Roman Catholic and Protestant Views of the Hereditary Effects of the Fall. Meaning of 'Total Depravity,'. . . . 197-246

VI

THE BIBLICAL DOCTRINE OF MAN AND SIN IN ITS RELATION TO THE CHRISTIAN REDEMPTION—RESTORATION AND PERFECTING OF THE DIVINE IMAGE

Still to be considered, 3. the *Physical* Consequence of Sin in Suffering and Death. Alleged Universality and Necessity of Death in the Organic World (Man included). Biblical View connected: (1) With its View of Man's Nature. Soul and Body not intended to be Separated. (2) With its View of Man's Primitive Condition. One of Moral Uprightness. Weismann's theory that Death is not a Necessity of Organisms. 'Immortality of the Protozoa.' Remarkable longevity in Animal World. Man's case stands on separate footing. He founds a New Kingdom; is destined for Immortality. Death a Contradiction of the true Idea of Humanity. *Posse non mori* and *non posse mori*. Harmony of previous Discussions with the Scripture Doctrine of Redemption. The Doctrines of Man and Sin implied: 1. In the *Presuppositions* of Redemption. (1) The infinite Value of the Soul. (2) Man's Capacity for Divine Sonship. (3) Man's Need of Redemption as a Sinner. 2. In the *End* of Redemption. The Restoration and Perfecting of the Divine Image. 3. In the *Means* and *Method* of Redemption. (1) In the Doctrine of Incarnation. The Divine Image the Ground of the Possibility of Incarnation. Christ the Perfect Realisation of the Divine Image in Man. (2) In the Doctrine of Atonement. Guilt the presupposition of Atonement. The Racial Aspect of Sin has its Counterpart in Redemption. The First and the Second Adams. The Penal Character of Death implied in Christ's Death for our Sins. (3) In the Doctrines of Regeneration and Renewal. Conformity to Christ's Image. (4) In the Doctrine of Resurrection and the Christian Hope of Immortality. Christ's Resurrection and ours. The Immortality of the Gospel, one in which the Body shares; an Immortality of the *whole* Person. Conclusion, . . 249-283

NOTES TO LECTURES

		PAGE
I.	Modern Naturalistic View of the World,	287
II.	The Creation Narrative and Science,	288
III.	Monistic Metaphysics—Reaction from Haeckel,	289
IV.	R. Otto on Present-Day Darwinism,	293
V.	Recent Views on the Descent of Man,	296
VI.	Modern Theories of Evolution and the Fall,	298
VII.	Retrogression among Savages,	301
VIII.	Professor Boyd Dawkins on Tertiary Man,	304
IX.	The End of the Ice Age,	305
X.	The 'New Race' in Egypt,	306
XI.	Otto on the Sudden Origin of Man,	308
XII.	The Lansing Skeleton,	309
XIII.	Weismann's Theory of Heredity,	311
XIV.	Heredity and Responsibility,	315

The Conflict of Biblical and Modern Views
of Man and Sin—The Issues stated

Aversion to Doctrines of the Gospel founded on altered views of their Presuppositions. The Biblical Views of God, Man, and Sin, met by a Counter-theory of the World and Man. Scientific Monism (Haeckel, etc.). Change on Doctrine of God. On Doctrines of Man and Sin. Effect on Christianity. Lectures to discuss Relations of Doctrines of Man and Sin to Modern Anthropological Theories. Extent of the Antagonism. Evolutionary View of the Origin of Man (Haeckel, Fiske). Conflict with Biblical Doctrine in respect: 1. of the *Nature* of Man; 2. of the *Original Integrity* of Man; 3. of the Origin, Nature, and Effects of *Sin*. Idealistic Evolutionism. Incompatibility with Christian View. Reply that while Ecclesiastical 'Dogmas' fall, the real Essence of Christianity is untouched. Fallacy of this: 1. Not Ecclesiastical Christianity alone, but the Christianity of the New Testament (Apostolic Gospel) falls; 2. Christ's own Teaching is subverted. Essence of Apostolic Christianity in Consciousness of Redemption through Jesus Christ. The Infinite Value of the Soul in Christianity. Humanity as receptive of the Divine in Christianity. The Cross and Human Sin. The opposing Views Irreconcilable.

I

THE CONFLICT OF BIBLICAL AND MODERN VIEWS ON MAN AND SIN—THE ISSUES STATED

IN studying the causes of the aversion undeniably felt in these times by many serious and thoughtful persons to the peculiar doctrines of the Christian religion, we are early led to the discovery that the real rock of offence lies, less in the doctrines themselves, than in what we may call the *presuppositions* of the doctrines—in certain views of God, man, and sin, which underlie them, and against which the modern mind is supposed to be in protest. Aversion to the doctrines of the Gospel, indeed—to its teachings on the ruin of man through sin, on redemption by the atoning death of Christ, and on regeneration by the Holy Spirit—is not special to any one age, and has often other than intellectual causes. No careful student, however, can be unobservant of the fact that Christianity is met to-day, not by piecemeal attacks upon its doctrines, or objections springing simply from moral dislike, but by a positively-conceived counter-view of the world, claiming to rest on scientific grounds, ably constructed and defended, yet in its fundamental ideas striking at the roots of the Christian system. The popularity of this counter-view of the universe—frequently described as the 'modern' view—is not to be denied. It commands wide acceptance; multitudes are attracted by its plausibility, and by the seeming cogency of its scientific proofs; many would deem it presumptuous, and a mark of ignorance, to call in question a view believed to have behind it so large a body of expert opinion; while perhaps a still greater number, with little first-hand knowledge, are powerfully influenced by the extent to which its theories and watchwords are, as the phrase is, 'in the air.'[1]

In truth, however, this modern view of the world, as expounded by its best-known representatives, does a great deal more than simply destroy belief in the doctrines we have been wont to call Christian. Carried through with unflinching consistency, it is as fatal to the primary

[1] See Note I. on Modern Naturalistic View of the World.

truths on which all religion rests as it is to the distinctive affirmations of the Christian Gospel. It is not without justification in the premises of his system that Haeckel, a foremost champion of the modern monistic view, speaks in his work on *The Riddle of the Universe*[1] of the ideas of God, freedom, and immortality, as 'the three great buttresses of superstition,' which it is the business of science to destroy. Still more significant, perhaps, of the currency which these theories have obtained, and of the influence they exert, is the fact that a writer like Mr. W. H. Mallock, in a work recently published, entitled *Religion as a Credible Doctrine: a Study of the Fundamental Difficulty*, should, while professing to defend the ideas of religion against Haeckel and others of his way of thinking, yet make abject and absolute surrender to Haeckel in nearly every one of his contentions. This capable writer spends six-sevenths of his book in showing, and all the skill of his resourceful intellect in establishing, that science, as Haeckel declares, demolishes the three great fundamental ideas of religion—God, free-

[1] More exactly, *The Riddles (Räthsel) of the Universe*. We quote from the English translation of M'Cabe (popular edition).

dom, immortality; leaves no place for them; that, as he puts it, there is an 'utter impossibility of intellectually reconciling religion with the essential doctrines of science.'[1] Then, in two closing chapters, he argues that we must still hold fast by these ideas on the ground of our moral convictions and of their practical value for life! The persons I have immediately in view in these lectures, however, do not, as a rule, go nearly so far as this. They are, on the contrary, neither hostile to Christianity as such, nor wish in principle to break with it; are concerned rather to find some way of preserving and vindicating the essentials of Christian faith. But they are at the same time profoundly influenced by modern conceptions, and are persuaded that, if Christianity is to survive, it must undergo an entire transformation and re-interpretation in harmony with modern theories, and must part with many of the doctrines hitherto regarded as distinctive of it. The only question left for them to consider is what form this re-interpretation is to take, and how much of the old creed must be thrown over, in order to effect the desired reconciliation.

[1] Pp. xiv. 270; cf. pp. 217, 242, etc.

I have hinted that the doctrines chiefly affected by the new cosmical conceptions are those of God, man, and sin; and it is obvious of itself that anything which seriously affects these important doctrines must vitally alter the complexion of our whole theory of Christianity. At the basis of all sound thinking in theology lies of necessity a right doctrine of *God*. The Christian system is an organism, every part of which is sensitive to change in any other;[1] but nowhere is change more determinative in its effects than here. As a man thinks God to be, so will his theology be. It is not too much to say that every crucial question in theology, almost, is already settled in principle in any thorough-going discussion of the divine attributes. God, in the Christian conception, is regarded as a personal, ethical, and self-revealing Being, infinite and eternal in all His perfections. He is thought of as subsisting in a threefold eternal distinction of Father, Son, and Spirit. He is righteous, holy, and loving. Any view, therefore, which, as in modern monistic and pantheistic systems, negates God's personality and consciousness; which, by limiting His attributes,

[1] Cf. below, p. 260.

denies to Him perfect wisdom and power; which, disrobing Him of holiness and righteousness, denies His moral government of the world and His judicial dealing with sin; which wholly merges either the judicial aspect of His character in the Fatherly, or the Fatherly in the judicial; which, going deeper, denies or tampers with the reality of the distinction of good and evil, and the ground of the good in God's essential nature; which, confining revelation to nature, refuses to acknowledge any *super*natural entrance of God in word or deed into history—such false or defective views of God react at once on any conception we can form of Christianity, and either compel its rejection altogether, or necessitate its transformation into something altogether different from the image we have of it in the New Testament.

If, however, our doctrine of God has this determinative effect on our general view of Christianity, it must now be said that the same is hardly less true of the doctrines of *man* and *sin*. These three doctrines of God, man, and sin, are indeed related, and in a manner mutually dependent. Our doctrine of God will manifestly in large measure determine our doctrine of man; while the Biblical view of God as holy Lawgiver and Judge is the necessary presupposition of any just conception of sin. On the other hand, the view we are led to form of man in his nature and origin inevitably reacts on our conceptions both of God and of sin, and through these, as well as more directly, affects our total view of Christianity. Suppose, *e.g.*, we agree with Haeckel and his following in denying to man the possession of a soul capable of bearing God's image, and of surviving death, or in denying to him moral freedom and the possibility of self-determining moral life: it is evident that we have destroyed at once the foundations of all religion, save as a baseless superstition, and have struck fatally at Christianity as the religion which most exalts man in his nature and destiny. The result is not very different if we deny to man the possession of a nature different in *kind* from that of the animals beneath him—say, *e.g.*, with Mr. Mallock, and with the greater number of the evolutionists, that 'the mental differences between man and the other animals are differences of degree only: it is impossible to show that they are differences of kind.'[1] For, on this hypothesis, to mention no other point at present, the dividing-line between impersonal and personal, mortal and immortal, vanishes. We are supposed to glide by insensible gradations from one into the other. But we have only to fix our thoughts on such a conception as immortality, to see that, in its very nature, immortality is not a thing of gradations into which a being *can* glide by development.[2] It must be there, or it must be absent, and there is infinity between the two conditions.

Still more obvious are the bearings of the views which we adopt of the nature and origin of man on the doctrine of sin. The consequences here are such as it is impossible to veil or minimise. If man be conceived of, as he is, in modern anthropological theories, as ascending by slow gradations from the stage of the brute—if his original condition is not one of purity and harmony, but of the foulness and ferocity attendant on emergence from the state of animalism—it is plain, and will be more fully established as we proceed,[3] that our whole conceptions of the nature

[1] Mallock, p. vii.   [2] See below, p. 192.   [3] Lecture V.

of sin, and of the degree of blame attaching to man in his existing moral condition, must be recast. It is at least my profound conviction that, on the basis of current anthropological theories, we can never have anything but defective and inadequate views of sin. This, again, vitally affects our conception of the Gospel, for it is a truism that, with defective and inadequate views of sin, there can never be an adequate doctrine of redemption. It is, in fact, precisely because so many superficial views of sin are abroad, that there is at the present time so general a recoil from the Biblical declarations on the need and reality of atonement. Not merely from particular modes of stating or explaining the atonement, but from the idea of atonement for sin altogether.[1]

These considerations will explain why, in the present course of lectures, I have chosen as my subject the Biblical doctrines of man and sin in their relations to modern anthropological theories. I have named the subject in the title 'God's

---

[1] It may be noted that, with the tendency to a break-up of naturalistic theories, and the revival of a more spiritual interpretation of the universe, there is being manifested an increasing disposition again to do justice to this central Christian doctrine.

Image in Man and its Defacement,' in order to bring into prominence the two ideas which will dominate my treatment: first, that man, as he came from the hands of God, visibly bore his Creator's image; and second, that sin is the effacement of that image of God in man—never wholly indeed, but to a degree that means for man moral and spiritual ruin, and necessitates a supernatural remedy if the Maker's image is to be restored. It is implied in what has been said that against these doctrines of Scripture and presuppositions of the Gospel, as I take them to be, much of what is called modern thought is in revolt. It does more than deny, as we shall see; it flouts them with scorn. It substitutes for them other doctrines incompatible with the Biblical, and claims to rest these on irrefragable grounds of science. The method of eclecticism which many adopt in trying to combine the one set of beliefs with the other, or by some ingenuity of re-interpretation to bring them into harmony, is, in my opinion, wholly unsuccessful. We have as the result a theology of patchwork—an unnatural compound of Christian ideas with thoughts borrowed from half a dozen alien philosophies—a new-fangled scheme sprinkled over with words taken over from evolutionary science, but sadly lacking in the ideas which are central in the theology of the Apostles. The cross, in short, that is attempted between these opposing conceptions is, I am convinced, an impossible one. Better that we face squarely the alternative presented to us, and make our choice. It will be my business to discuss frankly in these lectures the problems that arise from comparison of the modern with what I consider to be the genuinely Christian view, and to endeavour to show that the Christian solutions are, even at the present hour, the most rational and satisfying—the truest to fact and to experience.

It will now be my duty, in the remainder of this lecture, to expand the remarks already made, and to seek to place in as strong a light as I can the nature of the antagonism which I conceive to exist between the Christian and the so-called modern views. This will prepare the way for the special discussions of the succeeding lectures.

If, then, following the guidance of the modern

spirit, we put ourselves in the standpoint of dominant anthropological theories, we find ourselves at a stroke far removed from the doctrines we have been accustomed to call Biblical. The story of Eden, the picture of man coming upright and pure from his Maker's hand, and afterwards, by his wilful disobedience, falling from his first estate, and dragging down his posterity with him into spiritual ruin and death—this, it need hardly be said, is dismissed as baseless legend—the idlest of dreams.[1] They float down to us—or are supposed to do so—these fables of the world's infancy—from Babylonian antiquity, and, though purified, and made the vehicle of deeper moral teaching, still, in their childish *naïveté*, betray an age that knew nothing of science. Instead, we have the nineteenth-century gospel of evolution to tell us what man actually was, and how he has come to be what he is now. The myth of the *fall* of man is replaced by the scientific theory of the *ascent* of man. Man, as we now learn, is the last and highest product of the evolutionary process which has been going on for countless ages, first in the cosmic and inanimate, next in the organic, worlds.

[1] See Lecture IV.

His ancestry, starting from the primitive protozoon, is to be sought for proximately in the forms of animal life nearest to his own, viz., in the anthropoid apes. 'Sufficient for us,' says Haeckel, 'as an incontestable historical fact, is the important thesis that man descends immediately from the ape, and secondarily from a long series of lower vertebrates.'[1] Evolutionary science undertakes by the aid of embryology and palæontology to trace man's lineage through the successive forms of animal life, and to show, at the upper end of the scale, how, in both mind and body, he has developed from his original brute condition to his present splendid intellectual and moral pre-eminence. The nature of the process will engage our attention in a succeeding lecture.[2] Meanwhile, one glimpse may be taken from a popular book—Mr. Fiske's *Through Nature to God*. 'All at once,' says Mr. Fiske, 'perhaps somewhere in the upper eocene or lower miocene, it appears that among the primates, a newly-developing family already distinguished for prehensile capabilities, one genus is beginning to

---

[1] *Riddle of the Universe*, p. 30 (pop. edit.). See below, p. 82.
[2] Lecture III.

sustain itself more by mental craft and shiftiness than by any physical characteristic. Forthwith does natural selection seize upon any and every advantageous variation in this craft and shiftiness, until this genus of primates, this *Homo Alalus* [Haeckel's name is *pithecanthropus alalus*—" the ape-man without speech "], or speechless man, as we may call him, becomes pre-eminent for sagacity, as the mammoth is pre-eminent for bulk, or the giraffe for length of neck.'[1] By and by *Homo Alalus* invents speech, and his progress is thereby enormously accelerated. His condition, even at this stage, is naturally one on which that of the lowest existing savage represents a great advance. From the instincts and cunning of the animal, however, human reason and conscience are being gradually developed. Moral life in a rudimentary way has begun. The masses continue low and unprogressive; but by a happy accident of nature, which natural selection favours, some individuals in the crowd present higher qualities, and push a few degrees upwards. Ideas of right and wrong form themselves on the basis of experience; a moral ideal begins dimly to shape itself. So the

[1] Page 94.

race improves. Through this *nisus*, this impulse, this propensity to strive upwards, man has the leverage for advance within himself. Given his nature, suitable environment, and natural selection as a beneficent deity to help him at every turn, he is independent of every other aid.[1]

Already, I think, even on the basis of so meagre a sketch, the contrast must be apparent with the ideas of man we have been accustomed to associate with the Christian religion and its philosophy of salvation. The leading points have already been adverted to, but they will bear a little more elaboration.

1. The new theories are in conflict, in the most direct fashion, with the Biblical doctrine of the *nature* of man. Man is not, as the Bible asserts, a being made in the image of God, and bearing from the first His rational and moral likeness, but is evolved into what he is through transformation of the ape-image.[2] God, in truth, is not recognised in the process of his production at all. The laws of evolution are competent for their own work, and God is superfluous. In the result no

[1] See further on Mr. Fiske's views below, pp. 142-3, 148-50, etc.
[2] Cf. Darwin, quoted by Dr. H. Stirling, *Darwinianism*, p. 157.

clear boundary is discernible between man and the animals from whom he sprang: none as respects the body; none between animal and human intelligence; none between animal and human morality. Instead, as we have seen, there is throughout the gradual shading of animal into man. No wonder that on such a basis Haeckel denies immortality to man. For, apart from the intrusion of a supernatural cause, which would disrupt the whole system, there is no point at which immortality can come in. This first aspect of the conflict between the Biblical and the so-called modern views of man will be discussed in the second and third lectures.

2. There is a not less direct negation by the modern theory of the Biblical view of *an original state of integrity* of man. For this, it has already been shown, there is no room left whatever on the new anthropological hypothesis. Man's history is that of an *a*scent—an ascent through inherent powers—not of a *de*scent. Man begins at the *foot* of the intellectual and moral scale, gradually emerging from the ape condition, and slowly working his way upwards. The idea embodied in the Bible and the creeds of a pure

beginning of the race—of the introduction of man upon the earth in a condition of moral uprightness, of fitness for the knowledge of, communion with, and service of, his Maker[1]—is discredited and flouted as beyond the range of rational consideration. The magnitude of the gulf between the old and the new is as little disputed on the one side as on the other. This subject of man's primitive condition will occupy us in the fourth lecture.

3. It is equally plain, as I have already tried to emphasise, that there is a fundamental contrariety between the modern hypothesis and *the Biblical doctrine of sin*, alike in regard to sin's origin, nature, and effects in humanity. There is, in fact, on the basis of this theory, no proper doctrine of *sin* possible at all. Sin loses its Biblical character as voluntary transgression of divine law, as something catastrophic in the history of the race, and as entailing guilt, condemnation, death, and spiritual corruption on mankind. And as the view of sin presented in the Bible is weakened and destroyed, so, correspondingly, the need for redemption through

---

[1] On Mr. Tennant's view that this is not a part of Biblical doctrine, see below, pp. 157, 198, 200, 219, etc.

Christ is taken away. How should a redeemer be necessary to relieve man from consequences which flow from his very nature as created, or to secure for him a gain which evolutionary processes infallibly secure for him without supernatural help?[1]

There is, however, it is just to acknowledge, a much higher and more spiritual type of evolutionary theory than that which I have just sketched. The naturalistic monism of writers like Haeckel, which, it is claimed, is the reigning one in scientific circles (though even that statement, as we shall find, needs much modification),[2] has not the whole field to itself. Idealistic philosophy—especially that which connects itself with Hegel—has another type of doctrine, which is not naturalistic, but rational. This higher view regards man as in his true nature spiritual. He is not a mere animal, though he arises out of animal conditions. It would be truer on this view to say that evolution in both the inorganic and the organic worlds in nature is the unconscious working of an immanent reason, than that self-conscious reason in man

[1] See below, pp. 205-6. [2] See below, p. 71.

is a product of purely natural factors. We are here admittedly on a higher plane, and one which might seem to present greater possibilities of reconciliation with Christianity. In point of fact, however, it hardly does so. In the hands of most of the apparent advocates of this philosophical evolutionism, the antagonism with Christian doctrine is nearly as great as before. There is an inner spiritual principle, we are rightly taught, which lifts man in nature above the animals, and renders him capable of rational, self-guided life, of moral ideas and ends, of education, science, and religion. But this image of God in man is regarded as, to begin with, only a potency. The picture given by this theory of man in his first appearance and original condition is not very different from that of the naturalistic school. Man, it is assumed, begins, as before, in lowest savagery, or somewhat below existing savagery, and gradually works his way upwards, through inherent powers of development. There is, as little as in the former case, a fall; or rather, the fall is held to be the expression of an eternal truth of spirit; the truth, viz., that man must eat of the tree of the knowledge of good and evil to know truly what either good or evil is. Sin, that is, is a necessary step in the transition from mere naturalness to true manhood, though one that needs again to be transcended. It is evident, I think, that this evolutionary scheme fits in with Christianity nearly as badly as the former. If it does more justice to man's essential nature, it errs as grievously, and with less excuse, in depicting sin as a necessity of human development, in robbing it of its tragic character, and in rendering superfluous the reconciling work of Christ and renewal by the Spirit. This subject of the relation of the modern doctrine to sin will be discussed in the fifth and sixth lectures.

There can be little doubt, then, I think, that whether in its lower or in its higher forms this current evolutionary philosophy means the negation of much that is vital to Christianity, at least as it has hitherto been understood among us. It dislocates the entire Christian system; alters, where it does not overthrow, every doctrine in it. Neither God, nor man, nor sin, nor redemption, can be conceived of as before. With the change of attitude to redemption goes necessarily a change in the estimate of Christ's Person. The estimate we form of Christ's Person will doubtless largely control the idea we form of His work; but Ritschl is surely so far right when he affirms that the estimate we form of Christ's work must mainly control the idea we form of His Person. The complete truth is that the two doctrines must always be held together in congruity; in their inner and scriptural connection with each other; and, whenever one is tampered with, the other is certain ere long to suffer also. But in the evolutionary scheme there is, as said earlier, no place for a supernatural redeemer. Great personalities no doubt retain their place; Christ may remain as the crown of the evolutionary movement, and redemption as aid rendered to the race in its upward march of progress by a great and good character—One in whom the religious principle comes to its highest expression. But even this the more thorough-going monistic form of the philosophy will by no means concede. Spiritual life as a whole falls to ruin at its touch.

Thus far I have been looking at the conflict between the Christian and the modern views from the so-called scientific or modern standpoint. It may be well, before I close the lecture, that I look at it for a few moments from the side of positive Christianity. The answer that will naturally be made to most of the considerations I have advanced is that, even granting it to be as I say, it is only the *ecclesiastical* view of Christianity that falls—the real, the original, the essential Christianity remains. It is not, I will be told, a question of parting with Christianity, but a question of re-interpreting it, so as to do justice to its real essence, in harmony with modern demands. The things which are stripped off, it will be said—fall in Adam, death as the result of sin, a supernatural incarnation, an atonement, regeneration by the Spirit—are *accidents*: the substance, a purer Christianity, abides. The modern evolutionary conception, it is taken for granted, must be accepted: the only question is, how is Christianity to be made to fit into it? And the pleasing discovery made—or supposed to be made—is that, when dogmatic wrappages are removed, Christianity is in deep and beautiful harmony with the modern conceptions—shines with a new light, and receives a new lease of life, from its association with them.

It is a pleasing illusion ; and if it were not that I am convinced it is only an illusion, I should not be now speaking to you on these subjects. We do well in this matter to deal with ourselves in all honesty ; and it should, I think, with perfect frankness be acknowledged that, in this endeavour to harmonise Christianity with the new philosophy, it is not the Christianity of the *Church* only that falls, but the Christianity of the *New Testament*. It is, it seems to me, only by a species of self-deception that any one can hide this fact from himself. Neither, in truth, do all thus deceive themselves. It is perfectly common to hear it acknowledged that, if the new premises are accepted, the Christianity of the Apostles— *their* doctrines of sin, of the Person of Christ, of atonement, of the new birth, of justification—fall to the ground. These doctrines, it is argued, were largely the result of their own thoughts, experiences, and training, coloured by the ideas of their age. But the caveat will probably be made : not the Christianity of Christ — *that* abides. Here again, however—that we may be quite exact—it is to be remembered that the Christianity spoken of is not that of the Christ of the

Gospels *as we have them*, but the Christianity of a Christ shorn of most of his actual claims and attributes, and reduced to the necessary natural dimensions by a process of critical recasting and expurgation of the records. This residuum may be *called* Christianity: it is, however, I take leave to say, a Christianity which the world has never historically known; which, therefore, I may be pardoned for refusing to identify with the Christianity for which we *have* historical attestation—Christianity as embodied in its original and only authoritative documents.

If, accordingly, we inquire into the essence of Christianity as it meets us in the writings of the New Testament, I shall not, I think, be challenged for describing it as, on its experimental side, consisting above all in the joyful consciousness of redemption from sin and reconciliation to God through Jesus Christ, and in the possession of a new life of sonship and holiness through Christ's Spirit. This undeniably, reduced to its simplest terms, is what Christianity meant for its first preachers and their disciples, and what it has meant historically for the Church ever since. But now mark carefully the essential implications of this Apostolic Gospel. Harnack, in his recent Berlin lectures, places the essence of Christianity in the three great ideas of the Kingdom of God and its coming; of God the Father, and the infinite value of the human soul ; of the higher righteousness, and the commandment of love. There is indeed more than this in Christianity— much more : the idea of redemption in particular is conspicuously absent. But at least it will be admitted that these ideas *are* in Christianity ; that, in particular, the ideas of God the Father, and of the infinite value of the soul, are there. But see how far this already carries us. It means that man is affiliated to God ; that, in his spiritual nature, he is a being made in the image of God ; that he is capable of knowing, loving, and obeying God, and is destined for fellowship with God. There may be disputes as to the sense in which we can speak of a universal Fatherhood of God and a natural sonship of man ; but there will be no dispute, at least, about this, that Jesus recognised in every human soul an infinite value, an essential kinship with God, a *capacity* for sonship and for eternal life.[1] But this implies a view of

---

[1] See below, pp. 190-3.

man diametrically opposed to the current evolutionary hypothesis with its insensible gradations from animal to man.

It is, however, peculiarly in the light of the Christian doctrine of *redemption* that the untenableness of the opposite hypothesis is seen. The Christian man is one who knows himself redeemed, saved, forgiven, renewed, restored to fellowship with God. He believes this to have been accomplished at the infinite cost of the incarnation, sufferings, and death upon the cross, of the Son of God. But this again implies a transcendent value attaching to the soul of man, such as only a being made in God's image could have; implies a view of sin which invests it with an unspeakably awful and tragic character; implies a view of Christ which means that our nature was receptive of the fulness of the Godhead. Sin is no longer, in the light which this cross of Christ sheds upon it, a necessity in the history of the race, but something unnatural and abnormal, the result of voluntary apostacy from God; something which entails curse and death, and which, because it is absolutely universal—the whole world having gone aside from original righteous-

MAN AND SIN

ness, and fallen a prey to corruption and mortality—must be traced back to the fountainhead of the race; that is, to a fall in the beginning of the history of humanity.[1] But all this, beyond question, is in deepest contrast with a view in which, as formerly explained, sin is depicted, if not as a metaphysical, at least as a natural necessity; in which its real heinousness as offence against God is taken away;[2] where its foundations are not wholly destroyed by the denial of man's spirituality, freedom, and immortality.

There seems to me, therefore, no evading of the issue between this new and widely-accepted theory of man's origin, nature, primitive and existing moral condition, and the Christian faith. The two theories stand opposed to each other in fundamental respects, and, in the experience of those who adopt them, inevitably drift apart. Like oil and water they refuse to blend; one or other must be parted with. Which of the two it should be, it is the purpose of these lectures to inquire. If the foregoing remarks suggest that any antagonism is to be shown to legitimate

---

[1] See more fully below, pp. 198 ff. Cf. Lect. VI. p. 274.
[2] See Lect. V. pp. 208-9.

scientific inquiry, or well-established results of anthropological research, I can only hope that the further course of the lectures will dispel that fear. My deepest conviction is that of the unity of truth; and just in proportion to the strength of my persuasion of the truth of God's revelation, and of the saving power of Christ's Gospel, is the firmness of my assurance that nothing that science can make good will ultimately be found to conflict with the grounds of our Christian certainty.

Scripture and Science on the Nature of
Man—The Image of God in Man

Connection of Questions of Origin and Nature. Monistic View of Human Nature (Haeckel). Biblical Doctrine: Man made in the Image of God. Creation Narrative in Gen. i. Agreement of Bible and Science on Man's Place in Creation. Man as Link between Natural and Spiritual Worlds. The Second Creation Narrative. Man as 'Living Soul.' Relation of terms: Soul, Spirit, Flesh. Man a Compound Being: Body and Soul. Bearing on Doctrine of Death. Image of God in Man. Not in Bodily Form. Essentially a Mental and Moral Image. Rationality of Man. Moral Nature and Freedom of Man. Religious Capacity of Man. Sovereignty over the Creatures. Opposition of Modern Theories. Denial of Man's Distinction in Nature from the Animals. This Distinction *Qualitative*, not simply in *Degree*. Attack on Man's Nature of the older Materialism. Change of Standpoint in Monism. The 'Parallel Series' Theory. Haeckel's Denial of the Soul, Freedom and Immortality. Theory practically Materialistic. Absurdity of Haeckel's Eternal 'Substance.' Stronghold of Monistic Theory: Dependence of Mind on Brain. Fallacies in this: 1. 'Parallel Series' untenable. 2. Erroneous to reason from Brain Conditions in Disease to Brain Conditions in Health. 3. Ignoring of Counter-class of Facts: the Influence of Mind on Brain and Body. The Biblical View unharmed.

II

SCRIPTURE AND SCIENCE ON THE NATURE OF MAN—THE IMAGE OF GOD IN MAN

THE questions of the origin and of the nature of man are inseparably connected. Theories of origin, it is soon discovered, control in practice the view taken of man's essential constitution, and need to be checked and corrected by careful consideration of what man is—this being into whose origin we are inquiring. Conversely, the study of man's nature is speedily found to be implicated with theories of man's mental and moral evolution, which drive us back on considerations of origin. It will be convenient that in the present lecture attention should be mainly given to the Biblical account of man's nature, or to the doctrine of the image of God in man, and to the opposition manifested to this doctrine from the side of a materialistic monism. The subject of origin in the light of evolutionary theories will occupy us in the next lecture.

How keen is the antagonism between the Biblical doctrine of man and the so-called modern view may be seen from a single passage which I shall quote from Haeckel. 'Our own human nature,' says this writer, 'which exalted itself into an image of God in its anthropistic illusion, sinks to the level of a placental mammal, which has no more value for the universe at large than the ant, the fly of a summer's day, the microscopic infusorium, or the smallest bacillus. Humanity is but a transitory phase of the evolution of an eternal substance, a particular phenomenal form of matter and energy, the true proportion of which we soon perceive when we set it on the background of infinite space and eternal time.'[1] It is the truth of these allegations we are to test. We begin with the Biblical doctrine, and in the second part of the lecture will consider the materialistic and monistic negation.

The foundations of the Biblical doctrine of

[1] *Riddle of the Universe*, p. 87; cf. pp. 5, 6 (pop. edit.).

man are firmly laid at the very commencement of his history in the accounts given of his creation. In the narrative of creation in the opening chapter of Genesis—the so-called Priestly or Elohistic narrative—we have already that noblest of possible utterances regarding man: 'God created man in His own image.' The manner in which this declaration is led up to is hardly less remarkable than the utterance itself. The last stage in the work of creation has been reached, and the Creator is about to produce His masterpiece. But, as if to emphasise the importance of this event, and prepare us for something new and exceptional, the form of representation changes. Hitherto the simple fiat of omnipotence has sufficed—'God said.' Now the Creator — Elohim — is represented as taking counsel with Himself (for no other is mentioned): 'Let us make man in our image, after our likeness';[1] and in the next verse, with the employment of the stronger word 'created' (*bara*), the execution of this purpose is narrated: 'So God created man in His own image, in the image of God created He him, male and female

[1] Gen. i. 26.

created He them.'[1] This grand declaration that man is made in the image (*zelem*) of God, after His likeness (*d^emuth*)—I follow the best exegetes in assuming that no distinction is intended between the two terms[2]—is, as Haeckel also recognises, determinative of the whole Biblical idea of man. It is the conception, tacit or avowed, which underlies all revelation: is given, *e.g.*, in Gen. ix. 6, as the ground of the prohibition of the shedding of man's blood; is echoed in Psalm viii.; is reiterated frequently in the New Testament (1 Cor. xi. 7; Eph. iv. 21; Col. iii. 10; James iii. 9): is, in truth, the presupposition of the history of God's dealings with man from first to last.

In basing thus on the Creation narrative in Genesis i., I do not feel that it falls within my province to discuss the questions raised by criticism as to the origin and date of this

---

[1] Ver. 27. Dr. Driver remarks: 'The creation of man is introduced with solemnity: it is the result of a special deliberation on the part of God, and man is a special expression of the divine nature' (*Genesis, in loc.*). The plural is best explained as the plural of majesty. There is no allusion to a council of angels: critics note that angels are not introduced in the P narrative.

[2] See below, pp. 54, 58. Calvin already (*Instit.* I. xv. 3) and most Protestants reject the idea of a distinction.

narrative; nor is it necessary that I should do so. Enough for my present purpose that the narrative is *there*, and that the doctrine it enshrines is that which underlies all Scripture; is, besides, a doctrine which is verifiable and capable of vindication from the nature and history of man. In view, however, of its fundamental character, and the importance of the whole subject, I may offer the following brief remarks regarding it :—

1. While it may be in itself a secondary question at what period the narrative received its final literary shape or was incorporated in the book of the law, I am, in agreement with many able scholars, not persuaded of its late date; am disposed rather, with Delitzsch and others, to look on the account as one of the oldest we have, and as coming down to us from pre-Mosaic times.[1] A cosmogony with certain resembling features, resting, no doubt, on old Babylonian tradition, but defaced by polytheism and many absurdities—beginning, indeed, with the genesis

[1] On the different views held as to this narrative (Delitzsch, Schrader, Dillmann, Gunkel, Kittel, Oettli, etc.) see my work, *The Problem of the Old Testament*, pp. 405 ff. 530-1.

of the gods themselves—is found, I know, on Assyrian tablets. There is, however, to my mind, a supreme improbability in the idea that any writer, living, say, in the Exile, should borrow such an account from his heathen neighbours, and, after purging it from its polytheistic accretions, should place it in the forefront of his Scriptures. The earlier character of the narrative seems indicated by the references made to it in the Decalogue and in such Psalms as the 8th and 104th.[1]

2. With reference to the supposed borrowing of the narrative from Babylonian or similar myths, I think the first thing that must strike the impartial reader is not the alleged resemblance to, but rather the entire difference in spirit and structure of the Genesis narrative from, all other legends and cosmogonies which religion and literature present. These are, without exception, polytheistic, mythological, fantastic in character in the highest degree. The Biblical story is the opposite of all this: serious, orderly, monotheistic, rational, the vehicle of the very noblest ideas about God and His world. It has upon it a stamp of

[1] Cf. Delitzsch, *Genesis*, 1. pp. 63-66 (E. T.).

THE NATURE OF MAN

grandeur and individual character which speaks against its being an expurgated edition of the heathen fables from which it is supposed by some to be derived.[1]

3. With relation to science, while I grant at once that it is not the object of this narrative to teach what *we* call science, or to anticipate nineteenth-century discoveries, I confess again that what impresses me most about this ancient narrative is not its alleged disagreements with science, but its sobriety, rationality, and marvellous *general* congruence with the picture of creation, even as modern science presents it to us.

4. If, finally, we look at the *ideas* which the inspired record is intended primarily to convey— the ideas, viz., that there is one God, who is the Almighty Creator of the world; that the world is not a natural and necessary emanation of the divine Being, but originated in a free act of God's will ; that creation was not the result of a single act, but was accomplished in an ascending series of acts, culminating in man, in whom the creative

---

[1] In the work above-named I have argued that the relation of Hebrew to Babylonian tradition is probably one of 'cognateness' rather than of 'derivation.

activity came to rest [1]—I say, if we look at these ideas, it may be claimed for them that there is not one which comes into conflict with science, while, in respect of details, so true is the insight yielded by the Spirit of revelation into the orderly progress of nature, that there is marvellously little one requires to revise even in this primitive picture of creation in order to bring it into harmony with what our own advanced science has to teach us.[2]

On one point, at least—and that an all-important one—there will, I think, be general acknowledgment that the Biblical account is in complete agreement with science; that is, in placing man at the summit of creation, as the last and highest of God's works and the goal of the whole creative movement. Even evolutionary philosophy has no cavil to make here. For in it also man is the last and highest product of nature, the terminal point of organic development. It is not, so far as I know, seriously contended by any one—though some in the past have spoken in

---

[1] Cf. Driver, *Genesis*, pp. 32, 33.
[2] See Haeckel, quoted in Note II. on The Creation Narrative and Science.

THE NATURE OF MAN

that way—that humanity will evolve into something specifically different from, and higher than, the humanity we know. Whatever future development there may be, it seems always assumed that it will be development *within* humanity. As Mr. Fiske puts it in his *Through Nature to God*: 'In the long series of organic beings, man is the last; the cosmic process, having once evolved this masterpiece, could thenceforth do nothing better than perfect him.'[1] The unity of the human species seems also, in harmony with the Biblical representation, to be a necessary corollary from the doctrine of evolution.[2]

There is, however, another side to the complete Scripture doctrine of man's place in creation which requires likewise to be taken into account. While man is linked on the lower side of his being with organic nature, and in a manner, physiologically and otherwise, sums it up in himself, and is the microcosm of it, he not less clearly stands above nature—is in a true sense *supra*natural—and on this side of his being is linked with a higher *spiritual* order. Mr. Fiske, in his own way, admits this also; for it is to the possession of intelligence

[1] Page 85. [2] See below, p. 154.

by man, to the fact that henceforth variations of intelligence are more profitable to him than variations of body, that he attributes the cessation with him of further organic development.[1] Mr. Fiske's argument, we shall see after, is more specious than solid; but it will not at least be doubted that it is in virtue of his powers of mind, including under this his whole spiritual endowment, that man holds the unique position he does in creation. In the words of Herder, man is 'the middle link between two systems of creation intimately connected with each other'[2]—on the one hand, the highest of nature's products, crowning the long ascent from lower to higher forms of organic life; on the other, the starting-point of a new order of spiritual existence, or kingdom of intelligence. Nature, indeed, as we can now see, would have remained incomplete had not such a being appeared to crown its formations. For, with all its order and beauty, nature, without man, is unconscious of itself; is incapable of turning its eye back upon itself; and of contemplating what it has brought forth; has no proper final cause. Only when man appeared, with faculties capable of

[1] As above, pp. 83-85.   [2] *Ideen,* bk. v. 6.

THE NATURE OF MAN 43

surveying the scene of his existence, of understanding its processes and laws, and of utilising its vast resources, was the Riddle of the Universe (to use Haeckel's phrase) solved; only then was an adequate end—an end for self—found in it.[1]

Scripture, therefore, represents the truth with perfect accuracy when it speaks of man as the crown of nature, and as made in the image of God. Before considering more precisely what is covered by this last expression it will be proper to look briefly at the second and more anthropomorphic narrative of man's creation in Genesis ii., which also has its contribution to offer to our subject. This second narrative is sometimes spoken of, but without sufficient reason, as in contradiction with the first. Its standpoint, grouping, and mode of representation are, however, different from those of the previous chapter. The interest concentrates now specially in man, who is, as before, the centre and head of creation, brought into being by a special supernatural act of God. The object is to show how man was dealt with by God at his creation; how he was placed in suitable surroundings, provided with a helpmeet

[1] Cf. *The Christian View of God and the World*, p. 135.

in woman—'bone of his bone and flesh of his flesh'—made capable of fellowship with God, and of immortal life; but how, afterwards, listening to the tempter, the newly-created pair disobeyed the divine command imposed on them, and brought death into our world and all our woe. In this narrative the creation of man is thus described: 'And the Lord God [Jehovah Elohim] formed man of the dust of the ground, and breathed into his nostrils the breath of life (lit. the breath of lives, *nishmath ḥayyim*) and man became a living soul (*nephesh ḥayyah*).'[1] It would be a misreading of this pictorial description of the making of man to take it as meaning literally that Jehovah first moulded the shape of a human body from inanimate dust, then by a subsequent act breathed life into it. For one thing, such a lifeless shape would not be in any true sense a body—much less a 'man.' A body is not a lump of dead matter, but is a thing of flesh and blood, has its parts and organs, is built up of living tissue. The idea of the passage is fully satisfied by assuming that man's body—the organic frame—was produced by God, by whatever processes,

[1] Verse 7.

THE NATURE OF MAN 45

from lower elements, and that through the inspiration of the Almighty there was imparted to, or awakened within, the newly-created being that higher life which makes man what he truly is—a personal, self-conscious, rational and moral being. As much as in the previous case the narrative implies a distinctive act of God in man's production; but it is important to notice in what precisely the assertion of this distinctiveness lies. It does not lie in the simple expression, 'Man became a living soul,' for the same words are used in Ch. i. 20, 24, 30, to denote purely animal life. Animal, as well as man, is 'living soul.' Neither does it altogether lie in the expression 'breath of lives,' taken by itself; though it is to be observed that the term here employed for 'breath' (*neshamah*) is, with the single exception of Gen. vii. 22, always in the Old Testament confined to man.[1] Even in the passage named, when read with the close of the preceding verse: 'And every man: all in whose nostrils was the breath of life [lit. the breath of the spirit of lives], of all that was on the dry land died,' it is not quite clear that it is not man who is specially in

[1] Cf. Oehler, *Theol. of the O. T.*, i. p. 217.

view in the interpolated clause.[1] The true uniqueness in man's formation, however, is expressed by the act of the divine inbreathing, answering somewhat to the *bara* of the previous account. This is an act peculiar to the creation of man; no similar statement is made about the animals. The breath of Jehovah imparts to man the life which is his own, and awakens him to conscious possession of it. The same idea of the origination of the spiritual life of man in a divine inbreathing appears in other parts of Scripture, *e.g.*, in Job xxxii. 8, and xxxiii. 4; Isa. xlii. 5. In the first of these passages, for instance, we read: 'There is a spirit in man, and the breath (*nishmath*) of the Almighty (*shaddai*) giveth them understanding.'

This second narrative of creation affords the natural transition to another question arising out of the Scripture doctrine of man which at this point demands attention. It follows from all that has been stated, and from the facts of his constitution, that man is a *compound* being—related to nature and the lower organic world through his body, and to God and the higher spiritual world

[1] Cf. Delitzsch, *Genesis, in loc.*

through his spirit. We are accustomed to express this by saying that man has a body and a soul. This is substantially the Biblical view also; but the Biblical standpoint is nevertheless different from ours. We emphasise the *distinction* of the sides of man's nature—the material and the spiritual; the Bible regards man rather in the *unity* of his person as made up of these two elements. We shall see this best by looking at the meaning of the term 'soul' (*nephesh*, ψυχή) in its relation to the term 'spirit' (*ruah*, πνεῦμα) with the connected terms 'flesh' (*basar*, σάρξ) and 'body' (σῶμα; the Old Testament has not here a proper equivalent). There have been, and still are, elaborate discussions and different theories as to the relations, in the Biblical usage, of soul and spirit, and of both to flesh; but it will be sufficient to confine attention to main points.

The principal question is as to the relation of soul and spirit, and on this subject opinions run, perhaps, mainly into two groups:—[1]

---

[1] The different views may be seen fully expounded and discussed in Laidlaw's *Bible Doctrine of Man*, with arts. on 'Soul,' 'Spirit,' 'Psychology,' in Hastings' *Dict. of Bible*; in Dickson's *St. Paul's Use of the Terms Flesh and Spirit*; and in the various works on Biblical Theology. See also the author's *Christian View of God*, Lect. IV.

1. There is the view of those who take 'spirit' (*ruaḥ*) as the more general term, and regard it as denoting the originating *cause* or *principle* of life, and 'soul' (*nephesh*) as the *result* of the creative inbreathing of spirit, or as 'constituted' life. Thus, God's Spirit is the source of life or soul in all living beings, animals and men; and soul is the constituted life of these beings, the seat of all vital functions, that which makes them individual living beings—in the case of man that which makes him a person. It is perhaps not sufficiently noticed in this view that the inbreathing of the divine *nᵉshamah* (=*ruaḥ*) in the creative narrative is something peculiar to man. 'Flesh' (*basar*), in turn, is the body as animated by the soul; and the seat of the soul or life in the flesh is peculiarly the blood (cf. Lev. xvii. 11). The flesh is therefore in man, at least as he now is, connected with weakness, frailty, perishableness (cf. Gen. vi. 3). Man as flesh stands opposed to God whose Spirit gives him breath.[1]

---

[1] Thus Wendt in his work, *The Ideas of Flesh and Spirit in Biblical Usage* (see in Dickson as above), and, in the main, Laidlaw. A sentence or two from the latter may make the point clearer. '*Nephesh* is the subject or bearer of life. *Ruach* is the principle of life; so that in all the Old Testament references to the origin of

THE NATURE OF MAN 49

2. Another view—that which seems to me more correct—agrees with the former in regarding 'soul' as derived from 'spirit'—the divine Spirit—and as denoting 'constituted life' in the individual; but differs from it in its mode of conceiving of the soul itself, and of its relation to spirit *in man*. On the former theory soul and spirit in man are the same thing under different points of view. Viewed in relation to its origin, the vital, conscious principle in man is spirit (*ruah*); it is God's breath in man making him what he is. Viewed as something constituted and individual, as part of the individual being, it is soul (*nephesh*).[1] On the second view *nephesh* is the

living beings we distinguish *Nephesh* as life constituted in the creature from *Ruach* as life bestowed by the Creator. . . . A usage which is practically uniform, of putting "spirit" (*ruach* or *neshamah*) for the animating principle, and "soul" or "living soul" (*nephesh hayyah*) for the animated result' (*Bib. Doct. of Man*, rev. edit., p. 88). 'All through Scripture "spirit" denotes life as coming from God; "soul" denotes life as constituted in the man' (*Dict. of Bible*, iv. p. 167).

[1] 'The purpose of the double phrase, "soul and spirit,"' says Laidlaw, 'is, at most, to present the one indivisible thinking and feeling man in two diverse aspects, according as these two terms originally suggest his life viewed from two different points' (as above, pp. 91-92; cf. pp. 126-7). 'The two conceptions,' says Wendt, 'denote the same quantity (*Grösse*), but with a different estimate of value, *because from different points of view*. . . . The mental life-powers are called *ruach*, so far as they connect the

vital or animating principle in animals and men, and in man is the seat and source alike of animal and of spiritual life. It is, in the first instance, the animating principle of the body, the source of the vital functions, the seat of the animal appetites, desires, and passions. The body, as animated by the *nephesh*, is, as in the other view, *basar*, flesh. But in man the soul or *nephesh* is the source also of higher activities—those which we distinctively call rational and spiritual—which belong to man as a personal, moral, and religious being. It is these higher activities of the *nephesh* which, in the Biblical phraseology, are peculiarly denominated 'spirit.'[1] The soul, therefore, on this theory, is the source of two classes of activities: the animal, connected with the body, and the spiritual, in which lies man's proper affinity to God. It is the principle of life in man which manifests itself, on the one hand, in the corporeal functions; on the other, in the conscious activities of the mind.

creatures with God and place them in dependence upon Him: they are called *nephesh*, so far as they separate the creatures as animate individuals from one another and from the lifeless, impersonal world of sense' (in Dickson as above, p. 419).

[1] Hence such expressions as a spirit of wisdom, of knowledge, of understanding, of discretion, a free spirit, a humble spirit, etc.: on the contrary, a proud, perverse spirit, etc.

It is the bond between the natural and spiritual sides of man's life—is that, therefore, in which lies the centre of his personality.[1]

It will be seen from these remarks that the modern distinction of soul and body is not quite the Biblical—at least the Old Testament—one, as describing the elements of man's personality. Soul, in the Old Testament, is not opposed to body; it is *in* body, its animating and informing principle. It is the possession of a soul which makes a body; as, on the other hand, there is no soul which does not imply a body. It follows that soul, in Scripture, has always this connotation of a body. There may be spirits, *e.g.*, angels or demons, which have no bodies, but they are not 'souls.' On the other hand, souls, as having a spiritual origin, and as spiritual in nature, can be properly called 'spirits.' The 'spirits in prison' in 1 Pet. iii. 19, *e.g.*, are spirits or souls of *men*. But spirits that never had bodies could not, similarly, be called 'souls.' If this view of the relation of soul and spirit be accepted, it will be felt that it precludes the idea, which some

[1] Cf. Oehler, *Theol. of O. T.*, i. pp. 218-19; *Christian View of God*, pp. 137-38.

have entertained, that the Bible sanctions a doctrine of 'trichotomy,' or of three separable parts of man's nature: body, soul, and spirit. Spirit, we have just seen, is not something distinct from soul as a third separable element, but denotes the higher, self-conscious activities of the soul—to which also, in Biblical speech, special names are given.[1] The usage indicated may not be carried through quite uniformly in Scripture —what verbal usage is?—but examination will show, I think, that it is the prevailing one.

The view just explained as to the constitution of man's nature is, as we shall come to see afterwards, of extreme importance in its bearings on general Biblical doctrine. It brings man before us as a personal unity—a being composed of body and soul in a unity not intended to be dissolved. The body is as really a part of man's personality as the soul is. It is not, as philosophy is apt to teach us, a mere vesture or accident, or, still worse, temporary prison-house, of the soul, but is part of *ourselves*. Not, indeed, in the sense that the soul cannot survive the body, or subsist in

[1] On these cf. Laidlaw, pp. 131 ff., and the various works on Biblical Psychology.

some fashion without it, but in the sense that man was not created *incorporeal spirit*. His soul was made and meant to inhabit the body, and was never intended to subsist apart from it. Hence death, in the true Biblical point of view, is not something natural to man, but can only be regarded as something violent, *un*natural, the rupture or separation of parts of man's being that were never meant to be disjoined. The soul, in virtue of its spiritual, personal nature, survives the body; but, in separation from the body, it is, as many things in Scripture (*e.g.*, its doctrine of Sheol) show, in a mutilated, imperfect, weakened condition. This view is not only important in itself as giving its due share of honour to the body, and harmonising with the close relation between soul and body on which modern psychology lays increasing stress; but will be found to shed much light on other doctrines of Scripture —for instance, on death, on immortality, on resurrection, on the full scope of Christ's redemption. These relations will be considered in the concluding lecture.

I return now to the more fundamental declaration that man is made in the image of God, and proceed to inquire in what this image of God, which we have found to be determinative of the Biblical idea of man, distinctively consists. Generally, it is evident from the context in Genesis that the image of God denotes that in which, in distinction from all lower creatures, man *resembles* God—in which the print of likeness to God is stamped upon his nature. I have already stated that the terms used in Genesis i.— 'image' (*zelem*) and 'likeness' (*d^emuth*)—are not held to denote any real distinction (in verse 27 the one word 'image' covers both):[1] I do not therefore spend time in discussing older theories which imply that such a distinction is intended.[2] In what, then, I go on to ask, does the image of God, or likeness to God, in man, actually consist?

On this point the following remarks may be made:—

1. Negatively, it is plain that the image does not lie essentially in material form. There have indeed been anthropomorphites who held that God had visible form, and that man was His

[1] Cf. Laidlaw, p. 142; Driver, *Genesis*, p. 14; art. 'Image' in *Dict. of Bible*.

[2] Cf. Laidlaw, pp. 151-52; Oehler, *Theol. of O. T.*, i. p. 211; and see below, p. 58.

image in this respect. Swedenborgians and Mormons still entertain this fancy; but I need hardly stay to refute their notions. The God of whom it was declared that He had 'no similitude,' and of whom, on this very account, the people of Israel were forbidden to make 'any graven image, or likeness of male or female,'[1] was not a Being whom the monotheistic writer of Genesis i. could think of as creating man in His outward shape.[2] The idea of some of the Fathers that man was made in the image of Christ afterwards to come (*Christi futuri*, Tertullian), or that his bodily form was prophetic of the incarnation, is likewise fanciful, and inverts the true relation. The Son of God took on Him our Adamic nature;[3] man was not made in the image of the humanity of Christ. Yet in a certain sense it may be truly held that even in his bodily form man reflects, and is an image of, the glory of his Creator.[4]

[1] Deut. iv. 16; cf. the Second Commandment.

[2] Some writers (*e.g.*, Kautzsch) think that in pre-prophetic times Jehovah was conceived of as having bodily form; others (*e.g.*, H. P. Smith) that even the great prophets 'no doubt conceived God as existing in human form.' This seems quite unwarranted.

[3] Cf. Heb. ii. 14. Calvin (*Instit.* I. xv. 3) combats the views of Osiander on the above points. His whole section on this subject is interesting and valuable. [4] Cf. Calvin, as above.

The body is the temple of the rational spirit—is destined to be the temple of the Holy Ghost—and in its erect posture, its intelligent countenance, its quick-glancing eye, bears the stamp of its spiritual dignity upon it.[1] In that sense only is it the visible image of the invisible God.[2]

2. Positively, therefore, this image, or resemblance to God, must be supposed to lie primarily in man's nature, and secondarily, in the relation which through that nature he sustains to the lower creation, and to the world as a whole. As respects his *nature*, the resemblance cannot be looked for, as just said, in his body, nor in the animal functions of his soul. It must be looked for, therefore, in that higher constitution of his being which makes him spiritual.[3] It is in the

[1] In this sense some of the Fathers (as Justin and Irenæus) referred 'image' to the bodily form of man, and 'likeness' to his spirit. The saying of Novalis may be compared, as quoted by Carlyle in his *Heroes*: 'There is but one temple in the Universe, and that is the Body of Man. Nothing is holier than that high form. Bending before men is a reverence done to this Revelation in the Flesh. We touch Heaven when we lay our hand on a human body' (Lect. I.).

[2] The above refers only to bodily form. In a deeper sense, as will be shown later (Lect. VI. p. 269), man's nature, as grounded in the Eternal Word, sustains a relation to Christ—the Image of the Father.

[3] 'It relates,' says Driver, 'from the nature of the case, to man's immaterial nature.' See his whole suggestive note, *Genesis*, p. 15.

powers and activities of man as personal spirit that we are to seek his affinity to God and resemblance to Him. The image of God intended in Scripture, in other words, is a mental and moral image. It is to be sought for in the fact that man is a person—a spiritual, self-conscious being; and in the attributes of that personality—his rationality and capacity for moral life, including in the latter knowledge of moral law, self-determining freedom, and social affections; highest of all, in his capacity for fellowship with God. To these points I return below.

3. As respects his relation to nature *beneath* him, these attributes confer on man a dignity and sovereignty analogous to God's own: he had, as Genesis declares, a delegated power in creation, dominion over the creatures.[1] Some, as the Socinians, have placed the whole image of God in this dominion;[2] but plainly this sovereignty was something derivative. It depended on the fact that man possessed powers and attributes

---

[1] Gen. i. 26, 28; cf. Ps. viii., and, as regards the fulfilment of this destiny of man in Christ, Heb. ii. 5-9.

[2] F. R. Tennant, in his *The Fall and Original Sin*, seems to favour this interpretation (p. 104).

of soul qualifying him to take this place, and exercise this authority.[1]

Two further questions arise in regard to the divine image, which fall afterwards to be considered in their proper place.

1. Did the divine image in man include, not simply the possession of the elements or powers of a rational and moral nature, potencies to be subsequently developed, but likewise actual conformity to the divine image—holiness or righteousness of nature? In other words, was man from the first constituted a pure and holy being, and was this a necessary part of the divine image?[2] This raises the question of man's original condition, or of what is called the *status integritatis*, to be discussed in the fourth lecture.

2. A kindred question is—how far does man as fallen possess the divine image? Is it utterly destroyed, or to what extent does he retain it?[3]

[1] The different views of the divine image may be seen in Laidlaw (ch. vii., viii.) and in the other works and articles referred to. Jewish and patristic views are referred to by Tennant, as above, *passim*.

[2] On the different views here, cf. again Laidlaw, Tennant, etc., and see below, pp. 156, 187.

[3] A good deal depends in the patristic and mediæval discussions on this point on the untenable distinction between the 'image' and 'likeness' of God—the former denoting man's inherent natural and moral endowments, the latter a 'superadded' gift of righteousness.

THE NATURE OF MAN

The answer to that plainly is, in part to anticipate, that so far as the divine image answers to an indestructible element in man's constitution—reason, conscience, freedom, etc.—it still remains, but in a broken and impaired condition. As respects the actual exhibition of that image in moral resemblance to God, it is largely destroyed; even natural virtues are at best only a shadow of it, for they lack the spiritual element and true quality of holiness in not springing from the love and fear of God. The nature is not in true subordination to God, and does not shine with the lustre of His Spirit.

At the stage we have thus reached, we are already far within the confines of the territory where every step we can take is fated to be stoutly contested by the adherents of modern theories. One important question which arises immediately from the foregoing exposition is—Are we justified in assuming that the self-consciousness and

The latter was generally supposed to be lost by the fall; the former not, or not completely. Cf. Laidlaw, pp. 152 ff. Tennant, in the work above cited, tends unduly to minimise the teaching of Irenæus and others on the spiritual effects of the fall. If both image and likeness are represented by this Father as lost in the fall (p. 288), it is difficult to see that a spiritual ruin is not involved.

rationality we have attributed to man really constitute a distinction between him and the lower animals? Is the higher not simply, as the evolutionary theory asserts, the result of a gradual, but perfectly natural, development from the lower? The question will have to be carefully considered when we come to discuss origins; but the general grounds on which it is held that the distinction now assumed *is* qualitative, and not simply a distinction of degree, may here be fittingly indicated.

The actuality and breadth of the gulf between the mental powers of man and those of the lower animals is, of course, denied by no one. It is described by Mr. Fiske as 'immeasurable'; he even goes so far as to say that, 'while for zoological man you can hardly erect a distinct family from that of the chimpanzee and the orang; on the other hand, for psychological man you must erect a distinct kingdom; nay, you must even dichotomise the universe, putting man on one side and all things else on the other.'[1] This is

---

[1] As above, p. 82. Haeckel says: 'Reason is man's highest gift, the only prerogative that essentially distinguishes him from the lower animals' (*Riddle*, p. 6).

THE NATURE OF MAN 61

a remarkable admission, and others, equally striking, will meet us later. The difference, indeed, is supposed to be bridged over by processes of evolution; this, however, is mere hypothesis, and we shall find that evolution here has to encounter insuperable difficulties.[1] Meanwhile the broad distinction between man as a spiritual, rational being, and the lower animals, remains.

1. We found resemblance to God, first of all, in the fact that man, like his Maker, is a *personal, self-conscious* being. In this one fact he stands apart from, and above, all orders of the inferior creation. Man is not only conscious, but *self*-conscious. He can turn his mind back in reflection on himself; can apprehend himself; can speak of himself as 'I.' This consciousness of self is an attribute of personality which constitutes a difference, not in degree, but in kind, between the human and the merely animal.[2] No brute

[1] Cf. Lect. IV.

[2] Cf. again Dr. Driver's note on Gen. i. 26: 'It [the image of God] can be nothing but the gift of *self-conscious reason* which is possessed by man, but by no other animal. In all that is implied by this—in the various intellectual faculties possessed by him; in his creative and originative powers, etc. . . . man is distinguished fundamentally from other animals, and is allied to the divine nature' (*Genesis*, p. 15).

has this power. None, however elevated in the scale of nature, can properly be spoken of as a person. The sanctity that surrounds personality does not attach to it.[1]

2. This self-conscious, personal life of man, however, is itself but a manifestation of something deeper—what we are accustomed to call *rationality*. We speak sometimes of animals also as possessed of reason, and in a spontaneous, instinctive way, within limits, it is not denied that they do perform acts analogous to human reasoning. Yet reason in man, as a little reflection on its nature and results speedily shows, is something *qualitatively* different, and not merely different in degree, from what we find in animals.[2] The difference is seen, for one thing, in this, that man alone possesses the power of *abstraction* and *generalisation*. Even Haeckel, apparently, distinguishes the 'power of conceptual

[1] Gen. ix. 6.

[2] 'It is true,' says Dr. Driver, 'that some of the faculties mentioned are possessed, in a limited degree, by animals; but in none of them are they coupled with self-conscious reason; and hence do not form a foundation for the same distinctive character' (*Genesis*, p. 15). So far as reason appears in animals, we may perhaps say that it is rather reason that possesses them—the reason that is operative in all nature, even in plants, and in purely instinctive operations—than they who possess and wield reason.

thought and abstraction' in man from 'the non-conceptual stages of thought and ideation in the nearest related animals.'[1] By the power of abstraction man can take his experience to pieces, and hold apart in thought the various elements composing it; by the power of generalisation he can combine resembling qualities, and from them form general notions, or ideas of classes. The animal has no such power. It sees, *e.g.*, redness in objects, but it is wholly beyond its power to separate this attribute from the object, and form the abstract notion of 'redness.' As little is it able to separate this quality from a number of objects, and group the latter into one class under the general notion 'red.'[2] It is because he pos-

[1] *Riddle*, pp. 38, 45.

[2] There seems very general agreement that the distinction between human and animal intelligence reveals itself peculiarly at this point. Mr. G. H. Lewes says: 'The animal feels the cosmos and adapts himself to it. Man feels the cosmos but he also thinks it'; and he admits that brutes have 'no conceptions, no general ideas, no symbols of logical operations' (*Problems of Life and Mind*, i. pp. 123, 124, 157). Cf. Mivart, *Lessons from Nature*, chap. vii.; an able Roman Catholic work on *Psychology* by Father Maher ('Stoneyhurst Philosophical Series'), cited and reasoned against by Mr. Mallock; Iverach, *Evolution and Christianity*, pp. 170-71; more recently, Henslow, *Present-Day Rationalism Critically Examined*, pp. 209, 212-13, 219, etc. The last-named author says in his Preface: '*Man alone has acquired the power of making abstractions objects of*

sesses this power of abstraction that man is able to turn back his thoughts upon himself in self-consciousness, and know himself as person. But even this, when we probe the matter deeper, is only a phase of that more fundamental quality of thought in which its true essence as rationality consists—its capacity for the *universal*. Thought in this relation, as I have said elsewhere,[1] may be defined as the universalising principle in human nature. It is that which negates limits, which rises above the individual, which apprehends the general in the particulars, the law in the phenomena, the finite in the infinite. It is the ground of man's capacity for rising to general truths, and of framing such highest ideas as infinity, eternity, God, duty, religion. This power, almost every psychologist will acknowledge,[2] the animals do not possess. It belongs to that true, self-conscious rationality in which man is the image of God.

thought. This lies at the basis of all his superior "God-like" powers. It forms the sharp line of demarcation between him and the animal world' (p. vii.).

[1] *Christian View of God*, p. 113.

[2] 'Man,' says Max Müller, 'alone employs language, he alone comprehends himself, alone has the power of general ideas—he alone believes in God' (*Chips*, iv. p. 458). See further below, Lecture IV.

THE NATURE OF MAN 65

3. Should doubt still remain as to the essential character of this distinction between man and animal, the doubt should, I think, be removed if we look at the *consequences* of the presence of this power of rationality on the one hand, and of the absence of it on the other. Rationality is the ground, as already said, of the possession by man of *self-consciousness*, of *religion*, and of *morality*—of none of which the animals are capable. It is the ground of the faculty of intelligent speech—of *language*: another faculty possessed only by man. It is the foundation, therefore, of the possibility of education and *progress*; of all arts, institutions, and sciences. The animals are wholly unprogressive. As rational, man sets ends before him and anticipates the future; as moral, he not only knows and wills, but *loves*—using that term in its widest sense, to embrace the whole sphere of affection. He founds *societies*. Highest of all, he has the capacity for the knowledge of *God*, for fellowship with Him, and for loving obedience to Him: his thoughts touch the infinite and reach out to eternity. In all these and in many other respects the possibilities of merely animal life are absolutely transcended. A

potentiality is discerned in man which proves in him the presence of a *spirit* of which the highest of the animals are destitute.

Such then, briefly sketched, is the Biblical view of man's nature, and it might seem at first sight as if nothing could be more reasonable in itself, or more consonant with human experience. Man's whole history, with its splendid creations in arts, sciences, morality, institutions, religion, might appear to bear witness for it. Any lower view might seem to involve the negation of man's moral and spiritual dignity, and, as a consequence, the destruction, not only of Christianity, but of every elevating conception of man's calling and destiny. Yet, as we have had occasion to see, this view is now keenly, eagerly, almost fanatically assailed, and that, too, in the name of science. The whole force of what is proclaimed as 'the modern view of the world' is directed against it; pæans are already sung in many quarters over its overthrow; even such a writer as Mr. Mallock, as I mentioned at the beginning, in *defending*, too, the credibility of religion, ventures to speak of the assault as on scientific grounds everywhere victorious. Postponing for the present, as I proposed, the consideration of the attack from the side of evolution, I would now offer a few remarks on the aspect the assault assumes at the hands of philosophical monism.

Monism, particularly the naturalistic monism we have to do with here, may be defined in general as the affirmation of the unity of the power which manifests itself in nature in the production alike of material and of mental phenomena. Formerly the attack on the existence of a distinct spiritual principle in man came chiefly from the side of *materialism*. The materialistic hypothesis might be coarse, but it was at least intelligible. Mind was brain, and brain mind. Thought was simply cerebral change : matter in motion. The newer philosophy prides itself somewhat on the rejection of this crude materialism.[1] Conscious phenomena, it is forced to admit, are distinct from the phenomena of matter. Mental action and brain action represent two series of facts which cannot by any verbal 'hocus-pocus' (the phrase is Huxley's) be resolved into one another. The passage from brain-action to the conscious phenomenon which

[1] Cf. Mallock, *Religion as a Credible Doctrine*, p. 13.

attends it—say, a flash of light, an agreeable odour, a feeling of pain, the idea of a relation—is allowed to be unthinkable.[1] Yet, though distinct, the two series of phenomena are not held to be unrelated. They are in fact at bottom but two manifestions of the same original force which is the sole self-subsisting principle of the universe. This force, power, substance, or whatever we please to call it, however, is not immediately to be identified with matter. It has this double form of manifestation, and appears, now as matter, now as spirit. The two series of phenomena are not identical; they are simply parallel: they appear side by side, and one and the same power is represented in both.

It would take too long to attempt to trace the history of this monistic conception in its changeful shapes from Spinoza, its modern parent, down to recent times. What we are entitled to affirm of it is—that in one form or another it is (or has been till lately) the reigning conception in scientific circles; and that, in the hands of its more thorough-going representatives, it is applied to discredit entirely the spiritualistic view of man—

[1] See below, p. 125.

to prove that there is no distinct entity such as we call the soul, but only a series of perishable mental phenomena, the correlates of a parallel series of cerebral changes,[1] and another form of the same force that is displayed in these; that mind or soul, therefore, has no unity of its own, in virtue of which it can survive death; that freedom is an utter illusion—'the human will,' says Haeckel, ' has no more freedom than that of the higher animals, from which it differs only in degree, not in kind'[2]—more generally, that the mind has no spontaneous activity of any kind, is a mere reflex of the physical changes of the brain. The whole spiritual view of man thus falls, and, before the unanswerable 'demonstrations' of the new theory, Christian conceptions, it is confidently proclaimed, are to vanish, as spectres disappear at daybreak. Haeckel, I should perhaps say, is nearer unabashed materialism than some of the others, though he too in name rejects it. He speaks even of the 'parallel' theory as a species of heresy; a departure from true monism.[3]

[1] On this theory, now commonly called 'psychophysical parallelism,' see further below, pp. 74 ff.
[2] *Riddle*, p. 47.
[3] *Ibid.*, pp. 33-37, 64, etc.

His own formula is matter and *force*—mind, apparently, being a form of the latter.[1]

Two things must strike every one at the outset about this monistic theory. 1. That the Bible idea of man is only got rid of through getting rid of the Bible idea of God—a fresh illustration of the truth that the Bible doctrines of God and man stand or fall together; and (2) that, while professing to discard the older materialism, the theory in its naturalistic form, is, in procedure and results, indistinguishable from materialism. It *ought* not to be so, at least in the 'parallelism' form of it; for, in the first place, if one of the two series is to be made dependent on the other, it should, by admission of much in the system itself, be matter that is made dependent on mind, rather than mind on matter;[2] and secondly, if mental facts and physical facts really constitute

---

[1] 'Monism,' he says, 'recognises one sole substance in the universe, which is at once "God and Nature"; body and spirit (or matter and energy) it holds to be inseparable' (p. 8). Again: 'Our own naturalistic conception of the psychic activity sees in it a group of vital phenomena which are dependent on a definite material substratum, like all other phenomena. . . . Our conception is, in this sense, materialistic' (p. 32). He blames Virchow and others for discarding their earlier 'materialistic' conceptions (p. 33). See further Note III. below.

[2] Huxley and Spencer would admit this.

two parallel series, not causally related, then plainly each is as much entitled to speak for itself as the other is, and it is as illegitimate to sacrifice mental facts at the shrine of physical causation, as it would be to sacrifice the latter at the shrine of mind. In practice, however, in all these theories, it is the physical series of facts which is allowed to rule. Mental facts are interpreted in terms of molecular changes, and the laws of physics and chemistry are applied to rule out freedom and mental spontaneity. Thus materialism after all claims man for its prey, as truly as on the older view.

This leads to another general remark that must be made on the monistic theory as bearing on its assault on the doctrine of man. I refer to the exceeding *crudeness* of its metaphysics. I have observed that the denial of the spiritual dignity of man by the new monism has for its correlative the denial of personality and self-consciousness to God. The Power which manifests itself as matter and spirit—or which is itself identified with matter and force—in the universe, is supposed to be destitute of consciousness, intelligence, and will. Whether this conception is adequate to the explanation of a universe filled with evidences of wise and benevolent purpose, I do not now stay to discuss. But I may at least remark on the curious delusion that any real difficulty is escaped by postulating an infinite, eternal, unknowable, energising substance, source of all the variety of material and spiritual forces—which is Haeckel's view—while denying to that ultimate, self-existing Somewhat intelligence and purpose. How, indeed, on the monist's theory, are such conceptions arrived at, and what validity belongs to them? What business has a mind subsisting as the mere reflex of brain changes to be occupying itself with such ideas as those of eternity and infinity, of substance and cause, of force and energy, and where does it get them? Substance, as every tyro in philosophy knows, is one of the most difficult and obscure of metaphysical categories, and force and energy are hardly behind it in obscurity. Yet these notions are played with as if their meaning was clear as sunlight, and as if a theory of the universe could be built up by their aid without more ado![1]

[1] It is not, therefore, to be wondered at, and is a significant fact that, as Haeckel has to admit, nearly all his weightier supporters have, within the last quarter of a century, deserted him. His views are, in the higher thinking of his own country, already out of date. See Note III. on Monistic Metaphysics—Reaction from Haeckel.

The avowed stronghold of the theory, however, as respects man—still reserving its evolutionism—is its supposed demonstration of the dependence of mind on bodily, and specially on brain conditions. Here monism believes itself to have an irrefragable case. Life, it is pointed out, originates in the cell; consciousness is a manifestation of life; there are no mental changes which have not their counterparts in cerebral changes. Physical changes in the brain, on the other hand, and the general health conditions of the body, powerfully affect the mind. Brain disturbance means disturbed consciousness; brain disorder produces insanity or frenzy; injuries to brain tissue destroy or impair mental powers—sometimes change character; the action of drugs like alcohol or opium exhibits marked effects on mental conditions, etc. In view of such facts, how, it is asked, can it be held that the soul has a life of its own independently of the brain, and capable of surviving it? Is not the theory of *one* life which manifests itself in both mind and brain functions the only reasonable one? Must we not fall back on the 'parallel series' view of mental and brain phenomena, or some other phase of monism?

On this theory, so far as it takes the form of psychical and physical 'parallelism,'[1] or involves the sole dependence of mental phenomena on brain conditions, I would make in conclusion the following remarks :—

1. The alleged parallel series of mental and physical phenomena is, when narrowly scrutinised, a palpable absurdity. Grant that there is a series of physical changes in the brain; grant that there is a train of conscious phenomena in the mind; it is still most evident that the laws of physical causation supposed to explain the one give no account whatever of the other. Leaving free-will for the moment aside—though that is an essential part of man's consciousness of himself—we have still the fact to face that the train of thought in the mind proceeds on the principles of rational connection of ideas, with which physical

---

[1] For effective statements and criticisms of this theory in its different and often inconsistent forms, reference may be made to Professor Ward's *Naturalism and Agnosticism*, Lecture XI.; to an acute book by Professor C. A. Strong of Columbia University, New York, *Why the Mind has a Body* (with article in criticism by the present writer in *Princeton Theological Review*, October 1904); to a valuable German book by Von Ludwig Busse, Königsberg, *Geist und Körper, Seele und Leib* (1903 : defends interactionism); and to an older work, Herbert's *Modern Realism Examined.*

causation has nothing to do. In thinking out a demonstration in Euclid, *e.g.*, the steps of the reasoning are determined by the mental perception of the necessary relations of ideas, while changes in the brain, so far as due to purely physical causes, have no relation to rational successions, but proceed blindly under mechanical and chemical laws. The two series, in their respective determining principles, are thus quite disparate, and cannot be put alongside of each other as 'parallels.'

2. The reasoning, I observe next, so largely employed from diseased or impaired brain-conditions fails in validity when applied to the relations of mind and brain in a state of health. It is an argument from a pathological condition to a healthy one. The influence of brain disorder on the disturbance of mental conditions is not denied. Science makes no new discovery in informing us that a blow on the head destroys consciousness; that disease of the brain produces insanity; that when the brains are out a man will die. But unless it is maintained that there is no distinction between a healthy and unhealthy condition of brain, these phenomena of disease are

no disproof of the fact, which everybody also knows to be true, that in ordinary, normal conditions the mind is master of itself—perceives justly, reasons soundly, acts rationally—behaves, in every respect, as a sane mind should. The question is not, how will the mind act in the absence or disturbance of the appropriate brain conditions? but, how does it act when these appropriate conditions are present, and reason is securely seated on its throne? It is the last inquiry only that is relevant.

3. The gravest fallacy of the monistic argument, however, in this connection, is that, while heaping up evidence of the dependence of mind on brain, it takes no account of the vastly larger range of facts which show that brain and body generally are not less habitually influenced by mind. The dependence of mind on brain is, after all, only one side of the matter. It cannot even be said to be the most important one, for, on any just view of their relations, it must surely be held that brain exists to serve mind, not mind to serve brain. Multiply illustrations as one may of the dependence of mind on brain, it is equally certain that mind, on its side, is continually

THE NATURE OF MAN 77

effecting changes in brain, and controlling and dominating its action. The assumption—for it is nothing more—that the changes in brain accompanying mental action are wholly due to physical and chemical causes neither is nor can be proved to be true. All *prima facie* evidence is against it. The mind frames and executes carefully-considered plans; it receives advice from others, and acts in consequence; it collects information, and takes steps determined by that information. Here the mental link—the link of *idea*—is indispensable in a full statement of the train of causes and effects. Instances are continually afforded in experience of the powerful influence which mind exerts on body. A start of joyful surprise is occasioned by hearing a piece of good news; a shock given to the system by a letter or telegram announcing a bereavement or disaster may issue in death; the martyr is lifted by his faith above the pain of his torture; the soldier is unconscious of his wounds in battle. Mind-cure is even being erected into a pseudo-science. Take, however, the single instance of an act of will in a series determined by some conscious plan or end. How is that to be explained on any materialistic theory? Could we scrutinise the brain at such a moment, should we not find that changes were taking place in its cells, and in the distributions of its energy, for which it was necessary to postulate some invisible cause? Just as in the phenomena of life we see changes taking place in the speck of protoplasm for which physical and chemical agencies are utterly inadequate to account.[1] Science, in such cases, must do justice to all the facts. It must not allow them to be ruled out by *a priori* theorems about conservation of energy, though it might easily be shown that they imply no violation of any law of conservation which science has established. Mind, in brief, must be interpreted through study of itself. When this is done, the facts of intellect, of moral freedom, of religious aspiration, which Monism would overthrow, will be found reinstated in more than their former honour. The Biblical view stands unharmed by monistic speculations.

[1] Cf. the discussion in Henslow's *Present-Day Rationalism Critically Examined* (1904), chaps. vii., viii.

Scripture and Science on the Origin of Man
—The Image as a Creation

Biblical View of Man's Origin. Counter-theory of Monistic Evolution (Haeckel). Present-Day Influence of the Doctrine of Evolution. Extensions and Ambiguities of the Doctrine. Evolution and Creation. Evolution not necessarily Darwinism. Sketch and Criticism of Darwinian Theory. Fortuity invoked to do the work of Mind. Change of Attitude of Evolutionists. Inadequacy of Natural Selection to explain Evolution. Principal Objections. Revised Evolutionary Theories. Evolution and Involution. Evolution and Teleology; Directive Intelligence. Evolution not necessarily by Insensible Gradations. Creative Cause involved in Founding of New Kingdoms. 'Enigmas' of Science (Origin of Life, of Consciousness, of Man). Bearing on the Doctrine of the Origin of Man. Failure of Evolution to account for the mental and moral *Differentiæ* of Man. Unbridged Gulf between Man and the Lower Animals in a physical respect. The Missing Links yet Undiscovered. *Pithecanthropus Erectus.* Result: Higher Cause implied in Man's Origin.

III

SCRIPTURE AND SCIENCE ON THE ORIGIN OF MAN—THE IMAGE AS A CREATION

IN last lecture the Biblical account of man's origin was considered in its connection with the subject of man's nature. It was then shown that, in the account in Genesis, man's creation is referred to a special, supernatural act of God; that, while in it man appears as the head and crown of nature—the goal and resting-point of the whole creative movement—he is yet not a mere creature of nature, but stands in a peculiar relation to God, as bearing His rational and moral image, and standing under moral and religious responsibilities to Him. It was seen that this view of the spiritual nature and dignity of man is not overturned by what is advanced against it from the side of a materialistic monism, with its crude doctrine of a universal Substance, its denial of a distinct spiritual principle in man, its theories of psychical and physical parallelism, and its other forms of naturalistic negation. I am in the present lecture to consider the Biblical account of man's origin in relation to theories of natural evolution.

The monistic doctrine on this point may be sufficiently summed up for our present purpose in the following propositions, derived from Haeckel:—

1. There has been a slow and unbroken process of evolution from the lowest forms of organic life to the highest achievement of nature—Man. In Haeckel's view this 'biogenetic process, the slow development and transformation of countless organic germs, must have taken many millions of years—considerably over a hundred.'[1]

2. This evolution is the result of natural causes which do not imply intelligence or purpose.[2]

3. The immediate ancestors of man are the anthropoid apes. To quote our authority again: 'Sufficient for us, as an incontestable historical fact, is the important thesis that man descends immediately from the ape, and secondarily from

[1] *Riddle of Universe*, p. 5. [2] See below, pp. 90 ff.

a long series of lower vertebrates.'[1] More fully: 'The most perfect and most highly developed branch of the class mammalia is the order of primates, which first put in an appearance, by development from the lowest prochoriatæ, at the beginning of the tertiary period—at least three million years ago. The youngest and most perfect twig of the branch primates is man, who sprang from a series of man-like apes towards the end of the tertiary period.'[2]

4. This law of evolution applies to the mental and moral endowments, not less than to the physical structure of man.

5. The doctrine of the evolution of man from lower animals, by excluding belief in his essential distinction from the animals, is fatal to the assumption of a higher spiritual nature in man, and to belief in personal immortality.

In his advocacy of these views, Haeckel, if a somewhat extreme, may be taken as a fairly

[1] *Riddle of Universe*, p. 30.
[2] *Ibid.*, p. 5. Not, of course, from any species of *existing* ape (cf. Haeckel, *History of Creation*, ii. p. 277). So Weismann in his most recent work: 'There can be no question that man has evolved from animal ancestors, whose nearest relatives were the Anthropoid Apes' (*The Evol. Theory*, E. T., ii. p. 393). But see below, pp. 129, 136.

representative exponent of a very prevalent type of opinion.

Here, then, it might seem, we reach a sufficiently clear issue. The boundaries of our discussion, however, are far from being yet adequately defined. There is no subject on which writers in these days wax so easily eloquent as the universality of the great law of evolution; yet there is none in regard to which there is a louder call for careful discrimination and cautious statement. Evolution has, since Darwin's time, become invested with an omnipotence which, it may safely be affirmed, belongs to it only through a haze in the ideas of those who so exalt it. It receives extensions and applications which carry it far beyond the bounds of established fact. From the organic world it is extended to the inorganic; from our planet and the solar system, to the cosmos; from nature, to the creations of man's mind—arts, laws, language, institutions, religion. We speak in the same breath of the evolution of organic beings—plants and animals—and of the evolution of the steam-engine, of the printing-press, of the newspaper; now, even, of the evolution of the atom.[1] But pause for a moment to analyse any one of these ideas. We know where we are when we speak of organic evolution—of the evolution of organic species. We mean to imply a genetic relationship—a parental tie—between the successive orders of being—the derivation of one from the other in unbroken descent, so as to exclude what are called 'special creations.' Obviously, however, we are on a quite different plane when we speak of the evolution of arts, of language, of institutions, of religion. These things do not go on independently, reproducing themselves by genetic descent. Behind them all is the omnipresent creative agency of the human spirit. It is a still greater divergence from the original idea when we descant, as is sometimes done, on the evolution of such outward things as the steam-engine or the printing-press. There is nothing here in the least analogous to the derivation of one organic being from another. You have a

[1] Valuable remarks are made on this point in an important series of articles by R. Otto on 'Darwinismus von Heute und Theologie' (Present-Day Darwinism and Theology), in the German *Theologische Rundschau*, 1902-4, to which fuller reference will be made below. See also Note IV. on Otto on Present-Day Darwinism.

succession of gradually improved forms of the locomotive, beginning, say, with George Stephenson's rude 'Puffing Billy'; you can put these in a row; and you can, if you please, call the series an evolution. But these successive engines did not produce one another, were not derived from one another, were not perfected by natural selection, or any process of the kind. The sole bond that unites them is the invisible bond of idea in the successive inventors' minds. It is there, and nowhere else, that the evolution takes place. Each new engine, as it comes into existence, is a product by itself, the result of a new inventive act—in that sense, a special creation. It is the same with language. You can make a genealogical tree of the various families of human speech. But this tree does not grow of itself. Behind the whole development, as above observed, is the human mind, with its teeming world of ideas and feelings, all struggling for expression; and each new word, as it comes into existence —say this very word 'evolution'; or the word 'utilitarianism,' brought in by J. S. Mill; or the word 'solidarity,' struck out, I think, by Comte; or the word 'Agnosticism,' introduced by Professor Huxley—is a special coinage of some mind, the felicitous embodiment of some thought for which a word was needed. Yet it takes its place in what is called an 'evolution.' The idea suggested—to which, indeed, I have been working up—is that neither 'evolution' nor 'special creation,' as ordinarily understood, is an ultimate conception;[1] that what we need is some higher notion which will be seen to be the synthesis of both—in which, in fact, the supposed contradiction between them will disappear.[2]

Reverting now to the case of organic evolution and of man, it will be found that here also, before we can proceed profitably, it is necessary to define carefully the sense in which we speak of evolution. No religious interest, I may take it for granted, is imperilled by a theory of evolution,

[1] The contrary is the usual assumption. Thus in Art. 'Evolution' in *Ency. Brit.*, viii. p. 752: 'It is clear that the doctrine of evolution is directly antagonistic to that of creation. . . . The theory of evolution, by assuming one intelligible and adequate principle of change, simply eliminates the notion of creation from those regions of existence to which it is applied.' So Professor Huxley, in his New York *Lectures on Evolution*, etc.

[2] Cf. some remarks in Argyll's *Unity of Nature*, p. 272: 'Creation and Evolution, therefore, when these terms have been cleared from intellectual confusion, are not antagonistic conceptions mutually exclusive. They are harmonious and complementary.'

viewed simply as a method of creation, provided certain conditions are fulfilled, and certain limits are observed. It may be, I at least am not concerned to deny it, that, within limits which science must define for us, there has been organic evolution—genetic derivation of one order or species of living beings from another. The convergence of many lines of evidence has satisfied the great majority of scientific men at the present day that it is so. But our task, in considering the bearings of this fact on the Bible doctrine of man, does not end with this general acknowledgment. In truth it only begins. We have still to inquire what is the real nature of this process by which we assume organic forms to have been produced —what causes or factors are involved in it—and what limits attach to it as an explanation of the existing order, and specially of the appearance of such a being as man. And here it will be found on examination that science no longer speaks with a uniform or decisive voice; that there are, in fact, the widest divergences between the different schools of evolutionists; and that, when evolution is restricted within the limits which the best-established results of science at the present hour seem to impose upon it, the apparent antagonism between it and the Biblical view of man's origin largely vanishes. It is this position I desire to make good by a necessarily rapid, but I hope not altogether superficial, consideration of the actual state of the evidence.[1]

I begin with Darwin, whose theory of the origin of species by natural selection is universally acknowledged to mark the decisive turning-point in the history of modern opinion on this subject. Evolution and Darwinism, indeed, as we are constantly reminded nowadays,[2] are not synonymous. The fact is one which it will be a main object of this discussion to emphasise. It is the case, however, that by very many who speak and write on evolution the two are still practically treated as if

[1] The remarkable and increasing conflict of opinion in the evolutionary schools is well brought out by Otto in the series of articles above referred to (*Theol. Rund.*, 1902, pp. 489 ff. ; 1903, pp. 193 ff.; 1904, pp. 4 ff.). See Note IV., and cf. below, pp. 97, 110 ff.

[2] Cf. Fiske, *Through Nature to God*, p. 81. Spencer was a thorough-going evolutionist, but rejected Darwinism. Professor Huxley, much as he valued the Darwinian theory, repeatedly emphasised the distinction in articles and speeches. 'That the doctrine of natural selection presupposes evolution is quite true; but it is not true that evolution necessarily presupposes natural selection.' See his art. in *Nature*, 1895; lecture at Royal Institution, 1868; art. 'Evolution' in *Ency. Brit.*, vol. viii.; Darwin's *Life and Letters*, ii. p. 197, etc.

they were the same, and in the monistic philosophy I am combating this also is the constant assumption.[1] The distinction is important for this reason that, while evolution in itself has no necessary tendency of the kind, the peculiar merit of Darwinism in the eyes of its leading supporters is that, in words of Professor Huxley, it gives its 'death-blow' to teleology, or to the idea of purpose or design in nature.[2] It accomplishes this, it is supposed, by showing that what the old argument for design took to be *ends* in nature—to which the adaptations we see are then related as means—are in reality only *results*; appearances of design brought about by the operation of a few simple laws without the necessity of any assumption of intelligence.[3] That Darwin came to take

---

[1] Cf. *Riddle*, pp. 28, 90, 93, 134, etc. See also Henslow's *Present-Day Rationalism*, pref. p. vi. Henslow emphasises the above distinction (pp. 145, etc.).

[2] *Lay Sermons*, p. 330; cf. Henslow, *Present-Day Rationalism*, pp. 56, 74.

[3] Cf. Weismann, *The Evol. Theory*, i. pp. 55-56: 'But the philosophical significance of natural selection lies in the fact that it shows us how to explain the origin of useful, well-adapted structures purely by mechanical forces and without having to fall back on a *directive* force' (also p. 240). Thus also *Ency. Brit.*, art. 'Evolution,' viii. p. 764 (Sully): 'The philosophical significance of the hypothesis of natural selection, especially associated with Mr. Darwin, is due, as

the same view of the logical effect of his theory appears from his letters, in which he frequently combats the idea of Asa Gray and others that adaptation in nature implies design. 'The old argument from design in nature, as given by Paley, which formerly seemed to me so conclusive,' he says, 'fails now that the law of natural selection has been discovered . . . There seems to be no more design in the variability of organic beings, and in the action of natural selection, than in the course which the wind blows.'[1] The leading advocates of the theory, Huxley, Romanes, Helmholtz, Haeckel, Weismann, with many more, wrote—and write—in the same strain.[2]

Professor Helmholtz points out, to the fact that it introduces a strictly mechanical conception in order to account for those intricate arrangements known as organic adaptations which had before been conceived only in a teleological manner. . . . His theory, as a whole, is clearly a heavy blow to the teleological method.' R. Otto, in *Theol. Rund.*, 1902, p. 486, writes similarly: 'The most special significance of Darwin and his theory, that on account of which he is named the Newton of Biology . . . is the war against teleology.'

[1] *Life and Letters*, i. p. 309 ; cf. Dr. J. H. Stirling, *Darwinianism*, pp. 239 ff.

[2] Cf. Huxley above. Helmholtz, as quoted by Strauss (*Der alte und der neue Glaube*, p. 216), says : 'Darwin's theory shows how every adaptation of structure in organisms can originate without admixture of intelligence, through the blind operation of a natural law.' Romanes wrote : 'If [plants and animals] were specially created, the evidence of supernatural design remains unrefuted and

So, recently, it was replied to Lord Kelvin that by admitting a creative and directive force in organic nature we lose all the 'advantages' of Darwinism. This should be remembered when stress is laid on the supposed hostility of religion to science. If collision came about between Darwinism and theology, the blame does not rest altogether on the theologian, but must in part be borne by the original advocates of the theory, who openly boasted that by the theory of natural selection the foundations of theism were destroyed.

What, then, are these laws which, on the Darwinian view, enable us to dispense with intelligence in creation, and what is the theory proposed as a substitute? The laws in question are so well known that it is hardly necessary that I should do more than mention them. They are mainly these:—1. Indefinite variation; 2. Heredity; 3. The Struggle for Existence; and 4. Natural Selection, resulting in survival of the

---

irrefutable, whereas, if they were slowly evolved, that evidence has been utterly and for ever destroyed' (*Organic Evolution*, p. 13). On Weismann's views see fully in *Contemp. Review*, November 1894 (in reply to Lord Salisbury). Cf. also on this point, Otto, as above (*Theol. Rund.*, 1902, pp. 484-87; 1904, p. 2).

THE ORIGIN OF MAN 93

fittest. The theory based upon them may perhaps be briefly sketched thus. It lies in the nature of each organism to vary, and variations tend to be perpetuated from parent to offspring. These variations are fortuitous, accidental, 'chance' (a word frequently employed by Darwin) variations, not in the sense of being causeless, but that their causes do not imply any plan or design.[1] They are in themselves aimless, but some tend to the advantage of the individual or species; others militate against it. So keen, however, is the struggle for existence that each profitable variation, even the slightest, *tells*, and it is the fittest members of the species that on the whole survive. These favourable specimens hand down their advantage to their descendants, and the process is repeated with the result of still further improvements. Darwin emphasises the fact that the variations are exceedingly 'slight,'[2]

---

[1] Cf. Stirling, as above, p. 273.

[2] In the third edition of his *Origin of Species* Darwin wrote: 'Natural selection can act only by taking advantage of slight successive variations; she can never take a leap, but must advance by short and slow stages' (p. 214). A little earlier he had said (p. 208): 'If it could be demonstrated that any complex organ existed which could not possibly have been formed by numerous, successive, slight modifications, my theory would absolutely break

and that the time required for the accumulation of favourable variations is very long. 'I cannot doubt,' he writes, 'that during *millions of generations* individuals of a species will be born with some slight variation profitable to some part of its economy.'[1] Through this slow accumulation of profitable variations new organs are formed, new species are gradually produced; lower forms of life are changed to higher; till, at length, we rise to man. All this, as just said, is accomplished through the blind operation of the aforenamed laws. The *appearance* of intelligent adaptation is produced, but the real cause, in Darwin's words, is 'the action of selection on mere accidental variability.'[2]

Now the decisive objection to this theory of Darwin's, as an explanation of the origin of organic forms, apart from all special scientific difficulties, is that, as I have put it elsewhere,

---

down.' So Weismann to-day writes: 'Natural selection depends essentially on the cumulative augmentation of the most minute useful variations in the direction of their utility' (*The Evol. Theory*, i. p. 55). This shows, despite the argumentation of Romanes in his *Darwin and after Darwin* (II. chs. i. ii.; against Wallace), that Darwin at first laid practically the whole weight of his theory on natural selection. Cf. Mivart, *Lessons from Nature*, pp. 283 ff.

[1] *Life and Letters*, ii. p. 124.   [2] *Ibid.*, p. 369.

THE ORIGIN OF MAN

under a veil of words, it asks us to believe that accident and fortuity have done the work of mind.[1] To explain the adaptations which we find in nature by the adding of variation to variation in millions of successive generations is to miss the essential point. The real question is, how these variations happen to be there, how they come to persist in that particular line—say where an eye or an ear is being formed—and how, in combination with other variations, they come to make up in their totality a perfect organ which stands in correlation with the rest of that particular structure. The mere lengthening out of the process does not cast the least light on the ultimate production of a complex organ displaying in every part the marks of the most exquisite adaptation and design. I have already made the admission that there is no necessary antagonism between theism and a doctrine of organic evolution as such. That species should have arisen by a method of derivation from some primeval germ (or germs) rather than by unrelated creations, is not only not inconceivable, but may even commend itself as a higher and more worthy

[1] Cf. Martineau, *A Study of Religion*, i. pp. 278 ff.

conception of the divine working than the older hypothesis. Assume God—as many devout evolutionists do—to be immanent in the evolutionary process, and His intelligence and purpose to be expressed in it; then evolution, so far from conflicting with theism, may become a new and heightened form of the theistic argument. The real impelling force of evolution is now from *within*; it is not blind but purposeful; forces are inherent in organisms which, not fortuitously but with design, work out the variety and gradations in nature we observe. Evolution is but the other side of a previous *in*volution and only establishes a higher teleology. The case is totally altered, if, with Darwin and his more consistent followers, we substitute for intelligence the blind operation of natural selection. The question is not, it is to be observed, as to the existence of the laws on which Darwin relies—laws of variation, of heredity, of struggle for existence, of natural selection—but as to their sufficiency of themselves to explain the evolutionary process. It is here, as we shall immediately see, that the *crux* of the question lies as to the mode of origin of man; and, at the risk of

THE ORIGIN OF MAN

seeming—but only seeming—to delay in coming to my proper point, I must ask your attention a little longer to this fundamental issue in the doctrine of evolution.

It is, therefore, of the utmost interest for us to observe that it is precisely on this point of the sufficiency of the factors posited by Mr. Darwin to explain evolution that science itself has come to cast the strongest doubt. On every side we hear the admission made that while the *fact* of evolution, or doctrine of descent, stands secure, the *laws* which Darwin invoked to explain it —especially natural selection—are inadequate for that purpose, and that the real factors in evolution are yet to seek,[1] and must, to a larger

[1] The admission is so universal that only one or two testimonies need be cited. Weismann says: 'Even the much easier problem, how and by what forces the evolution of the living world has proceeded from a given beginning, is far from being finally settled: antagonistic views are still in conflict, and there is no arbitrator whose authoritative word can decide which is right. The *How*? of evolution is still doubtful, but not the *fact*, and this is the secure foundation on which we stand to-day: the world of life, as we know it, has been evolved, and did not originate all at once' (*The Evol. Theory*, i. p. 3).

Huxley, in *Nature* (Nov. 1, 1894), quotes from the great palæontologist Zittel: 'For the naturalist evolution offers the only natural solution of the problem of the development and succession of organic beings. But as to the causes which bring about the modification

extent than Darwin, even in his latest stage, acknowledged,[1] be sought *within* the organism. This leads to a curious result, the full bearings of which are not always apprehended. Mr. Darwin was not the first to put forward the hypothesis of development, and to support it from the facts of 'classification,' geological succession, homologies, embryology, and rudimentary organs.'[2] 'Nevertheless,' he tells us in the Introduction to his *Origin of Species*, 'such a conclusion, even if well-founded, would be unsatisfactory until it could be shown how the innumerable species

---

of species, and especially the change [continuously] in a given direction, opinions are yet greatly divided. That the principle of natural selection discovered by Darwin leaves many phenomena unexplained is no longer denied by even the warmest followers of Darwin.'

See also Huxley, Art. 'Evolution' in *Ency. Brit.*, viii. p. 751: 'On the evidence of palæontology, the evolution of many existing forms of animal life from their predecessors is no longer an hypothesis, but an historical fact: it is only the nature of the physiological factors to which that evolution is due which is still open to discussion.'

The same authority, in an address at Buffalo, August 25, 1876, said: 'The history of evolution, as a matter of fact, is now distinctly traced. We *know* that it has happened, and what remains is the subordinate question of how it happened.'

[1] On the later modifications in Darwin's views, cf. Mivart, *Lessons from Nature*, chaps. ix., x.; and see below, p. 104.

[2] *Life and Letters*, ii. p. 313.

inhabiting this world have been modified so as to acquire that perfection of structure and adaptation which justly excites our admiration.' In other words, the *fact* of evolution could not be regarded as satisfactorily established until the *method* of evolution had been shown; and it is the peculiar claim of Mr. Darwin's book to have put the hypothesis of evolution on a firm basis by the discovery of the method, viz., natural selection. Now, by a curious inversion, it is precisely Darwin's theory of the *how* which is placed in doubt, while the *fact* of evolution, which he thought could not be regarded as established till the method was discovered, is held to be the one thing certain.[1]

It would take me too far afield to attempt to summarise, with any fulness, the scientific grounds on which the Darwinian theory is held by an increasing number of evolutionists to be inadequate for the purpose of explaining the origin of species in nature, including man. They touch every point in the theory—variation, inheritance,

[1] Romanes, therefore, inverts the true order, when he explains 'the principal function of Darwin's work' by saying 'that in those days the *fact* of evolution itself, as distinguished from its *method*, had to be proved' (*Darwin and after Darwin*, ii. pp. 159-60).

struggle for existence, natural selection, insensible gradations, geological evidence, adequacy of geological time, etc. Only a few of the principal can be glanced at : [1]—

1. There is admittedly variation in organisms, but variation, it is confidently contended, is neither indefinite nor unlimited,[2] and in the state of nature there is a strong tendency to reversion to type. In each organism there is a limit beyond which variation cannot be pushed.[3] This puts a barrier in the way of the conversion of varieties into species.

Variations, besides, are not always slight and gradual. They may be, and sometimes are, of a

---

[1] Cf. with some of the points mentioned, Henslow's 'Summary of the False Data upon which Darwinism is based' in his (more recent) work, *Present-Day Rationalism critically examined*, p. 160, and see his whole section, pp. 145-60. This writer goes so far as to say: Darwinism 'is an *imaginary process* to account for evolution' (p. 145). For an older summary, see Mivart's *Genesis of Species*, p. 21.

[2] Huxley says, Art. 'Evolution,' *Ency. Brit.*, viii. p. 751: 'The causes and conditions of variation have yet to be thoroughly explored; and the importance of natural selection will not be impaired even if further inquiries should show that variability is definite, and is determined in certain directions, rather than in others, by conditions inherent in that which varies.'

[3] In the case of the pigeon, *e.g.*, there is a limit of size, in the number of tail-feathers, etc.

THE ORIGIN OF MAN

pronounced character, and involve correlated changes in the organism as a whole.[1]

2. There is struggle for existence, but where the struggle is severe it does not, it is argued, aid, but hinders, evolution.[2]

3. There is natural selection, but it is increasingly recognised that natural selection *creates* nothing. It only weeds out the weak, and preserves the strong. As A. R. Wallace says, in writing to Darwin, 'Nature does not so much select special varieties, as exterminate the most unfavourable ones.'[3] Given the fitter specimen (or organ), natural selection comes into play to preserve it, but it has no power of itself to produce the fitter specimen.

4. On various grounds the power attributed to natural selection of infallibly picking out infinitesimal favourable variations, and preserving them for many (perhaps millions of) generations till new favourable variations are added, is widely recognised to be untenable.[4]

---

[1] See below, pp. 113 ff.

[2] Cf. Otto, *Theol. Rund.*, 1904, p. 61; and see Note IV.

[3] *Life and Letters*, iii. p. 46.

[4] Thus, *e.g.*, H. Spencer, *Principles of Biology* (sec. 166); two papers on 'Factors of Organic Evolution'; Arts. in *Nineteenth Century*, February 1888 and November 1895; G. J. Romanes in *Nine-*

Here, perhaps, criticism of Darwinism is at its keenest, and is most obviously successful. It is forcibly pointed out that in its incipient stage an organ may be of no advantage to its possessor at all;[1] that variations do not occur singly, but many together, and in the complexity of life tend to balance and neutralise each other both in the individual and in the species;[2] that the forces destructive of life, especially in its lower grades, are often on a scale that puts slight variations out of the question as a means of protection;[3] that the chances of perpetuating variations are

teenth Century, January 1887; the Duke of Argyll, *Nineteenth Century*, March and April 1895; Mivart, Murphy, etc., with very many American and Continental naturalists (on latter, see Otto, *Theol. Rund.*, 1904, pp. 4 ff.).

[1] 'We should entirely fail to form any conception how a very slightly enlarged sebaceous follicle, a minute pimple on the nose of a fish, or a microscopic point of ossification or consolidation amongst the muscles of any animal, could give its possessor any superiority over its fellows; yet by the terms of the hypothesis such, and no other, must have been the origin of the mammary gland, of the powerful offensive weapons of the sword-fish or saw-fish, and of loco-motor organs generally amongst the higher animals' (Elam, *Winds of Doctrine*, p. 128. Arts. reprinted from *Contemp. Review*).

[2] Thus Spencer, etc.

[3] 'This wholesale destruction is effected by means which absolutely preclude any idea of "struggle," as influencing the result in the slightest conceivable degree. When clouds of locusts devastate an entire district; when countless millions of aphides destroy vegetation, and are themselves helplessly swallowed up in mass by ladybirds and

weakened by pairing, etc. The difficulty is increased by Mr. Darwin's insistence on the very slight—'infinitesimal'—character of the variations necessary for his theory. For instance, he speaks of a bird being born with a beak one-hundredth of an inch longer than usual.[1]

5. The acknowledged sterility of hybrids is a serious block in the way of the theory. This difficulty weighed strongly with Professor Huxley, and kept him from ever giving his unqualified assent to the theory of natural selection.[2]

other enemies, etc., . . . surely in all this the most vivid imagination can see no room for "struggle," or any possibility of "survival of the fittest." For what advantage could it afford to an insect that was about to be swallowed by a bird, that it possessed a thousandth fragment of some property not possessed by its fellows?' (Elam, pp. 123-4).

[1] *Life and Letters*, iii. p. 33: 'The more I work,' he says with reference to this instance, 'the more I feel convinced that it is by the accumulation of such extremely slight variations that new species arise.' But in the fifth edition of his *Origin of Species* he confesses: 'Until reading an article in the *North British Review* (1867), I did not appreciate how rarely single variations, whether slight or strongly marked, could be perpetuated' (p. 104).

[2] 'For all this, our acceptance of the Darwinian hypothesis must be provisional so long as one link in the chain of evidence is wanting; and so long as all the animals and plants certainly produced by selective breeding from a common stock are fertile, and their progeny are fertile with one another, that link will be wanting' (*Man's Place in Nature*, p. 107); cf. *Lay Sermons*, pp. 299, 302, 323-24, 337, and *Life and Letters* of Darwin, ii. p. 280.

6. Apart from the general impossibility of explaining the marvellous adaptations of organic beings by the action of unintelligent causes, there is the fact, as Darwin was led ultimately to acknowledge, that there are numerous organic structures which neither did originate, nor could have originated, from natural selection. This is the most remarkable of Mr. Darwin's later admissions. He had earlier stated that, if it could be shown that any complex organ could not be formed by numerous, successive, slight variations, his theory 'would absolutely break down.'[1] In his *Descent of Man*, however, he admits, after reading Nägeli and others, that he had 'probably attributed too much to the action of natural selection or the survival of the fittest.' 'I had not formerly sufficiently considered,' he says, 'the existence of many structures which appear to be, so far as we can judge, neither beneficial nor injurious; and this I believe to be one of the greatest oversights as yet detected in my work.'[2] He acknowledges the presence in man, as well as in every other animal, of struc-

---

[1] See above, p. 93.
[2] *Descent of Man*, i. p. 152; cf. *Life and Letters*, iii. p. 159.

tures which 'cannot be accounted for by any form of selection, or by the inherited effects of the use and disuse of parts.'[1] The cause in these cases, he allows, must lie in powers inherent in the organism.[2]

7. The geological record, while lending general support to the theory of descent, is in manifold conflict with the special Darwinian form of that theory. Its periods, as will be shown later, fall far short of the enormous duration required for the Darwinian processes;[3] it suggests that evolution did not proceed by slow, continuous changes, but was marked by 'critical periods,' when new forms appeared in great abundance;[4] apart from one or two hypothetical pedigrees,[5] it fails to furnish evidence of the transmutation of one

---

[1] *Descent of Man*, ii. p. 387.

[2] The above structures are referred to 'unknown agencies' in the organism (*Ibid.*, i. pp. 154, etc.). These are the 'Lamarckian' elements in Darwin which the so-called 'pure Darwinianism' (Weismann, Wallace, etc.) would again purge out (cf. Weismann, *The Evol. Theory*, i. pp. 241 ff).

It is to be noticed that many hold the 'non-adaptive' characters in the higher groups to be fully as numerous as the 'adaptive' (cf. Romanes, *Darwin and after Darwin*, ii. pp. 174, 256).

[3] See below, pp. 175 ff.   [4] See below, p. 117.

[5] These, however, if granted (see note below), support only the doctrine of genetic descent, not the specific Darwinian theory.

species into another by gradual modification.[1] On this last point of transitional forms, it is difficult to prevent assertion from outrunning real evidence; but the evidence, up to the present moment, must be pronounced extraordinarily scant.[2] Zittel, the palæontologist, in an address in 1896 to the International Congress of Geologists, made the following weighty statements: 'Although an abundance of palæontological facts can be cited in the most convincing manner in favour of the theory of descent, on the other hand, we must not forget that we still know no point of origin for numerous inde-

[1] In 1862, Professor Huxley wrote of the geological evidence: 'It negatives these doctrines [of progressive modification], for it either shows us no evidence of such modification, or demonstrates it to have been very slight; and as to the nature of that modification, it yields no evidence whatever that the earlier members of any long-continued group were more generalised in structure than the later ones' (republished in 1870 in *Lay Sermons*, p. 249).

[2] For an interesting account of the so-called 'intermediate' forms, see Professor Huxley's New York *Lectures on Evolution*, (1876, Lectures II. and III.). The horse apparently is the only instance he regards as 'demonstrative' (of evolution, not of Darwinism). To this extent his judgment quoted above has to be modified. Even the horse, however, has not escaped criticism. See, *e.g.*, Fleischmann's remarks in Otto (*Theol. Rund.*, 1903, p. 191), and cf. Mivart, *Genesis of Species*, pp. 133-34. Owen is quoted as saying of the Hipparion and other extinct forms that they 'differ from each other in a greater degree than do the horse, zebra, and ass.'

pendently arising creatures, and that the connection between the larger divisions of the animal and vegetable kingdoms is by no means so intimate as the theory specially postulates. . . . The warmest adherents of the theory must at all events admit that extinct links between the different classes and orders of the vegetable and animal kingdoms are forthcoming *only in a small and ever-diminishing number*' (italics ours).[1] On the whole, therefore, the case for Darwinism does not stand very differently to-day from what it did when Professor Huxley wrote: 'It is our clear conviction that, as the evidence stands, it is not absolutely proven that a group of animals, having all the characters exhibited by species in nature, has ever been originated by selection, whether natural or artificial.'[2]

In view of these objections to evolution in its Darwinian form, we would seem compelled, either (1) to abandon the evolutionary theory altogether,

---

[1] See below, p. 131.

[2] Art. on 'The Origin of Species,' 1860; republished in *Lay Sermons* (p. 322) in 1870. It is, perhaps, still more striking to find both Mr. Darwin and his son and biographer announcing: 'We cannot prove that a single species has changed' (*Life and Letters*, iii. p. 25).

which, as we have seen, scientific men, on general grounds, are not prepared to do ; or (2) to revise our conception of evolution, and seek some other *rationale* of it than that offered by the theory of natural selection, while allowing to the latter factor whatever subordinate place may rightly belong to it. Adopting this second alternative, we have to ask what view of man and his origin, consistently with the facts of science, a revised evolutionism has to yield us.

We have seen that the Darwinian theory is characterised—

1. By the denial of teleology, for which it substitutes natural selection.

2. By the assumption that evolution proceeds by slow and insensible gradations.

3. By the assertion that organic advance has been absolutely continuous from the lowest form to the highest.

The newer evolution differs from the old—though the conflict of views really dates from the beginning [1]—in laying stress in the explanation

---

[1] Mivart, Asa Gray, Murphy, Owen, Carpenter, the Duke of Argyll, etc., contended for these views from the first. They are new only as coming into greater prominence and more general acknowledgment, as the difficulties of the other view become more apparent.

of organic advance mainly on causes *internal* to the organism, and in recognising that these operate, not blindly, but in definite and purposeful directions. This change in the point of view from outer to inner, from causes working fortuitously to a principle of inner teleology, has immediate effects on the rest of the theory. It is no longer necessary, *e.g.*, that variations should be regarded as slight, or progress as slow; that specific forms should be thought of as produced only by gradual and imperceptible modifications; that the ascent of life should be viewed as something absolutely continuous. These consequences all depend on the fundamental assumption that the effective agency in evolution is the fortuitous action of natural selection. When that is parted with, they lose their logical basis and justification. The causes of variation and progressive development being now placed chiefly within, there is no longer any reason why very considerable variations, or even new types, should not appear suddenly, struck out by the Creative Power in the plastic organism. And this is the view which, I shall try to show, scientific facts support.

The new evolutionism, then, so to designate it, in the hands of many of its ablest advocates, may be described, in contrast with the other, as characterised by the three following features :—

1. The recognition in the evolutionary process of directive intelligence—of the presence of 'idea.'

2. The denial that the only mode of progress is by insensible gradations.

3. The conception of nature as an ascending series of 'kingdoms'—the higher in each case involving new factors, and requiring a specific cause to account for it.[1]

I shall offer a few remarks on these points severally, then seek to show their bearings on the origin of man.

1. On the first of these points—directive intelligence—it is not necessary that I should say much. If the fortuity of Darwinism is rejected, there is but one alternative conception, whatever the precise phrase used to express it

[1] I am aware of the difficulty of finding a general expression for theories often so widely varying, but I think I am justified in regarding the above as fairly typical features. Cf. Otto on the New Evolutionism in Note IV.

THE ORIGIN OF MAN

(self-adaptation,[1] orthogenesis, or the like)—that the changes through which new organs are developed, and new types formed, have their origin from within, and are directed by the forces that produce them to an end. The process, indeed, is not fatalistic. On one side is the stimulus of environment; on the other, response to that stimulus, and adaptation to the particular need—with whatever assistance natural selection, use or disuse, or other so-called 'Lamarckian' factors can yield. But in and through all purposeful forces are at work. American students are familiar with this conception through the writings of Le Conte, Asa Gray, Dana; and it has been, and is advocated by theistic evolutionists, and others not avowedly theistic, in

[1] Cf. Romanes on these views, *Darwin and after Darwin*, ii. pp. 14 ff., 174. 'Self-adaptation' is the phrase of Henslow and others, concerning which Romanes elsewhere says: 'It simply refers the facts of adaptation immediately to some theory of design, and so brings us back again to Paley, Bell, and Chalmers' (*Life and Letters of G. J. Romanes*, p. 361). See more fully Henslow's own work already referred to, *Present-Day Rationalism Critically Examined* (1904), with its advocacy of 'directivity' (chaps. vii., viii.). We have such statements as these: 'Paley's argument, readapted to evolution, becomes as sound as before, and, indeed, far strengthened, as being strictly in accordance with facts' (p. 57); 'Paley's well-known argument of the watch only requires readjustment to be as sound as ever' (p. 94; on the eye, p. 96), etc.

Britain, and on the Continent.[1] Romanes, who had argued against design, would seem to have come round to belief in it, at least on the broad scale, before his death.[2] Lord Kelvin, in a recent memorable utterance, re-affirmed his faith in it, and cited the witness of other eminent scientific men; but in that pronouncement he only echoed his own words of thirty years earlier as President of the British Association. 'I feel profoundly convinced,' he then said, 'that the argument from design has been greatly too much lost sight of in recent zoological speculations. Overpoweringly

[1] Bronn, Darwin's German translator, separates himself from Darwin on this point.

[2] See *Thoughts on Religion*, pp. 30, 92-94. Somewhat earlier he wrote: 'Physical causation cannot be made to supply its own explanation, and the mere persistence of force, even if it were conceded to account for particular cases of physical sequence, can give no account of the ubiquitous and eternal direction of force in the construction and maintenance of universal order. . . . By no logical artifice can we escape from the conclusion that, so far as we can see, this universal order must be regarded as due to some one integrating principle; and that this, so far as we can see, is most probably of the nature of mind. At least it must be allowed that we can conceive of it under no other aspect; and that, if any particular adaptation in organic nature is held to be suggestive of such an agency, the sum-total of all adaptations in the universe must be held to be incomparably more so' (*Ibid.*, pp. 71-72). We attach little importance to the distinction Romanes is disposed to draw between design in the 'universal order' and design in particular structures (*e.g.*, the eye). The argument above is valid equally for both.

THE ORIGIN OF MAN 113

strong proofs of intelligent and benevolent design lie around us, and if ever perplexities, whether metaphysical or scientific, turn us away from them for a time, they come back upon us with irresistible force, showing to us through nature the influence of a free-will, and teaching us that all living things depend on one everlasting Creator and Ruler.'

2. The second point, viz.: the transformation of species by alleged insensible gradations, is one of cardinal importance in the theory of Darwin— one he is never weary of insisting on. Variations, he tells us, are slight, very minute, infinitesmal ; for how else could an organism built up by accumulation of variations have the fineness and continuity of structure it possesses? But is this really nature's method of advance? At least we must say, and Darwin had in the end to acknowledge,[1] not necessarily. A vast amount of evidence has been collected, and may be seen in the books, showing that very remarkable variations do appear, new forms, new structures, quite

[1] 'An unexplained residuum of change, perhaps a large one,' he says, 'must be left to the assumed action of those unknown agencies which occasionally induce marked and abrupt deviations of structure in our domestic productions' (*Descent of Man*, I. p. 154).

suddenly, in both animals and plants.¹ There has been, accordingly, an increasing disposition to admit, as best in harmony with the facts, that the changes giving rise to new varieties and species may not always have been, as the Darwinian theory postulates, slow and insensible, but may have been at times marked and sudden.² I may give two illustrations from unexceptionable authorities in support of this statement. Lyell,

---

[1] Cf. Huxley, *Lay Sermons*, pp. 290 ff. (the Ancona Sheep), p. 326; Mivart, *The Genesis of Species,,* ch. iv. (striking examples); *Lessons from Nature*, p. 339; Argyll, *Unity of Nature*, pp. 271-73. The most remarkable recent experiments, perhaps, are those of the Dutch botanist, De Vries, who claims to have produced new species from the evening primrose by *per saltum* mutations. His experiments have been confirmed by New York botanists. See some account of them in the *Princeton Theol. Review*, July 1904, pp. 439-40. The writer there points out that the result is produced, 'not by the Darwinian hypothesis of accumulating infinitesimal variations, but by the more definite route of considerable mutations; not by slow development,' but apparently by a more or less marked *per saltum* movement.' See below, p. 116.

[2] The Germans speak of this form of development as *sprungweise*. Professor Macloskie of Princeton University, referring to the experiments of De Vries mentioned in a preceding note, thus speaks of the origin of men in an art. in the *Bibliotheca Sacra*, April 1903, p. 267: 'Most of the biologists are of opinion, and justly so, that man has somehow been evolved. Most of them probably think that there has been something special in his case, perhaps a sudden or *per saltum* variation, or a decisive mutation, to use De Vries's term, which would leave few traces behind, and nothing of the "missing-link" kind.'

THE ORIGIN OF MAN

in his *Antiquity of Man*, in dealing with the difficulty of the time involved in the development of man, demurs to the assumption 'that the hypothesis of variation and natural selection obliges us to assume that there was an absolutely insensible passage from the highest intelligence of the inferior animals to the improvable reason of man.' He takes the analogy of 'the birth of an individual of transcendent genius,' and asks 'whether the successive steps in advance by which a progressive scheme has been developed may not admit of *occasional strides*, constituting breaks in an otherwise continuous series of psychical changes.' He goes on: 'If, in conformity with the theory of progression, we believe mankind to have risen slowly from a rude and humble starting-point, *such leaps* may have successively introduced not only higher and higher forms and grades of intellect, but at a much remoter period *may have cleared at one bound* the space which separated the highest stage of the improgressive intelligence of the inferior animals from the first and lowest form of improvable reason of man.'[1] The other quotation is from Professor Huxley.

[1] *Antiquity of Man*, p. 504.

'Mr. Darwin's position,' he wrote in his article on 'The Origin of Species,' 'might, we think, have been even stronger than it is if he had not embarrassed himself with the aphorism, *Natura non facit saltum*, which turns up so often in his pages. We believe, as we have said above, that nature does make *jumps* now and then, and a recognition of the fact is of no small importance in disposing of many minor objections to the doctrine of transmutation.'[1] And again, in his review of Kölliker: 'We have always thought that Mr. Darwin has unnecessarily hampered himself by adhering so strictly to his favourite "*natura non facit saltum*." We greatly suspect that she does make *considerable jumps* in way of variation now and then, and that these saltations give rise to some of the gaps which appear to exist in the series of known forms.'[2] Precisely, with the aid of rapid 'strides' and 'jumps,' we can accomplish much; but what then becomes of the theory of continuous evolution by natural selection of slight aimless variations? Still the 'jumps' do seem to be there in nature, and cannot be got rid of. The geo-

---

[1] *Lay Sermons*, p. 326.
[2] *Ibid.*, p. 342 (italics in the quotations ours).

THE ORIGIN OF MAN

logical record, with its unbridged gaps, and marked inrush of new forms at particular eras, alternating with periods of apparent quiescence, has always been a trouble to evolutionists. As G. H. Lewes wrote: 'The sudden appearance of new organs, not a trace of which is discernible in the embryo or adult forms of organisms lower in the scale—*e.g.*, the phosphorescent and electric organs—is, like the sudden appearance of new instruments in the social organism, such as the printing-press and the railway, wholly inexplicable on the theory of descent.'[1] It is not wonderful, therefore, that in recent developments of evolutionary theory, this undeniable fact of sudden change in organisms—carrying with it correlated changes[2]—should be deemed of essential importance.[3]

3. A still more important point is raised, when we come to the consideration of distinct *kingdoms* in nature. How is the gulf to be bridged over here—the gulf between the inorganic and the

[1] *Physical Basis of Mind*, pp. 110, 117. 'It is very noteworthy,' remarks Sir J. W. Dawson, 'that in the later Tertiary and modern times, with the exception of man himself, and perhaps a very few other species, no new forms of life have been introduced, while many old forms have perished' (*Modern Ideas of Evolution*, p. 107).

[2] Cf. Weismann, *The Evol. Theory*, i. pp. 79, 80 ff.

[3] Cf. Otto, *Theol. Rund.*, 1904, pp. 60-61.

organic, between the insentient and the conscious, between the animal consciousness, and the moral and spiritual personality of man? These are the true 'riddles of the universe,' which science in its highest representatives tells us frankly it is unable to solve—some of which it never hopes to solve. Du Bois-Reymond, in a famous lecture at Berlin,[1] specified seven such limits to a materialistic explanation of nature—among them the nature of matter and force, the origin of life, the origin of consciousness, rational thought and the origin of speech. In the forefront, in the development of nature, the origin of life stands as a blank wall in the way of any thorough-going theory of naturalistic evolution. Professor Huxley, while acknowledging that the verdict of science is wholly against a spontaneous origin of life, yet declares that were it given him to look beyond the abyss of geologically recorded time to a still more remote period, he would 'expect to be a witness of the evolution of living protoplasm from not-living matter.'[2]

[1] In his *Die Sieben Welträthsel*—so great a grief of soul to Haeckel (cf. *Riddle*, p. 34).

[2] *Critiques and Addresses*, p. 239. Weismann also, while admitting the impossibility of proof, 'holds fast' to belief in an original 'spontaneous generation' (*The Evol. Theory*, i., p. 370).

THE ORIGIN OF MAN

May I remark that, even if he did behold this first inflashing of life into the world, the miracle of its appearance would not be one whit less than before. It would still be something new, not capable of being explained out of purely physical and chemical combinations. Professor Ward, in his *Naturalism and Agnosticism*, comments on 'the light and airy way in which Mr. Spencer glides over this problem'—apologising for the omission of the two volumes of his system in which it would fall to be discussed—in contrast with 'the confidence of physicists like Lord Kelvin and Helmholtz, or of physiologists like Liebig and Pasteur, that mechanical theories as to the origin and maintenance of life are hopeless.'[1] Still, as the same writer observes, the great gap between the inorganic and the organic world is a less severe strain on naturalism than the passage 'from the physical aspect of life to the psychical';[2] and that, again, pales before the crowning difficulty of bridging the gulf between the animal consciousness and the rational intelligence and free-will of man.

---

[1] Chap. i. p. 262. Cf. the whole section.

[2] *Ibid.*, p. 9. Professor Ward forcibly draws attention to the difference between 'evolution without guidance and evolution with guidance' (p. 205).

To this last problem, as the goal of our whole discussion, I now confine myself; and would simply remark, in summing up here, on the altered aspect which evolution presents when transformed to meet these new demands upon it. It seems to me that the representatives of our modern theology, when they speak of 'evolution,' sometimes fail adequately to realise how entirely they have departed from the evolution of a Darwin, or Huxley, or even Spencer, under whose names they shelter themselves. Listen, *e.g.*, to Professor Sabatier discoursing on the philosophy of religion. 'At each step,' he says, 'nature surpasses itself by a mysterious creation that resembles a true miracle in relation to an inferior stage. What, then, shall we conclude from these observations, except that in nature there is a hidden force, an immeasurable "potential energy," an ever-open, never-exhausted fount of apparitions, at once magnificent and unexpected.'[1] True, but plainly, on this hypothesis, the antithesis between 'evolution' and 'special creation,' as said before, tends to disappear; call these 'apparitions' new species, and what are virtually

[1] *Phil. of Rel.*, E. T., p. 84.

'special creations' are taken up into evolution as phases of it. Sabatier draws from his theory the conclusion that miracles do not happen. Dr. Lyman Abbott sees more logically that, on this hypothesis, the door is open for any number of miracles. There is no *a priori* reason, as he says, why the Power constantly manifesting itself in usual ways should not, if need arises, manifest itself in unusual ways.[1]

Let us now examine how, as the result of these discussions, the evidence stands on the question of the origin of man. I suppose that, since the publication of Darwin's *Descent of Man*, there is no subject on which the modern mind is supposed to have a more entire conviction than on the evolutionary origin of man. So far as this doctrine is a corollary from the general doctrine of evolution, it falls under the remarks already made. The question is not whether homologies, embryology, and other physiological facts, establish a probability of some kind of genetic connection of man with inferior forms of animal life; on that point science may and must be left to pro-

[1] *Theol. of an Evolutionist*, p. 141.

nounce its own verdict. The vital question is whether that which constitutes the *differentia* of man—those bodily and mental characters in which he stands above, and is distinguished from, the animals, can be accounted for by unaided evolution; and especially whether they can be accounted for on the Darwinian theory of a gradual transformation of man from the anthropoid apes, through natural selection acting on slight unguided variations. And on this point no one can say that the voice of science is unanimous. The latter, or strictly Darwinian, theory, though it has still its influential advocates, our previous reasonings compel us to reject. In the light of science itself, we are, I believe, entitled to say with assurance that, however man has originated, he has not originated *thus*. But it is very important here to remember that, if the Darwinian theory of the origin of species by unaided natural selection is abandoned, there falls with it, as already seen, the necessity of supposing advance to have taken place by small, insensible gradations, or of denying the entrance, from point to point, of new and higher—what, from the theological point of view, we would call *creative*—forces, for

THE ORIGIN OF MAN

the production of new types of being, or the founding of new kingdoms or orders of existence. So far from the creation narrative being here in conflict with evolution, I think it may be said to furnish the complement and correction which certain theories of evolution need. It does this in three ways:—

1. By the recognition of the element of true *creation* in nature, or the production of something perfectly new by the direct act of God (expressed by the term *bara*[1]). Even Sabatier, as we saw, speaks of the hidden force, the immeasurable 'potential energy,' the ever-open, never-exhausted fount of apparitions in nature, which at each step 'surpasses itself by a mysterious creation that resembles a true miracle.'

2. In laying stress on the production and propagation of 'kinds'[2]—of specific forms. For it is a false conception of evolution which represents organic life as in constant process of flux, and

---

[1] This term is used in Gen. i. at the first creation of heaven and earth (ver. 1), the first origin of animal life (water creatures and fowl, ver. 21), the creation of man (ver. 27), and is *implied* in the description of the origin of vegetation (cf. vers. 11, 12 with vers. 20, 21).

[2] Gen. i. 11, 12, 21, 24, 25.

ignores the fixity and persistence of stable types as the goal of the process.[1]

3. Specially, in affirming the existence of distinct stages or kingdoms in nature, each of which needs a creative act of God for its introduction.

These conceptions, it has already been seen, science does not contradict, but in a remarkable way confirms. It, too, is compelled to fall back on the idea of evolution regulated from within, and to dispense with the idea of small and insensible changes as the instrument of advance. It, too, is compelled to recognise origins, and the appearance, fixation, and persistence of new types.[2] Above, all, it is compelled to recognise the rise, not only of new kinds, but of new orders of existence—of new *kingdoms* of nature—of 'gulfs,' as in the transition from the inorganic to the organic, from the insentient to the conscious, which no theory of evolution enables it to pass. I quoted before Du Bois-Reymond's admission of the seven riddles of the universe; we have the testimonies of Huxley, Tyndall, Helmholtz, Spencer, and

[1] Cf. the views of Reinke, Hamann, etc., in Otto (*Theol. Rund.*, 1903, p. 194 ff.).

[2] On persistence see Huxley's striking Essay in his *Lay Sermons*, p. 238 ff.

others, that the chasm between the physics of the brain and consciousness is intellectually impassable —'unthinkable';[1] we have, finally, the fact of such a thorough-going evolutionist as Dr. A. R. Wallace—in other respects a 'pure' Darwinian— astonishing his readers by the acknowledgment that 'there are at least three stages in the development of the organic world when some new cause or power must necessarily have come into action': viz., at the introduction of life, at the introduction of sensation and consciousness; and at the origin of man.[2] A similar view, you are aware, is held, as regards at least man's mental nature, by many evolutionists of repute.[3] Our question, therefore, regarding man resolves itself into this: Is man really an appearance of such a kind in nature that higher causes are implied in his origin?

Now, if the answer to this question is to be based on the pure *data* of science, apart from

[1] See references in my *Christian View of God*, p. 143. So Weismann: 'How the activity of certain brain-elements can give rise to a thought *which cannot be compared with anything material*, which is nevertheless able to react upon the material parts of our body, and, as Will, to give rise to movement—that we attempt in vain to understand' (*The Evol. Theory*, ii. p. 392).

[2] *Darwinism*, pp. 474-5. [3] See below, pp. 141 ff.

prepossessions derived from particular theories of development, I think candour will compel the acknowledgment that the balance of probability is in favour of man's exceptional origin. The Darwinian hypothesis of the origin of man by transformation from the apes by slow and insensible gradations belongs to the region of imagination, not to that of scientifically established fact, and even there, it is not too much to say, is being increasingly discredited. There is no need in evolutionism, we have just seen, apart from Darwinian assumption, for supposing such a gradual transformation. Even Lyell, as I showed, allows us, on the psychical side, 'rapid strides,' 'leaps,' which 'may have cleared at one bound the space' between highest animal and lowest man; and Professor Huxley allows us 'jumps'—'saltations'—on the organic side, which 'give rise to some of the gaps which appear to exist in the series of known forms.'[1] But the facts speak for themselves. The enormous distance that separates man from the highest of the animals, alike in a bodily and in a mental respect, is not to be gainsaid, nor, to do them justice, do the

[1] See above, pp. 115-16.

THE ORIGIN OF MAN

better class of evolutionists seek to gainsay it. Mr. Fiske, who is satisfied that man, both bodily and mentally, is evolved by natural selection, yet emphasises, in words formerly quoted, the 'immeasurable' gap between the minds of man and ape, and declares that 'for psychological man you must erect a distinct kingdom; nay, you must even dichotomise the universe, putting man on one side, and all things else on the other.'[1] Similarly Professor Huxley, while insisting on the minute structural and embryological resemblances between man and the apes,[2] goes on frankly to recognise an 'immeasurable and practically infinite divergence of the Human from the Simian Stirps.'[3] He indicates the essential superiority of man, as being 'the only consciously intelligent denizen of this world,' and

[1] See above, p. 60.

[2] *Man's Place in Nature*, p. 67: 'It is only quite in the later stages of development that the young human being presents marked differences from the young ape'—the real point being, however, that then it *does* exhibit these marked differences.

[3] *Ibid.*, p. 103. Yet he thinks 'some inconspicuous structural difference' may have been the 'primary cause' of this mighty divergence—a pure chance change, apparently, yet we are asked to believe that all this came out of it. A speck of rust, no doubt, will stop a watch (p. 103), but no number of specks will make the watch, or keep it going.

declares that 'no one is more strongly convinced than I am of the vastness of the gulf between civilised man and the brutes; or is more certain that whether *from* them or not, he is assuredly not of them.'[1] Even in regard to physical structure significant admissions are made. Professor Huxley repudiates the view 'that the structural differences between man and even the highest apes are small and insignificant'; asserts, on the contrary, 'that they are great and significant; that every bone of a gorilla bears marks by which it might be distinguished from the corresponding bone of a man; and that, in the present creation, at any rate, no intermediate link bridges over the gap between *Homo* and the *Troglodytes*.'[2]

When we examine more minutely into the character of this difference, we gain new evidence of the physical superiority of man. 'The differences between a gorilla's skull and a man's,' Professor Huxley informs us, 'are truly immense.'[3] 'It may be doubted whether a human adult brain ever weighed less than 31 or 32 ounces, or that

[1] *Man's Place in Nature*, p. 110.   [2] *Ibid.*, p. 104.
[3] *Ibid.*, p. 76.

THE ORIGIN OF MAN

the heaviest gorilla brain has exceeded 20 ounces'—'a difference which is all the more remarkable when we recollect that a full-grown gorilla is probably pretty nearly twice as heavy as a Bosjes man, or as many an European woman.'[1] Dr. A. R. Wallace, however, puts this more strongly. 'The average human brain,' he remarks, 'weighs 48 or 49 ounces, and if we take the average ape brain at only two ounces less than the largest gorilla's brain, or 18 ounces, we shall see better the enormous increase which has taken place in the brain of man since the time when he branched off from the apes'—assuming that he did so.[2] Dr. Calderwood says:

[1] *Man's Place in Nature*, p. 102. The force of this is sought to be broken after by the remark: 'Remember, if you will, that there is no existing link between Man and the Gorilla, but do not forget that there is no less sharp a line of demarcation, a no less complete absence of any transitional form, between the Gorilla and the Orang, or the Orang and the Gibbon. I say, not less sharp, though it is somewhat narrower.' But (1) this new absence of transitional forms only creates fresh difficulties for the Darwinian evolutionist (see below), and does nothing to solve that of the difference between man and the ape; and (2) the 'somewhat' surely needs qualification. Gorilla and Orang, Orang and Gibbon, stand in lateral relations, but man on an immensely *higher* level, and the *kind* of demarcation, as shown in the consequences, is incalculably different in the two cases.

[2] *Darwinism*, p. 458. It will be seen below (p. 136) that it is now a very debatable question whether man came through the line of the apes at all.

'The ape's brain, including the gorilla, with the chimpanzee, at its maximum weight is only 15 ounces, whereas the brain of man at its average weight is 49 ounces.'[1] If, as a last test, we take cubic capacity of cranium, the largest human skull, we find, contains 114 cubic inches, the smallest 63; the largest adult gorilla skull, 34; the smallest, 24; or, according to Mr. Wallace, the average proportions are: anthropoid apes, 10; savages, 26; civilised man, 32.

In light of these indubitable facts, we begin to understand what Professor Dana meant when he spoke of 'an abrupt fall from existing man to the ape level, in which the cubic capacity of the brain is one-half less.'[2] The next question which arises is: Has science been able to do anything to bridge over this gulf, and show how, from the lower forms, the higher have been gradually evolved? This question also, I take it, must, if we confine ourselves to facts, be answered in the negative. It was shown before[3] how hard it is, in the domain of palæontology, to prove the existence of transitional forms at

---

[1] *Evolution*, p. 277.   [2] *Geology*, p. 603.
[3] See above, p. 106.

THE ORIGIN OF MAN

any point in the animal kingdom.[1] It is stated by zoologists that there are at least five distinct types, or plans, on which members of the animal kingdom are constructed, which cannot be reduced to any general expression or formula.[2] Regarding these, Professor Huxley wrote in his lecture on 'The Study of Zoology,' included in his *Lay Sermons*: 'So definitely and precisely marked is the structure of each animal that, in the present state of our knowledge, there is not the least evidence to prove that a form, in the slightest degree transitional between any two of the groups *Vertebrata, Annulosa, Mollusca,* and *Cœlenterata,* either exists, or has existed, during that period of the earth's history which is recorded by the geologist';[3] and as an up-to-date testimony by one of highest authority in this department, we have the words of Zittel in 1896, already referred to: 'The warmest adherents of the theory must at all events admit that extinct

---

[1] See Professor Huxley above on apes.

[2] Others greatly increase the number of these irreducible classes. 'The zoology of to-day,' Fleischmann avers, 'points not merely to four, as Cuvier thought, but to *seventeen* typical forms (*stilarten*), which it is hopeless to attempt to derive from one another' (in Otto, *Theol. Rund.*, 1903, p. 101).

[3] P. 114: on a partial later qualification, see above, p. 106.

links between the different classes and orders of the vegetable and animal kingdoms are forthcoming only in a small and ever-diminishing number.'[1]

The difficulty here signalised of discovering transition links is at its maximum in the case of man. The palæontological evidence I shall consider in next lecture: meanwhile, it is sufficient to say that the oldest human skulls yet discovered furnish no support to the theory of transformation. They fairly equal in capacity the average skulls of the present day.[2] The state of the case

---

[1] In *An Address delivered before the International Congress of Geologists on 'Palæontology and Biogenetic Law'* at Zurich.

[2] Cf., *e.g.*, the interesting lengthy discussion of the Engis and Neanderthal skulls in Part III. of Huxley's *Man's Place in Nature*. The verdict arrived at on the Engis skull (of extreme antiquity) is: 'Assuredly, there is no mark of degradation about any part of its structure. It is, in fact, a fair average human skull, which might have belonged to a philosopher, or might have contained the thoughtless brains of a savage' (p. 156); and on the Neanderthal skull: 'In no sense, then, can the Neanderthal bones be regarded as the remains of a being intermediate between Man and Apes' (p. 157); and the general conclusion is: 'The fossil remains of Man hitherto discovered do not seem to me to take us appreciably nearer to that lower pithecoid form, by the modification of which he has, probably, become what he is' (p. 159).

On one of the most recent discoveries (1902), the Lansing skull, see below, pp. 182, 184. Cf. there also Professor G. F. Wright's remarks on the suddenness of man's appearance.

THE ORIGIN OF MAN

in this particular is not essentially altered from what it was when Sir Charles Lyell wrote in his *Antiquity of Man* in 1863: 'At present we must be content to wait patiently, and not allow our judgments respecting transmutation to be influenced by the want of evidence';[1] when Dana wrote in 1875: 'No remains of fossil man bear evidence to less perfect erectness of structure than in civilised man, or to any nearer approach to the man-ape in essential characteristics. . . . If the links ever existed, their annihilation, without trace, is so extremely improbable, that it may be pronounced impossible';[2] or since Virchow said in 1879: 'On the whole, we must readily acknowledge that all fossil type of a lower human development is absolutely wanting. Indeed, if we take the total of all fossil men that have been found hitherto, and compare them with what the present offers, then we can maintain with certainty that among the present generation there is a much larger number of relatively low-type individuals than among the fossils hitherto known.'[3] Sir Charles Lyell, quoted above, was

[1] P. 499. [2] *Geology*, p. 603.
[3] Address on *The Freedom of Science* at Berlin.

at first a keen opponent of transmutationism,[1] and never yielded fully to Darwin's influence. 'To the end of his life,' Huxley being witness, 'he entertained a profound antipathy for the pithecoid origin of man,'[2] and seems, even, from his correspondence with Darwin, to have continued to believe in a creation of 'distinct successive types.'[3]

I am, of course, well aware that announcements have been made from time to time of the discovery of the so-called 'missing links'; but, unfortunately, these have, up to this date, failed to get their credit established. The most famous of these discoveries—perhaps the only one deserving of notice—was that of Dr. Eugene Dubois, of Amsterdam, who, in 1891-92, found in Java the skull, thigh bone, and teeth of a great man-like mammal, which he forthwith designated *Pithecanthropus Erectus*, or the Erect Ape-Man. Dr. Dubois expounded his discovery at a meeting of the Ethnological Society at Leyden in 1895, but the chairman of that body, the redoubtable

---

[1] Cf. the earlier editions of his *Principles of Geology*.
[2] *Life and Letters* of Darwin, ii. pp. 190, 192.
[3] *Life and Letters*, ii. p. 340.

THE ORIGIN OF MAN

Dr. Virchow, reputed to be the chief craniologist in Europe, utterly refused to be persuaded. He argued that the supposed discovery was no discovery at all. He revised and disputed Dubois' measurements. The skull in question, he said, exactly resembled that of a large gibbon. He held that no reason had been shown for believing that it belonged to any other creature than an ape, while he was also in doubt whether the various bones had all belonged originally to one body. Scientific opinion has been keenly divided about these Java relics ever since—some holding with Virchow that the creature was an ape, others holding that it was human, but very few accepting it as an *intermediate* form. Professor Boyd Dawkins has expressed doubts whether the being walked upright.[1]

[1] See further in Otto (*Theol. Rund.*, 1903, p. 188). Otto, referring to the 'almost dramatic character' of the proceedings in the Ethnological Society, says: 'In the different opinions of Dubois, Virchow, Nehring, Kollmann, Krause, and others, one has almost an epitome of "the state of the Darwinian Question" to-day.' One cause of the ambiguity seems to lie in the difference of measurements. 'Virchow,' we are told, 'opposed to the highly striking drawings of Dubois his own drawing, according to which the curve of the Pithecanthropus coincided with that of a Hylobates (Gibbon).' He thus summed up: 'Up to the present no one has succeeded in making a diluvial discovery which can be held as referring to a man of pithecoid type.'

Cf. Henslow, in *Present Day Rationalism* (p. 209): 'We have not

The remainder of this discussion, relating to man's intellectual and moral nature, I must postpone to next lecture.

yet discovered the missing links to prove by objective evidence the genealogy of the genus *Homo* from the common stock with the existing ape-family.'

It must now be added that the fundamental premiss of this whole discussion, viz., that man has descended from some form of the anthropoid ape, is itself, on what seem to be valid grounds, brought into dispute by recent anthropology. See Note V. on Recent Views on the Descent of Man.

Scripture and Science on the Primitive
Condition of Man—The Image as
Actual Moral Resemblance

Evolution in its Bearing on Man's Mental and Moral Nature. Alleged gradual Development of Man's Mind from Animal Intelligence (Darwin, Romanes, Fiske). Failure to explain true Rationality in Man. Potentiality of Progress (Language, Education, Science, etc.) in Man. Free-Will and Morality in Man (Haeckel, Fiske, Huxley). Bearing on Origin of Body in Man. Mind and Body necessarily rise together. Creative Cause accordingly implied in both. Creation of Man 'male and female.' Unity of Race. Question of Man's Primitive Moral Condition. Does Creation in the Divine Image imply actual Moral Resemblance? Biblical View, and Contradiction of Evolutionary Philosophy. Darwinian Picture of Primitive Man. Support sought in Facts of Anthropology. 1. Argument from Existing Savage Races; fallacy of this. 2. Argument from Remote Antiquity of Man. Usshers's Chronology untenable. Former Exaggerated Estimates of Man's Antiquity. Revised Views. Post-Glacial Man. Physical Science on Age of Earth (Kelvin, Tait, etc.). Recent Beginnings of History (Babylonia, Egypt, etc.). Evolution does not establish this view of Man. 1. Evolution is not necessarily by slow gradations. 2. Palæontological Evidence: Cave Men, etc. High Character of Oldest Skulls. 3. High Character of Early Civilisation. 4. No proof that Civilisation has originated from Barbarism. Subject viewed in light of true Idea of Man. The Primitive Man of Evolution not simply in a Non-Moral, but in an Immoral and Wrong State. Contradiction of Divine Fatherhood. Destiny of Man to Divine Sonship and to Immortality. These Ideas Contradictory of Evolutionary Hypothesis.

IV

SCRIPTURE AND SCIENCE ON THE PRIMITIVE CON-
DITION OF MAN—THE IMAGE AS ACTUAL
MORAL RESEMBLANCE

IN the previous lecture I was engaged in discussing the bearing of the doctrine of evolution, and especially of the Darwinian form of it, on the question of the origin of man. I come now to speak of the closely-related, and from the Biblical point of view, even more important subject, of man's primitive condition. The transition may appropriately be made to this inquiry in the consideration of a point left over from last lecture, viz., how far the theory of evolution, which we saw failed to bridge the gulf between man and the highest ape in a physical respect, is competent to the more difficult task of accounting for his intellectual and moral endowment. The question is: Is there a true dividing-line between man and the highest of the animals in respect of intelligence and moral nature which evolution cannot cross? Does man truly, on the mental, moral, and spiritual side, constitute a new order in nature, requiring a special cause for his origin? I tried to give some reasons for an affirmative answer to that question in the second lecture, but we must now look at it in connection with the attempts to break down the limits between human and animal intelligence, and show that man's mind, equally with his body, can be explained on principles of gradual development.

Here, to avoid misapprehension, it may be as well to say that, while it is a striking fact, the importance of which cannot be minimised, that no means have yet been found of bridging the gap between man and the forms of animal life most nearly related to him, it is in nowise essential to my position that there should not have existed forms which might be described as 'transitional.' There is no *a priori* reason why the creative plan should not have embraced beings showing much nearer approximations to man in structure, and even in a species of intelligence, than have yet been discovered. If, *e.g.*, the traces of flint-chipping apes supposed by some to be found in miocene deposits should be confirmed—though the evidence, as we shall see, is very doubtful[1]—there would be no ground for anxiety. This might be true, yet the dividing-line between man proper and his animal predecessors, based on the possession of rationality, might be as marked and impassable as before.

I need not say, then, that it is a very general assumption among evolutionists that man's intellectual and moral nature *can* be explained by slow evolution from the rudiments of intelligence and social instinct and affection observable in the lower animals. Darwin, Romanes,[2] Fiske, and many others, have attempted the task of showing how this can be accomplished. With monists of the standpoint of Haeckel the transformation is of course an article of faith.[3] Not all evolutionists, however, are of this opinion. Many, as Wallace, Mivart, Murphy, the Duke of Argyll, Professor Calderwood, with some American and Continental

---

[1] See below, p. 171. Cf. Dawkins, *Early Man in Britain*, p. 68 ; Mortillet, in Wright's *Man and the Glacial Period* (App. by Haynes), p. 367, etc.

[2] In his *Mental Evolution in the Animal World*.

[3] Cf. his *Riddle*, chap. vii. ff. Mr. Mallock supports him.

evolutionists, while allowing natural selection large, if not exclusive, play in the production of man's body, draw the line very decidedly at mind. And surely, as I sought to show in the second lecture, with abundant reason. Just criticism might be passed, at the outset, on the *method* by which the transition from animal to human intelligence is supposed to be made out—its essential assumptiveness, and continual drafts, in default of real evidence, on the resources of the inventive imagination. That brilliant writer, Mr. Fiske, *e.g.*, does wonderful execution by the single help of the little word 'comes.' A variation, or succession of such, needed to produce a new organ or faculty, has only to be called for, and it 'comes.' 'Presently'—thus he trips along—'the movements of limbs and sense-organs *come* to be added, and, as we rise in the animal scale, these movements *come* to be endlessly various and complex, and by and by implicate the nervous system more and more deeply in complex acts of perception, memory, reasoning, and volition.'[1] . . . 'To the mere love of life, which is the conservative force that keeps the whole animal

[1] *Through Nature to God*, p. 91.

world in existence, there now *comes* gradually to be superadded the feeling of religious aspiration, which is nothing more nor less than the yearning after the highest possible completeness of spirituality.'[1] No doubt it 'comes'; but the whole mystery lies in that 'comes'! Mr. Fiske finds the grand secret of human progress in 'the prolongation of infancy'; [2] Mr. Mallock finds it in the possession of a 'hand.' [3] But where does the 'hand' come from? More subtle, perhaps, is the constant *non sequitur* transition from what we are conscious of in our own minds to the explanation of seemingly like actions on the part of the animals—though slight reflection should convince us that the acts in the latter case must depend on quite dissimilar psychical processes.[4]

[1] *Through Nature to God*, p. 53. See below, p. 148. The hypothetical and assumptive character of much of Mr. Darwin's reasoning has often been remarked on (cf. Stirling, *Darwinianism*, p. 156; Mivart, *Lessons from Nature*, pp. 88, 327 ff., etc.). Here is a small example, begging the whole point: 'Any animal whatever, endowed with well-marked social instincts, would inevitably acquire a moral sense or conscience, as soon as its intellectual powers had become as well developed, or nearly as well developed, as in man' (*Descent of Man*, i. p. 71). [2] *Ibid.*, pp. 49, etc.
[3] *Religion as a Credible Doctrine*, p. 62.
[4] This is evidenced, for one thing, by the fact that many of the acts are performed perfectly from the hour of birth, prior to experience, training, or opportunity for reflection. The rational being has

Most of the evolutionary theories now indicated proceed, like Darwin's, on the assumption that the transition from animal to human intelligence is effected by natural selection operating on slight accidental variations, and, in so far as this is the case, the objections already urged against the sufficiency of natural selection to explain the evolutionary process hold good. They err also—so far as the connection of man with the ape is concerned—in too slight regard for the patent fact that animal intelligence does not exhibit a steady ascent towards man, reaching its maximum in the apes: the dog, *e.g.*, is more intelligent than the ape, and the ant, I presume, which has hardly a brain at all, is more intelligent than either.[1]

slowly to acquire his powers of observing, judging, comparing, connecting causes and effects, etc. Some remarks of G. H. Lewes on animal *versus* human consciousness are worth quoting. 'The animal world,' he says, 'is a continuum of smells, sights, touches, tastes, pains, pleasures; it has no objects, no laws, no distinguishable abstractions such as self and not-self. This world we can never understand, except in such dim guesses as we can form respecting the experiences of those born blind, guesses that are always vitiated by the fact that we cannot help seeing what we try to imagine them as only touching' (*Problems of Life and Mind*, i. p. 140; cf. pp. 123, 127).

[1] See the striking illustrations of this point in Professor H. Calderwood's *Relations of Mind and Brain*, chap. v. Professor Huxley (to meet, however, an objection) challenges 'the assumption that intellectual power depends altogether on the brain' (*Man's Place in*

PRIMITIVE CONDITION OF MAN

The chief point of weakness in these theories, however, is that they do nothing, really, to meet the proof, derived from the simple fact of man's susceptibility for education and progress, that there are barriers in their nature *impassable* between animal and human intelligence; which, accordingly, involve a distinction, not in *degree* only, but in *quality* and *kind*, between the two, and place man essentially in an order and kingdom by himself.[1] Lyell naïvely acknowledged this when he spoke of the space which separates the unprogressive intelligence of the inferior animals from the improvable reason of man.[2] Professor Calderwood laid his finger on the point when he said of the higher mammals that 'they give no signs of having at command a Reflective Intelligence such as men possess,'[3] and remarked: 'This funda-

---

Nature, p. 102). Yet Mr. Joseph M'Cabe, in an article in the *Hibbert Journal* for July 1905 (p. 751), ventures the assertion 'that the advance [in the evolution of the mind] is rigidly proportioned to the formation and distribution of neural cells.'

[1] Haeckel is content to rely on Romanes for 'demonstration' that human intelligence and speech differ only in *degree*, not in *kind*, from those of the brute (p. 45). Romanes, however, does not make an approach to 'demonstrating' that; as little do Lewes, Spencer, and Darwin.

[2] *Antiquity of Man*, p. 504; see above, p. 115.

[3] *Evolution and the Nature of Man*, p. 99.

mental difference is such as to place the orders of life at vast distance from each other. This appears under every test that can be applied—emotional, industrial, literary, artistic. These facts show that the evolution theory is inapplicable to mind, and thereby insufficient to afford a scientific view of its genesis.'[1]

I need not go back, except in a word, on what was said in the second lecture on man's distinction from the animals in an *intellectual* respect. It was then sought to be shown that the real root of the peculiarity of the human mind, in its distinction from the animal, lay in its proper *rationality*—its power of thought, its faculty for the universal.[2] Man, in virtue of this endowment, allying him with his Maker, is, as the animals are not, a personal, self-conscious being; capable of conceptual thought, of rational speech, of education, of development, of progress; capable also, therefore, of moral, self-regulated life. The enormous difference of *potentiality* involved in all this points to a dis-

[1] *Evolution and the Nature of Man*, p. 161.
[2] Mr. Mivart puts the distinctiveness of man in the possession of 'self-consciousness, reason, and will, with rational speech' (*Lessons from Nature*, p. 198).

PRIMITIVE CONDITION OF MAN 147

tinct cause, and puts a gulf between man and the animals which no evolutionary theory has proved itself capable of bridging. New effects imply new causes; and here is a world of new effects!

Some attention must, however, now be given to the *ethical* aspect of man's nature in its relation to this doctrine of evolution. What applies to the intellectual prerogative of man applies to morality, and in a peculiar way to man's attribute of freedom. It is very significant to observe how determinedly the apostle of monism — Haeckel — assails this citadel of man's spirituality, moral freedom.[1] The implication of his argument throughout is that, if free-will is conceded, his theory breaks down. This, however, is no mere matter of speculation. Man *knows* himself to have, within limits, the power of determining his actions; of affecting the outward world; of regulating his conduct in the view of ends. As

---

[1] Cf. *Riddle*, p. 47. I do not here enter into the difficult psychological and philosophical questions regarding freedom. It is enough for my present purpose to take the word in its common, well-understood acceptation; that man is, within limits, a true, self-determining cause of his own volitions and actions, and takes responsibility to himself for such acts as his own.

Professor Huxley, with all his theories of automatism, illogically allows: 'Our volition counts for something as a condition of the course of events.'[1] Freedom in man, however, is connected inalienably, as Kant so well showed, with the consciousness of a moral law; with ideas of right and wrong; with the idea of an 'ought' in life. What has evolution to say to this, or how does it propose to account for ideas of the kind? Mr. Fiske, whom we may again consult, seeks to show the origin of these ideas, and of the moral sentiments generally, from *sympathy*, but with the usual result that he puts into the process the ideas he professes to evolve from it, or deftly changes the idea in the course of the discussion. Mark the procedure. 'There is thus,' he says, 'a wide interval between the highest and lowest degrees of completeness in living that are compatible with maintenance of life. . . . Now it is because of this interval . . . that man can be distinguished as morally good and morally bad. . . . Morality *comes* upon the scene when there is an alternative offered of leading better lives or worse lives. . . . This rise from a bestial to a moral plane of exist-

[1] *Lay Sermons*, p. 159; *Evolution and Ethics*, p. 79.

PRIMITIVE CONDITION OF MAN 149

ence involves the acquirement of the knowledge of good and evil. Conscience *is generated* to play a part analogous to that played by the sense of pain in the lower stages of life, and to keep us from wrong-doing.'[1] Again: 'Egoism has ceased to be all in all, and altruism has begun to assert its claim to sovereignty. . . . This conception of ought, of obligation, of duty, of debt to something outside of self, resulted from the shifting of the standard of conduct outside of the individual's self. Once thus externalised, objectivised, the ethical standard demanded homage from the individual. It furnished the rule for a higher life than one dictated by mere selfishness. . . . It appears to me that we begin to find for ethics the most tremendous kind of sanction in the nature of the cosmic process.'[2] What is all this, we are constrained to ask, but the process of 'coming' over again? the simple observing of the ideas as they arise, and saying that they are there? As to *how* ethical laws obtain the character of an absolute authority—of a *right* to command—there is not a scintilla of explanation. As regards the 'cosmic process,'

[1] *Through Nature to God*, pp. 51-52. [2] *Ibid.*, pp. 106-7.

refreshing light is thrown on its 'tremendous sanction' by Professor Huxley in his Romanes Lecture on *Evolution and Ethics*, the thesis of which is that the cosmic process of natural selection and survival of the *fittest* is the direct antithesis of the ethical process, which combats the law of natural selection, and has for its aim the survival of the *best*. 'The ethical process,' he says flatly, 'is in opposition to the principle of the cosmic process, and tends to the suppression of the qualities best fitted for success in that struggle.'[1] If evolution is divided against evolution, how shall its kingdom stand?

A fortiori what applies to morality applies to religion—to the capacity of the soul for relations with an unseen Spiritual Power, and for the various exercises of love, trust, worship, obedience, which such relations call forth; but this I leave over for the present. I would only register that the outcome of my argument, so far as it has gone, is this: that the features in man's nature for which we find evolution inadequate to account

[1] Pp. 31, 81. Mr. Huxley seems to feel he has gone far enough, and in a note to the lecture remarks that, in strictness, the ethical process as well as the other is to be included in 'the general process of evolution.'

PRIMITIVE CONDITION OF MAN

are precisely those in which we found the natural image of God in man to consist: his rationality, his moral nature, his religious capacity. The need of creative action to account for man's spirit, stamped with its attributes of rational intelligence and moral freedom, is on these grounds, it seems to me, established.

The way is now clear to proceed to other parts of the subject; but, before I do this, let me ask attention to one important corollary from the conclusion now reached. I mentioned before that not a few evolutionists admit the necessity of a special supernatural Cause, or, from another standpoint, of a higher exercise of the creative cause *within* nature, to account for man's mind, who do not feel that the same necessity applies to his body. That, they think, may be left to the ordinary evolutionary processes. Dr. Calderwood appears to adopt this view in his work on the subject; Dr. A. R. Wallace, in his *Darwinism*, seems also to adopt it.[1] I say 'seems'; for in his earlier unretracted work on *Natural Selection in Relation to Man*, he adduced strong arguments to prove that man's body likewise, in its erect

[1] P. 478.

posture, its potential capacity of brain anticipating future requirements, and other physical peculiarities, shows marks of special origin, and many have followed him in these reasonings. I would put the matter, however, on another ground. I confess it has always seemed to me an illogical and untenable position to postulate a special origin for man's mind, and deny it for his body. I base here on the close relation which every one now admits to subsist between man's mental and physical organisation. Mind and body constitute together a unity in man. Mind and brain, in particular, are so related that a sudden rise on the mental side cannot be conceived without a corresponding rise on the physical side. Evolution, it will be admitted, cannot outrun actual acquirements, and produce in advance, say, from the ape-stock, a brain fitted to receive the higher mind afterwards to be put into it. You could not put a human mind into a simian brain. It follows that, if you assign to man mental attributes qualitatively different from those of the animals —self-consciousness, rationality, self-determining freedom—you must provide an organ adapted to their manifestation and exercise. If you have a

PRIMITIVE CONDITION OF MAN 153

rise on the one side, due to a special cause, you must have an equivalent rise on the other. In full accordance with this is the fact already emphasised, that, so far as scientific evidence goes, man's appearance on the earth does represent a rise even on the physical side. The 'missing link' of theoretical evolution has often been sought for, but, as I showed, has not yet been found;[1] and here we seem to see the reason.

The result we reach, then, from this protracted discussion of man's origin, is, I think, one singularly in harmony with the Biblical doctrine, viz.: that man, alike in his physical structure and in his spirit, in which he bears the stamp of the divine image, is not, as naturalistic theories assert, a mere product of evolution, but has, in a peculiar sense, his origin in a direct creative act. I might adduce, in corroboration of this, the fact that, on the Biblical view, and also, of course, in the view of science, man was created 'male and female.' Do we always consider the difficulty which this creates for a purely evolutionary theory?—that it is not *one* being only evolution has to produce,

[1] See above, pp. 134-5.

but a *pair*; a first pair; the male and female counterparts of each other.[1] To some it may seem a simple matter: to me it appears that, with all our philosophy, the production of a first human pair remains as much a mystery of the laboratory of nature as before evolution was heard of!

Having thus completed, as far as my limits permit, the consideration of man's origin, I now return to the question specially proposed as the subject of this lecture—the primitive condition of man. I have already hinted that on certain important points the latest verdict of science and the Biblical doctrine seem absolutely to agree—*e.g.*, in regard to the *unity* of the human race. If doubts could be raised before, and even scientific men like Agassiz could be found speaking of 'distinct centres of creation' for the human species, it is one thing we may put to the credit of the evolutionary philosophy that it has for ever banished such speculations. No true evolutionist will allow that the evolution of two or more beings

[1] The difficulty applies in lesser degree to all species; it is at its maximum in the case of the rational and moral being.

such as man, along distinct and independent lines, is for a moment to be contemplated. What Scripture said from the beginning, that God 'made of one every nation of men for to dwell on all the face of the earth,'[1] science, in the nineteenth century, with halting foot confirms. Even as to the *where* of man's origin a certain measure of agreement may be observed between science and Scripture. The subject is one, naturally, on which different theories have been propounded; but I think I am right in saying that the lines of scientific opinion tend increasingly to converge on just that region which is the historical cradle of the principal races, and where the Bible also places approximately the site of Eden. It is a curious fact that even Haeckel and others of the evolutionary school trace man's affiliations from the neighbourhood of the Persian Gulf—somewhat further south, however, in a supposed submerged continent.[2] The Biblical Eden in the region of the Tigris and Euphrates thus begins to loom out into something more substantial than myth!

[1] Acts xvii. 26 (R.V.).
[2] Cf. Haeckel, *Hist. of Creat.*, ii. pp. 325-6, 399.

It stands very differently with the Biblical description of man's original moral condition. It will be remembered that, when discussing the subject of the image of God in man, there was one important question which I reserved, viz.: Is it enough to constitute the image of God in man that he should possess simply the *elements* of that image in the powers of a rational and moral nature—potencies to be subsequently developed? Or is it not also requisite that he should be in a state actually *conformable* to that image—a state of moral purity and harmony? In one sense, certainly, it will be allowed by all that the image of God in the first human beings was, and must have been, largely potential. Their powers were undeveloped; the glorious possibilities that lay in them, awaiting their unfolding in history, were undreamt of. But a dewdrop may reflect the sun; and man, in one sense in his childhood, may yet have reflected in a clear intellect, harmonious affections, and an uncorrupted will, the undimmed image of his Maker. This also, it will scarcely be denied, is the picture given us in the Bible, and implied in its later doctrine of the apostacy and guilt of man, and of the divine provision for his redemption.[1] Man is pictured in Genesis, indeed, as beginning his existence under the simplest conditions. His intelligence is not developed. On the contrary, he has everything to learn. But he is neither a child nor a savage. He is capable of knowing, understanding, conversing with, worshipping and obeying his Creator. His nature is undefiled by sin. He has the power to remain obedient. He is not under the law of death.

How complete the contrast of all this is to the doctrine of modern evolutionary science I need not remind you. It is here, in fact, as I formerly said, that the opposition of the modern and the Biblical views of the world and man comes to its sharpest point.[2] It is for this reason that I have

[1] See next Lecture, pp. 199 ff. Mr. Tennant and others, however, do deny that this is the presentation in the Bible (*The Fall and Original Sin*, pp. 10 ff.). See below, pp. 198, 200, 219, etc.

[2] In a note on 'Adam, the Fall, the Origin of Evil,' Romanes says: 'These, all taken together as Christian dogmas, are undoubtedly hard hit by the scientific proof of evolution (but are the *only* dogmas which can fairly be said to be so), and, as constituting the logical basis of the whole plan, they certainly do appear at first sight necessarily to involve in their destruction that of the entire superstructure' (*Thoughts on Religion*, p. 176). He thinks the difficulty is got over by treating the narrative as 'allegorical'—'a poem as distinguished from a history.' But is it got over? See below.

dwelt so long on the subject of man's origin. The question of origin has its chief interest and importance from its bearing on the doctrine of man's nature and condition, and through that on the doctrine of sin. I make no attempt, therefore, to minimise the seriousness of the issue that is involved. Nor can I agree with those theologians who, sometimes with a light heart, make capitulation of the whole position to the evolutionist, and accept the consequences in a weakened doctrine of the origin of sin and of guilt. These writers doubtless act in fullest loyalty to what they regard as the settled teachings of science, and their theories are valuable as illustrating the best possibilities of a reconciliation of evolutionary teaching with fundamental Christian conceptions.[1] Still I cannot regard their efforts as successful. Inevitably they seem to me to minimise the awful evil of sin; nor do I think that some of the writers, at least, realise the full gravity of what they are giving up. What is of immensely greater moment, I do not think there is any necessity for this capitulation. I feel very certain, on the

---

[1] See Note VI. on Modern Theories of Evolution and the Fall; and see below, pp. 209-10.

PRIMITIVE CONDITION OF MAN

contrary, that, so far as science is concerned, there is, for any sincere believer in the incarnation, and in the *new* creation of man in Jesus Christ, no such necessity.

Our question then is: How did man appear upon the earth? In what condition? We know what the Adam of the old theology—with, perhaps, some traits of exaggeration—was: to make clear how strangely different is the picture presented by modern evolutionism, two extracts will suffice. Here is Mr. Darwin's description of the genesis and primitive condition of man. 'Man,' he says, 'is descended from a hairy quadruped, furnished with a tail and pointed ears, probably arboreal in its habits, and an inhabitant of the Old World. . . . At the period and place, whenever and wherever it may have been [he suggests the eocene period], when man first lost his hairy covering, he probably inhabited a hot country, and this would be favourable for a frugiferous diet, on which, judging by analogy, he subsisted.'[1] On the moral aspect, Sir Charles Lyell cites with approval the description of Horace (no mean precursor, it will be seen, of the evolutionists):

[1] *Descent of Man*, ii. p. 372; cf. p. 192.

'When animals first crept forth from the newly-formed earth, a dumb and filthy herd, they fought for acorns and lurking-places with their nails and fists, then with clubs, and at last with arms, which, taught by experience, they had forged. They then invented names for things, and words to express their thoughts. After that they began to desist from war, to fortify cities, and enact laws.'[1] This view for the present prevails. It is accepted even by many who reject pure Darwinism, but still seem to hold it as a necessary implication of evolution that man should begin at the lowest point possible to humanity, and gradually work up. Support for it is thought to be found in the facts of anthropology and palæontology, taken in connection with the evidences of man's remote antiquity. We are pointed to the savage races that still inhabit the earth as object-lessons of what man was before he attained to civilisation; to the remains of prehistoric man —the men of the river-drifts and caves—as proof at once of man's great age and rude primitive condition; to the accumulating evidences that, while our civilisations are but of yesterday, man's

[1] *Antiquity of Man*, pp. 379-80.

existence on earth can be traced back to a period incredibly remote—a quarter of a million, or half a million, years.[1] These facts, to many minds, are incontestable, and it is held to be the sheerest theological prejudice that prevents any one from drawing from them their legitimate conclusion. Is it so? Let us try to look at the matter dispassionately.

1. The argument from existing savage races is one that need not long detain us. Taken by itself, it rests on the unproved assumption that the condition of existing savage races represents (or most nearly represents) that of primitive man. That, I am warranted in saying, is an assumption which, in its proof that behind many, if not most, savage races there stood a state of higher culture and civilisation, science itself is increasingly discrediting.[2] 'We now know,' as Max Müller says,

[1] See the argument from these facts as presented by Driver in the Introduction to his *Genesis* (1904), pp. xxxi. ff.

[2] A large body of evidence on this point may be gathered from writers, like Spencer and Tylor, who, on the whole, represent a different point of view. See a number of instances in Mivart's *Lessons from Nature*, ch. vi., and Note VII. on Retrogression among Savages. Mr. Spencer himself says of savages: 'Probably most of them, if not all of them, had ancestors in higher states; and among their beliefs remain some which were evolved during these higher states' (*Sociology*, i. p. 106).

'that savage and primitive are very far from meaning the same thing.'[1] Still less tenable is the Darwinian assumption that savages of low grade represent an arrested stage in the ascent from the ape-condition to the human. No weaker argument has ever been offered than that which one sometimes meets with even in books of repute —that the difference between animal and human intelligence is not greater than that which subsists between the baby and the philosopher, between the savage and the cultured races. This argument is a favourite one with Haeckel,[2] and after him by Mr. Mallock. 'If there is no break,' argues the latter, 'between the consciousness of the full-grown man and the baby's, how can we pretend that, as an actual and demonstrable fact, an impassable gulf yawns between the baby's consciousness and the dog's.'[3] 'We may assume that the terrier is not a Hegel, a Sir William Hamilton, or a Kant. But no more is an Andaman Islander; no more is an English baby.'[4] The fallacy here is too transparent to impose on any one. The obvious reply is, that in the baby's consciousness

---

[1] *Anthrop. Rel.*, pp. 149, 150.
[2] *Riddle*, p. 65, etc.
[3] *Religion as a Credible Doctrine*, p. 52.
[4] *Ibid.*, p. 54.

there lie all the *potentialities* of the grown man, whereas in the dog's there do not. Similarly the savage, left to himself, may be rude and unprogressive; but, when touched by higher civilisation, still more by Christian influences, he exhibits likewise, often in remarkable degree, all the powers—intellectual and moral—of high manhood.[1] Permit but one illustration. Captain Cook gave the name Savage Island to one of a group in which the inhabitants were so fierce that it was impossible to land amongst them. John Williams tried to evangelise them, and was driven off. By and by a converted Samoan took a journey of three hundred miles to try to do them good. In twelve years, out of 5000 on the island, only eight remained heathen. They became transformed into a proverbially kind and loving people.

[1] The aborigines of Australia were placed by Prof. H. Drummond at 'almost the lowest level of humanity' ('Though the settlements of the Europeans,' he says, 'have been there for a generation, he will find the child of nature still untouched, and neither by intercourse nor imitation removed by one degree from the lowest savage state'); and the statement of old books that those natives are so low intellectually as to be unable to count five is still sometimes quoted. I was recently assured, however, by a local educationist, that the children of such of these natives as have been Christianised show themselves quite as alert and capable as the children of white parents. At a recent examination in a State school in Victoria, a girl, daughter

Every year they sent (at the time of my reading the account) £400 to the London Missionary Society. When a ship was wanted for a New Guinea Mission, costing £500, they voluntarily undertook to raise the whole amount. The Sydney people sent £50 to meet some extra expenses, but the islanders sent it back with thanks, preferring to complete the work they had begun. Thirty married teachers had gone from that island to New Guinea. Can we doubt it?—these are not semi-animals, but children of the kingdom of God.[1]

2. The weight of the argument, however, for the original semi-brutish condition of man rests,

of aboriginal parents, who was in the sixth class, took the first prize. Most are familiar with the changes on the (seemingly hopelessly degraded) Tierra del Fuegians, which so deeply interested Mr. Darwin as to lead him to become a subscriber to the Missionary Society which had wrought the wonder.

[1] Perhaps I should have given consideration here to the argument from the time necessary for the evolution of the various *races* of men. I cannot see, however, looking to the facts of rapid variation among animals under climatic and other influences (cf. *e.g.*, Mivart, *Genesis of Species*, p. 160), that the time required for these changes need have been so long, or the changes themselves so gradual, as many suppose. It may be presumed that early man would show greater plasticity, and be more susceptible to new influences, than his successors; and in historical times there have been instances of very remarkable changes. Dr. Livingstone tells us that the negro type occurs rarely in Africa, and that the tribes in the interior differ greatly in hue and colour.

not so much on the condition of existing savages, as on the facts of palæontology and geology, which are believed to establish an immense antiquity, and rude primitive state, of the human race. To these palæontological facts, accordingly, I now turn—and, first, of the question of the extreme *antiquity* of man.

It is well known that the chronology of Archbishop Ussher, framed from comparison of the numbers of the Hebrew text, placed the creation of the world and of man about 4004 B.C., while the Septuagint numbers enlarged this period to 5508 years.[1] This calculation, however, is plainly erroneous. Discovery has shown that the civilisation of Babylonia and Egypt of themselves go back considerably beyond Ussher's date for the Creation, and this, in Egypt at least, is many long centuries after the Flood, and leaves no room for the whole antediluvian period. It is now generally acknowledged that the good Archbishop's method of reckoning, though natural at the time, is based on data that do not really yield it with any certainty. The genealogies of the

[1] Ussher's real date was 4138 B.C.; the dates for the Deluge on the two reckonings are respectively 2348 and 3246 B.C.

patriarchs before the Flood, and of the descendants of Noah after it, are not of a character that admit of precise calculations being based on them. They precede strictly historical times; it is not improbable that they represent to some extent clan successions; in any case they offer no guarantee of completeness.[1]

On the other hand, the tendency in modern scientific speculation has been to claim for man an almost fabulous antiquity. Common estimates are 100,000 or 200,000 years; some, as Dr. A. R. Wallace, would go back half a million.[2] The evidence on which such computations are based may be seen in Lyell's *Antiquity of Man* and similar works. Now it cannot be denied that, if such an immense antiquity could really be made out for man, it would involve a revolution in our whole mode of conception of man's original condition and subsequent history.[3] But here, now, comes in the

[1] It is a fault of Dr. Driver's argument that he seeks to fix the Bible reader down to the Ussher chronology. See a valuable article by the late Professor W. H. Green in the *Bib. Sacra* for April 1890.

[2] In *Nature*, Oct. 2, 1873, pp. 462-463; cf. his *Darwinism*, p. 456.

[3] The difficulty, however, is perhaps even greater for the evolutionist, for the skulls referred to that remote period are as good as those of modern men. See below, pp. 183 ff.

remarkable fact that the *original* contentions, at least, on this subject have proved incapable of being maintained, and that on scientific grounds alone it has been found necessary to retrench enormously the periods claimed for man's existence on the earth.[1] One after another of the evidences relied on has been shown to be fallacious. No evidence, *e.g.*, was deemed more striking than that derived from the stalagmite formations in Kent's Cavern, Torquay. Professor Boyd Dawkins, however—himself an advocate of a great antiquity for man—takes the ground from this by remarking : 'The value of a layer of stalagmite in measuring the antiquity of deposits below it is comparatively little. The layers, for instance, in Kent's Hole, which are generally believed to have required a considerable

[1] Professor G. F. Wright says, in an article in *Bib. Sacra*, 1903, on the Lansing discovery (p. 31), 'Geological time is not that enormous quantity which it was supposed to be twenty-five years ago. During that period there has been a revolution of opinion respecting geological time which is as yet scarcely appreciated by anthropologists and theologians. . . . Geological time is not one-hundredth part so long as it was supposed to be fifty years ago. The popular writers who glibly talk of the antiquity of man upon the basis of the old geologic ratios are behind the times, and are ignorant of the new light that, like a flood, has been shed upon this whole question during the last few years.' See below, pp. 173 ff.

lapse of time, may possibly have been formed at the rate of a quarter of an inch per annum'—at which rate '20 feet of stalagmite might be formed in 1000 years.'[1] Mr. Pengelly's estimate for the deposit was 5000 years for one inch, and 60 times 5000, or 300,000 years for 5 feet! The same authority, in an address at the British Association, said: 'The question of the antiquity of man is inseparably connected with the further question, is it possible to measure the lapse of geological time in years? Various attempts have been made, and all, as it seems to me, have ended in failure. Till we know the rate of causation in the past, and until we can be sure that it is invariable and uninterrupted, I cannot see anything but failure in the future.'[2]

I am saved, however, from the necessity of going into the evidences in detail, for there is one

---

[1] *Cave Hunting*, pp. 39-41.
[2] *Report*, September 6th, 1888. I may cite the remarks of Professor Huxley on the Somme deposits—another leading evidence: 'The question as to the exact time to be attached to alluvial remains in the valley of the Somme could not be settled satisfactorily. . . . There had been enormous changes during the last five hundred years in the north of Europe. The volcanoes of Iceland had been continually active; great floods of lava had been poured forth, and the level of the coast had been most remarkably changed. Similar causes might have produced enormous changes in the valley of the

point to which, I think I am right in saying, the whole question now nearly reduces itself, and on which it is becoming possible to form some definite judgment. This crucial point is the relation of the earliest-known traces of man to what is called in geology the Glacial Period. I think I am within the mark in affirming that there is a considerable—probably growing—concensus of opinion among competent authorities that the earliest *certain* traces of man are post-glacial,[1] or at least not much earlier than the *close* of the glacial period.[2] I go back to an

Somme, and therefore any arguments based, as to time, upon the appearances of the valley, were not to be trusted' (*Brit. Assoc.* 1877). On the probable age of the deposits, see Prestwich's *Geology*, ii. p. 533, and Wright's *Man and the Glacial Period*, p. 355 ff.

[1] Less certain, because depending on differing interpretations of the phenomena, are the few evidences adduced of *inter*-glacial man (see below). A certain ambiguity, unfortunately, rests on the use of these terms 'post-glacial,' 'inter-glacial,' etc., which gives rise to some confusion (see below, p. 173). Sir J. W. Dawson writes: 'Whether attributed, as by some, to the latest inter-glacial period, or to the post-glacial—a mere question of terms, not of facts' (*Geol. and Hist.* p. 21).

[2] I observe from an article in *The Liberal Churchman* for June 1905 (pp. 222-223), that Professor G. Henslow is of a very different opinion. 'The abundant evidence,' he says, 'of the existence of prehistoric man in wellnigh all quarters of the globe, proves him to have been on a uniformly low level of barbarism for an incalculable length of time; for the vast antiquity of the human race is seen in the all but undeniable proofs of his pre-glacial existence.' And in a

important meeting of the British Anthropological Institute held in 1877 to discuss the question of whether man's appearance was pre-glacial, inter-glacial, or post-glacial. Sir John Evans, Professors Huxley, Prestwich, Rolleston, Dawkins, Hughes, and many other notables were present, and the almost unanimous conclusion of the meeting, says the editor of *Nature*, was that 'the fossil mammalia of the pleistocene tell us nothing of the relation of man to the glacial period. . . . The general question of the antiquity of man in Europe was not discussed, though we gathered that the evidence of man in the Italian pliocene was not considered satisfactory. The general impression left upon our minds is that in Britain there is no evidence of any palæolithic man, either in caves or the river deposits, of an age older than post-glacial.'[1] Not much is to be

note: 'Astronomical considerations would place the glacial epoch some 100,000 years ago.' The reader must judge. What could set man, we may only ask, after these untold ages of unprogressive barbarism, suddenly on a career of development to brilliant civilisation? Has this verisimilitude?

[1] *Nature*, June 7, pp. 97-8. A chief evidence of pre-glacial man, which Professor Boyd Dawkins had at first accepted, though with misgiving, was a fragment of bone, believed to be human, found under glacial clay in Victoria Cave, near Settle, Yorkshire, in 1872.

added in modification of this verdict from subsequent discovery.[1] There are, I know, some eminent geologists who think that relics of man or of his handiwork have been discovered in pliocene deposits of the tertiary period—*e.g.*, the Calaveras skull in California about which, from its very high type, even evolutionists are sceptical[2] —but their inferences are contested by others of equal distinction, and the general view perhaps is

At the meeting in 1877 above referred to, Professor Dawkins gave his reasons for believing that the bone was not human but ursine, and held that the clay was not proved to be glacial clay.

[1] The American evidence is very clearly given in Dr. G. F. Wright's *Man and the Glacial Period*, ch. viii. The deposits incorporating human relics, with one doubtful exception (Claymont, Delaware), he places 'well on towards the close of the great Ice Age' (pp. 254, 258). [Even these, however, especially the 'finds' at Trenton, N.J., have since been very effectively challenged by Mr. W. H. Holmes, of the American Geological Survey. See *Science*, November 1892, etc.]. By far the most recent important discovery in this connection is that of the Lansing Skeleton in Kansas in 1902, which has been the subject of keen discussion. 'The Lansing Skeleton,' we are told, 'affords probably our oldest proof of man's presence on this continent' (*Bib. Sacra*, 1902, p. 741). See Note XII. on the Lansing Skeleton, and cf. below, p. 184.

[2] See below, p. 184. On this, and on the evidence for tertiary man generally, see Appendix by Professor H. W. Haynes to Wright's *Man and the Glacial Period*. Professor Haynes remarks on the Californian relics (pp. 372-374): 'No archæologist will believe that, while palæolithic man has not yet been discovered in the tertiary deposits of Western Europe, the works of neolithic man have been found in similar deposits in Western America.'

very fairly summed up in an able article on the subject in the *London Quarterly Review* for July 1896. 'We need no longer,' the writer says, 'discuss the problem of tertiary man, as man's existence in these distant ages has been most emphatically denied by many of the leading geologists in England, France, and America. In England Sir John Evans, Sir Joseph Prestwich, and Professor Hughes all refuse to accept it; and Professor Boyd Dawkins, in his greatest work, rejects the idea that man lived during the tertiary period.[1] Even in France—where the theory is more favourably regarded—so able an archæologist as M. Carthaillac rejects the evidence for tertiary man. In America also, Sir J. W. Dawson will not accept the theory, and Professor Haynes, after having examined all the evidence for tertiary man, at length rejects the idea completely.'[2]

The question, then, as to the age of the known

---

[1] See Note VIII. on Professor Boyd Dawkins on Tertiary Man.

[2] Cf. the confident assertions of a writer like Mr. S. Laing: 'The evidence for the existence of man, or for some ancestral form of man, in the tertiary period, has accumulated to such an extent (!) that there are few competent anthropologists who any longer deny it' (*Human Origins*, pop. edit. pp. 421-422). Even Mr. Laing, however, is doubtful about the Calaveras skull, which shows no approach to an 'ancestral form.'

remains of man, resolves itself pretty much into this: what period of time has elapsed since the close of the Ice Age? Formerly hypothetical calculations were made which put the close of this age a very long way back indeed. Fortunately the means exist, especially on the American Continent, of putting these calculations to a very precise test, and large numbers of eminent scientific men have devoted their attention to the subject with remarkable and, in the main point, singularly accordant results. One of the best accounts of these computations, and of the facts and theories on the Ice Age generally, is found in Professor Wright's book, *Man and the Glacial Period*, in the International Scientific Series. The conclusions there reached are in harmony with those of Professor Prestwich, the greatest English authority on pleistocene geology.[1] One impor-

[1] Professor Prestwich estimated the duration of the glacial period itself at about 25,000 years (in Wright, p. 364). There are considerable differences in the interpretation of glacial and post-glacial phenomena, some affirming, others disputing, inter-glacial periods, and many contending for a great post-glacial submergence constituting a distinct break between palæolithic and neolithic man. The latter is brought by many into relations with the Biblical Flood. Thus Howarth, Prestwich, the Duke of Argyll, G. F. Wright, Sir J. W. Dawson, etc. See Howarth's *Mammoth and the Flood*; three articles on 'Geological Confirmations of the Noachian Deluge,'

tant chronometer is Niagara Falls, which are of post-glacial origin. Lyell computed the age of the Falls at about one hundred thousand years; but a series of accurate surveys have since been made by the New York State Geologists, and by Mr. Woodward, of the United States Geological Survey, extending from 1842 to 1866, which have resulted in showing a rate of retrocession of two and a half feet per annum, and much more at the centre. The whole excavation, in the opinion of these experts, cannot have occupied longer than seven thousand years.[1] Exactly similar results have been yielded by a long series of observations on the Falls of St. Anthony at Minneapolis. The length of time since the commencement of cutting of the gorge in the post-glacial age is reckoned by Professor Winchell at eight thousand years.[2] To these a large number of corroborative calculations have

by Professor G. F. Wright in *Bib. Sacra* for 1902, with the literature there mentioned; Dawson's *Meeting-Place of Geology and History*, etc.

[1] Wright, pp. 338-339. Allowing for an outlet from the Great Lakes in a different direction in early post-glacial times, the time may be a little longer (see art. referred to below by Professor Wright on 'The Revision of Geological Time' in *Bib. Sacra*, July 1903).

[2] *Ibid.*, pp. 340-341.

since been added, based on careful observation, and overthrowing old extravagant estimates. Such are the measurements of Professor Hicks in a river-valley in Ohio; of Professor Wright in Andover; and of Dr. E. Andrews, of Chicago, on the rate of erosion of Lake Michigan. These, again, yield the result that 'the post-glacial time cannot be more than ten thousand years, and probably not more than seven thousand.'[1] How entirely revolutionary these views are of the older calculations, and how completely they bring the age of man within limits easily reconcilable with the Biblical representations, need not be dwelt on. Their bearings also on the primitive condition of man are great, and will presently be indicated.

Another cause, however, which has necessitated the revision of the extravagant estimates of time formerly current, and demanded by the Darwinian theory, came from another quarter than geology —viz., physical science and astronomy. There seemed practically no limits to the drafts which evolutionists, with the sanction of geologists, were prepared to make on the bank of time.

[1] *Bib. Sacra*, July 1903, p. 346. See further, Note IX. on The End of the Ice Age.

Darwin, in the first edition of his *Origin of Species*, estimated the time required for the erosion of the Wealden deposits in England alone at 306,662,400 years (!), and spoke of this as 'a mere trifle' at his command for the purposes of his theory.[1] It was a rude blow to these millionaires in time when another Darwin—Dr. George H. Darwin, of Cambridge—demonstrated that the physical conditions were such that geology must limit itself to a period inside of 100,000,000 years. Lord Kelvin, Professor Tait, and Professor Newcomb approach the subject from another point, and, on grounds that seem cogent, bring down the whole period that can be given to the geologists much further—to 20,000,000, 15,000,000, or even to 10,000,000 years.[2] In fact, in a lecture

[1] Ed. 1859, p. 287. In a paper read to the Congress of Zoologists at Cambridge in 1898, Professor Haeckel spoke of 1000 millions of years as necessary for his evolution tree! When reminded that physical science would not allow him more than 25 millions of years, he said that he had got the time from an eminent geologist, and that he himself 'had no intuition of the length of time.' In his *Riddle* he considerately asks no more than 48 millions of years (p. 97).

[2] 'Lord Kelvin is willing, I believe,' said Sir Archibald Geikie in his President's Address to the British Association in 1892, 'to grant us some twenty millions of years, but Professor Tait would have us content with less than ten millions.' Professor Tait himself says: 'Physical considerations from various independent points of view render it utterly impossible that more than ten or fifteen millions of

PRIMITIVE CONDITION OF MAN 177

on the sun's heat, Lord Kelvin, assuredly our highest authority on purely physical questions, declares that the age of the *sun* is not more than 20,000,000 years[1]—which, if correct, would not give more than possibly 6,000,000 years to geology. These conclusions have, of course, been contested by geologists and biologists, but assuredly have not been overthrown. While they stand, or presuming them to be even approximately correct, they carry with them consequences fatal alike to the Darwinian slow development of species, and to the extremely remote antiquity claimed for man. For geologists are in the main well agreed as to the relative periods of time to be devoted to the palæozoic, mesozoic, and cænozoic periods which they distinguish. Dana's ratio is 12 : 3 : 1; others suggest 13 : 3 : 1.[2] This means that the

years can be granted. . . . From this point of view we are led to a limit of something like ten millions of years as the utmost we can give to geologists for their speculations as to the history even of the lowest order of fossils' (*Recent Advances in Physical Science*, pp. 167-168).

[1] More strictly, of the sun's *light* (*Lects. and Addresses*, p. 390).

[2] Haeckel in his *Riddle* gives the proportions slightly differently for the organic period: primary, 34,000,000; secondary, 11,000,000; tertiary, 3,000,000—the last still, however, it will be observed, one-sixteenth of the whole (48,000,000).

cænozoic or newest period, in the most superficial portions of which alone man's remains are found, has only one-sixteenth of the whole, or considerably less than 1,000,000 years: if Lord Kelvin is right as to the age of the sun, hardly a quarter of that period. Of these the eocene, miocene, and pliocene will require six-sevenths, or even seven-eighths, leaving only a very small fraction of time, perhaps 100,000 years—it may be much less—for the pleistocene period, including the glacial age and the period of man. This agrees, it will be seen, with approximate accuracy, with the foregoing calculations as to the late date and comparatively recent close of the glacial period.

There is one consideration more to which I would briefly advert. The results thus far reached, not by Biblical apologists, but by men of science working on their own *data*, agree in a remarkable way with the general evidence afforded by history. It is well known that recent discoveries in Babylonia and Egypt carry back man's appearance in history several thousands of years beyond the traditional Biblical date; still, however, not apparently beyond 5000, 6000, or at

PRIMITIVE CONDITION OF MAN 179

most 7000 years B.C. The history of civilisation, as we now read it, begins with Babylonia. It bursts upon us there, however, as all these ancient civilisations do, in something like maturity. We have not yet been able to reach a period in the development of these nations when we leave behind us letters and arts.[1] Behind stands, we shall suppose, the age of palæolithic man—sharply separated, some believe, by the post-glacial submergence (Deluge) from that of neolithic man—but it is in no way proved that this older age was not, in part, contemporary with a (or *the*) higher civilisation. Neither the recollections nor the traditions of these oldest civilised peoples know anything of a past which would be compatible with those enormous stretches of blank, unprogressive savagery which the opposite theory assumes. There is much justification for the view that, if we allow, say, from 12,000 to 15,000 years since

[1] This was true till recently of both Egypt and Babylonia. The case is partially altered as regards Egypt by the remarkable discoveries between 1894 and 1901 of the graves and other remains of a race distinct from the dynastic Egyptians—the so-called 'New Race' of Professor Petrie. A full account of these discoveries and of the theories to which they have given rise may be seen in Budge's *History of Egypt*, I. ch. i. They do not essentially affect our conclusions. See Note X. on the 'New Race' in Egypt.

the time of man's first appearance on our globe, we do ample justice to all the facts that are available, and probably the lower figure is nearer the mark than the higher.

There is but one answer to all this, and it forms the real ground on which, in so many quarters, a long antiquity and semi-brutish origin is still claimed for man. It is the theory of *evolution*. Man, it is said, *must* have been hundreds of thousands of years upon the earth to give time for his slow development upwards to the stage at which we find him on his earliest historical appearance.[1] It is wonderful to observe the hold which this idea of man's extremely slow ascent from an animal condition has on the imaginations even of those who decline to accept the unmodified Darwinian hypothesis of his origin. I spoke before on the relation of evolution to man's origin; I make now the following remarks on its bearing on man's primitive condition:—

[1] Thus Wallace argues: Man 'must therefore have diverged from the common ancestral form before the existing types of anthropoid apes had diverged from one another. Now, this divergence almost certainly took place as early as the miocene period,' etc. (*Darwinism*, pp. 455-456). So Geikie in British Association Address (above).

1. Negatively, I would say first, that it is a false issue to represent the view just stated as following necessarily from the principles of evolution. From the Darwinian theory of evolution it does follow; but that view, which transforms man from the apes by slow and insensible gradations, through natural selection, has been shown to be without sufficient warrant, and is widely discredited among naturalists themselves. The time for it, as we have seen, cannot be allowed; the agencies invoked—fortuitous variation, natural selection, and survival of the fittest—could never have brought it about; chief of all, it is contradicted by the facts of man's mental and moral nature, which show him to stand on a different platform altogether from the animals, and to require a special cause for his origin. But if such a special cause is postulated, and it is allowed that man represents, mentally and physically, a *rise* on the previous orders of nature—that with him there is the introduction of something new, the founding of a new kingdom — then there is nothing to require that, on his first appearance, man should answer to the degrading descriptions that are given of him. It is a mistake, therefore,

on the part of those who reject pure Darwinism to think, as they often seem to do, that evolution commits them to assume that man must begin at the lowest savage state, or a degree below it. The logical ground for such a contention is parted with, when it is granted that man is not an evolution by slow and insensible gradations from the ape, but is the beginning of a new order. If Professor Huxley's 'jumps' in nature are warrantable anywhere, surely it is here.[1] If the idea of slow transition is discarded as a necessary implicate of a theory of evolution—and I think it must—man may have been in his origin as pure and upright as the most orthodox theory requires.[2]

2. Palæontology, as before shown, bears this out: on the one hand, in failing to furnish any evidence of intermediate forms between man and

---

[1] Prof. G. F. Wright, in his article on the Lansing Skull (*Bib. Sacra*, 1903, p. 30) says: 'There is not adequate scientific evidence going to show that the origin of man, even on the evolutionary hypothesis, was not a sudden leap, which might well involve a divine interference, and might properly be called a miracle. Those evolutionists who maintain that the passage from the physical development of the lower members of the anthropoid family to that of man was by infinitesimal stages have few facts to go upon, and are taking an immense leap in the dark.'

[2] See passage quoted from Otto (*Theol. Rund.*, 1903, p. 233), in Note XI. on The Sudden Origin of Man.

PRIMITIVE CONDITION OF MAN 183

the ape; and, on the other, by the accumulating evidence it affords that in brain capacity and physical characteristics, primeval man stood on as high a level as the average man of to-day. This is the disconcerting thing for evolutionism, that, however far the remains of man are carried back, we never get any nearer a being not man: the oldest skulls are quite as good as the new. Professor Huxley's testimony was cited in last lecture to the high and human character of the Engis and even of the (somewhat more degraded, but less ancient) Neanderthal skulls.[1] The famous 'Old Man of Cro-Magnon' (palæolithic) is described as 'of great stature, being nearly six feet high' (other specimens of the race are seven feet) '. . . The skull proper, or brain case, is very long—more so than in ordinary skulls— and this length is accompanied with a great breadth ; so that the brain was of greater size than in average modern men, and the frontal region was largely and well developed.'[2] The higher the antiquity of these skulls, the greater

---

[1] See above, p. 132. Cf. Wright's *Man and the Glacial Period*, pp. 275-276.
[2] Dawson, *Meeting-Place of Geology and History*, pp. 53-54.

the difficulty for the evolutionist; it is not infrequently, therefore, from the anthropological side that the stoutest opposition comes to the admission of their age.[1] So we read in the article of the *London Quarterly Review*, formerly quoted, on the Calaveras skull, attributed by some to the pliocene period: 'Mr. Laing is doubtful: and well he may be, for the skull is of a very high type, resembling those of the modern Eskimo, and if it be a genuine pliocene relic, it deals a death-blow to the idea that man was developed from an ape, or any ape-like creature.' Dr. Dawson writes of a European skeleton found in pliocene beds at Castelnedolo, near Brescia: 'Unfortunately the skull of the only perfect skeleton is said to have been of fair proportions and superior to those of the ruder types of post-glacial men. This has cast a shade of suspicion on the discovery, especially on the part of evolutionists who think

[1] This has been anew exemplified in the case of the Lansing Skull, of which Professor Wright says: 'The skull does not differ, in its shape and capacity, to any appreciable extent, from that of some of the modern Indian tribes, or at any rate of individuals of these tribes.' He remarks that 'the most persistent *a priori* objections to a recognition of this skeleton as of glacial age comes from the anthropologists' (*Bib. Sacra*, 1903, p. 29). Professor Chamberlin, *e.g.*, assigns to it 'a very respectable antiquity, but much short of the glacial invasion.' See Note XII. on The Lansing Skeleton.

PRIMITIVE CONDITION OF MAN

that it is not in accordance with theory that man should retrograde between the pliocene and the early modern period, instead of advancing.'[1] The state of the case seems well summed up by the *London Quarterly Review* writer, of whose words I again avail myself. 'On reviewing the whole period of prehistoric times,' he says, 'the idea which strikes us most forcibly is the high intellectual character of the earliest men. The palæolithic men—the first revealed to us by science—had heads as large as, or even larger than, the average inhabitant of Western Europe in the present day, and they must have possessed brains at least equal in size to any men now living, while in strength and stature and form they were as far removed from apes as are the modern Europeans. . . . It is therefore certain that geological and archæological research has given a verdict strongly opposed to the idea that man has been developed from an ape, or from any ape-like creature whatever.'

3. The facts already adverted to as to the high

---

[1] *Geology and History*, p. 29. It seems now commonly agreed that the presence of the skeletons in these beds is due to interment (*Man and Glacial Period*, App. p. 366).

character of early civilisation are adverse to the theory of the slow evolutionary origin and original brutishness of man. Instead of finding man more savage as we push his history backward in Egypt and Babylonia, we find him possessed of most of the elements of civilisation—and I shall add of purer ideas of divine things—than he subsequently entertained. The progress of discovery here in recent years has been a continual series of surprises. We are taken back 6000 or 7000 years B.C., probably more than half the total period of man's existence; and still we find arts, letters, laws, religion, cities, temples, and most of the things we identify with progress. This, too, in those regions which most now acknowledge to be the original centres of the distribution of the populations of the world. The rude and degraded races, on the other hand, are, as a rule, not found near the centre of distribution, but in outlying parts. 'It is a fact,' says the Duke of Argyll, in a chapter which deserves study in his *Unity of Nature*, 'that the lowest and rudest tribes in the population of the globe have been found at the farthest extremities of its larger continents, or in the distant islands of its great oceans, or among the hills and forests which in every land have been the last refuge of the victims of violence and misfortune.'[1]

4. To all which I may add, that there is yet no evidence of a really degraded or savage tribe having raised itself out of its degradation without contact with a prior higher civilisation. The statement of Dr. Whately stands yet unrefuted. 'Facts,' he says, 'are stubborn things, and that no authenticated instance can be produced of savages that ever *did* emerge unaided from that state is no *theory*, but a statement, hitherto never refuted, of a matter of fact.'[2]

And now, in concluding this discussion, I would have you look at the matter again in the light of *the true idea of man.* I put the question earlier: Is it enough to constitute the image of God in man that he should possess these essential attributes —personality, rationality, morality?—or is it not also required that he should be in a moral state actually conformable to rectitude? I mean, if man is a moral being by nature and destination,

[1] Page 426. See his examples, and the evidence in a former note to the fact of degradation among savages.
[2] Exeter Hall Lecture on *The Origin of Civilisation.*

is it reasonable or allowable to suppose that he would be launched on time in a *non-moral* or *immoral* condition? For it cannot be overlooked that if a moral being is in a state unconformable to moral law—a state in which passion has the ascendency over reason and conscience, in which the latter are a mere glimmer or potentiality, while wild, ungoverned impulses rule—he is not merely in an *immature*, but is in a *wrong* moral state. Moral law requires not merely the *presence* of the elements of a moral nature, but the due harmony of the elements of the nature, the due subordination of desire and passion to reason— it requires moral clearness, moral purity, moral freedom; and of all these things the state described is the negation. I do not mean, as I said before, that the moral conditions are not satisfied by a state of great simplicity—of relative childlikeness —but that it requires the pure nature and inner harmony of soul which gives the possibility of sinless development. Where that is absent, and fierceness, cruelty, and lust rule instead—made worse, not better, by self-consciousness—you have, not a moral being in the true sense, but a being whose nature is a self-contradiction. In consistency with His very aim, therefore, of introducing upon the earth a being fitted to be its lord—the rational and moral image of Himself—it would seem that the Creator could not introduce man in the condition supposed. It shocks our ideas of God's holiness, of His real care and interest in man, of His *Fatherhood*—of which many who hold these views I am combating make so much—to think that He would do so. What kind of a father is it—we are entitled to ask—who would launch his children into the world, as God is supposed to have launched man, and would have left them for uncounted ages to struggle upwards as best they could out of bestial conditions? The Fatherhood that is compatible with such a theory is not the Fatherhood of the Gospel.

I take it, then, that the view which accords best with the Biblical doctrine, and with the Christian gospel of redemption, is also that which accords best with the facts of man's nature, and with what we are entitled to expect from just views of God. It is not unreasonable to believe —and I for one do believe it—that man was introduced into the world in a manner and state conformable with his moral nature, his destination to sonship with God, and his glorious prerogative of immortality—through which features he is distinguished from all below him; that, not in name only, but in reality, he was made in the image of God. He need not have been mentally developed in any high degree; but, as a pure being, he would stand in a relation to God, and would be the recipient of communications from Him, suited to start him on his high career. He would not be left an *orphaned* being; God in some way would be around him, near him, taking him in hand as his teacher and guide. We are, after all, wonderfully near the old story of the Book of Genesis in this; and that book, I take it, gives us in essence more sound philosophy on this point than all the sages we can consult.

My treatment would still be incomplete if I did not ask you further to observe how, from this whole subject we have been considering, there emerge the two grand truths which enter so deeply into our Christian view of man—the *divine sonship* of man, and his *immortal destiny*. Sonship, I grant, is an idea to which, as respects the individual, we find only approximations in the Old Testament;[1] it is in its perfection a revelation of the Gospel. Yet already it lies in principle in the fact that man is made in God's image, has rational and ethical resemblance to Him, and through this spiritual affinity is capable of knowing, loving, and serving Him. This, at least, we must surely say of sonship—that it lay in man's destiny, even as created, to be a son of God ; to sustain a filial relation to Him. I mean by that, that we must assume it to have lain in God's purpose to take this being He had created, as the goal of His dealings with him, into that relation of free, loving, trustful fellowship with Himself, which we properly describe as filial. And in that destiny—in that capacity, and in the destination itself—there already lies the pledge of *immortality*. How this is related to the subject of physical death I shall consider in a future lecture. But that man, in the make and constitution of his being, as bearing the image of God, is adapted for a larger and more enduring life than that of time, I am entitled to assume. That mind of his, looking before and after; that spirit, awed with thoughts of the infinite and

[1] *E.g.*, Ps. ciii. 13.

eternal, capable of infinite growth, endowed for relations of fellowship with the Infinite One, aspiring, through every faculty, to a knowledge, an activity, a blessedness, greater than any which earth can yield—would be an inexplicable riddle, a hopeless self-contradiction, if immortality were not his destiny. It is here, as I have already urged, that we perceive most clearly the bearings on our Christian faith of naturalistic theories of evolution. If man, by the make of his being, has an affinity to God which gives him the capacity for sonship, does not this constitute a deeper line of demarcation between him and the animals than any we have yet considered? On the other hand, on the theory of insensible gradations, where does the potency for sonship come in? Is God the God of the man, or is He of the ape also? The difficulty is even greater, as I emphasised before, with respect to immortality. It is a loose way of thinking which conceives the immortality which is man's prerogative as only the natural life indefinitely prolonged. A being made for immortality, destined for it, and having the potency of it within him by creation, is on a plane of things as much above the animal as heaven is above the earth. The Gospel brings life and incorruption to light;[1] but the basis in man's nature on which that great hope is built is laid in the first utterance about man in the Bible. I claim, then, that the Biblical view of man, in his nature and original condition, is the only view entirely coherent with itself, and in agreement with its own presuppositions in the character of God. Nor has it been shown to be contradicted by any real truth or discovery of science.

[1] 2 Tim. i. 10.

Scripture and Science on the Origin and
Nature of Sin—The Defacement of
God's Image

Defacement of God's Image Matter of Experience. If Man Created pure, a 'Fall' is presupposed. Idea of Sin as Apostacy from God underlies all Scripture. Counter-theory that Man has not *Fallen* but *Risen*. Objections to this View. On Evolutionary Theory Sin loses its 'Catastrophic' Character. Alleged necessity of Sin (Fiske, Sabatier, etc.). Evolutionary theory robs Sin of its Gravity. Effect on Idea of Guilt. Insufficient to speak of Realisation of Moral Ideal. Moral Law demands an Upright Nature and Pure Affections from the first. Biblical Doctrine of Sin: that which absolutely Ought not to be. Contrast of Religious and Philosophical Ethics. Sin as violation of Duty to God. Religion recognises Duties to God as well as to Man. Inmost Principle of Sin: Self-Will, Egoism. Sins graded on this Principle. Narrative of Fall. Connection with Superhuman Evil. Effects of Sin. 1. The *Spiritual* consequence of Sin in Depravation. Bond cut with God. Ascendency of Lower Impulses. Sin as Anarchy and Bondage. 2. The *Racial* Consequences of Sin. Organic Constitution of Race. Relation to Doctrine of Heredity. 'Ape and Tiger' Theory of Original Sin. Objection to Doctrine from Non-transmissibility of Acquired Characters (Weismann). Effects of Ethical Volition on Mind and Body *are* transmissible. Roman Catholic and Protestant Views of the Hereditary Effects of the Fall. Meaning of 'Total Depravity.'

V

SCRIPTURE AND SCIENCE ON THE ORIGIN AND NATURE OF SIN—THE DEFACEMENT OF GOD'S IMAGE

THE conclusions reached in the foregoing discussion have evidently important bearings on the doctrine of sin. If man was created in the image of God, and if that image included a pure and harmonious state of the moral nature, it is certain that man does not bear that undimmed image now. From its first pages to its last, Scripture assumes that man is not in a condition corresponding to his being's end and aim, but is in a state of apostacy from God, and morally impure. The indestructible elements of that image—rationality, self-consciousness, conscience, faculty of choice—he indeed continues to possess, else he would not be man.[1] But the realisation of the divine image in actual moral likeness to God is no longer his.

[1] Cf. Gen. ix. 6; James iii. 9.

He is no longer a being over whom the Creator could pronounce the words 'very good.' But if man was made good, and now is evil, the inference is irresistible that he has become so by voluntary departure from rectitude. And if this condition is universal, as Scripture and experience unite in showing it to be, this can only mean that the defection must be carried back to the fountainhead of the race: in other words, is due to what we are accustomed to speak of as a *fall*.

This doctrine that sin has its origin in man's voluntary act, and entered at the beginning of the race, is, it may be confidently said, the only one that puts sin on a right basis. The assertion, indeed, is not uncommon that, while the doctrine of a fall from original uprightness is found in the beginning of Genesis, and reappears in the theology of Paul, it is not a doctrine recognised elsewhere in the Old Testament—for example, in the prophets.[1] This, however, is a contention which I think it will be found difficult to maintain. Even on the principles of the critics, it can hardly be doubted that the story

---

[1] Cf. Tennant, *The Fall and Original Sin*, pp. 90 ff.

of Eden and of the sin of man was known to the prophets. It formed part of the sacred tradition of their nation, and is found in that part of the narrative of Genesis (the Jehovistic) which is generally admitted to have been drawn up, and in circulation, before written prophecy began.[1] But a deeper argument is that based on the whole tenor of the Scriptural representation of man. At no point in Scripture history does man appear as standing in right or normal relations with God. His condition is invariably pictured as, naturally, one of rebellion against God, and of great and deepening corruption.[2]

[1] The JE narrative of the critics is usually dated '*before* Amos or Hosea' (Driver, *Genesis*, p. xvi.). The newer form of the critical theory also, in putting P later than JE, presupposes that P was acquainted with the contents of JE. Thus Wellhausen writes: 'In JE the flood is well led up to ; in Q [= P] we should be inclined to ask in surprise how the earth has come all at once to be so corrupted, after being in the best of order, did we not know it from JE ' (*History of Israel*, p. 310). Even Carpenter, after informing us that P 'knows no Eden,' etc., writes: 'If the *Toledh'oth* [P] sections do not describe the origin of evil and the entry of sin and suffering, they are not indifferent to them, rather does the method of Genesis v. presuppose them, and Chap. vi. 13 records their consequences' (Oxford *Hex.* i. p. 132).

[2] Dillmann, in his *Alttest. Theol.*, while attributing the story of the fall to the deeper insight of the prophetic narrator (J), nevertheless holds that the Old Testament everywhere presupposes the rule of sin and death in humanity, in contradiction to its original destiny,

What language could be stronger than that in Genesis of the race before the Flood: 'God saw that the wickedness of man was *great* in the earth, and that *every* imagination of the *thoughts* of his heart was *only* evil continually.'[1] Could the universality of human transgression be more vividly depicted than in Psalm xiv. 2 : 'The Lord looked down from heaven upon the children of men, to see if there were any that did understand, that did seek after God. They are all gone aside : they are together become filthy ; there is none that doeth good, no, not one' ? The prophets depict a moral condition in Israel and in the surrounding heathen peoples in the highest degree abhorrent to Jehovah, and bringing down on them His severest judgments. I need

---

and the presence of an inborn evil tendency (pp. 368, 376, ff.). 'So,' he concludes, 'we are brought back to the doctrine of the prophetic narrator of an original state [of integrity] and fall of the first man, who, from an uncorrupted nature, giving entrance to sin, did that which had fatal consequences for the whole race' (p. 380).

[1] Gen. vi. 5; cf. viii. 21. Mr. Tennant will not allow that even in the 'Jahvist' writer this evil imagination is connected with the fall which that writer narrates, and even holds it to be 'expressly implied' in Chap. viii. 21 (God's compassion) 'that such an evil inclination is partly due to the constitution which man received at the hand of his Maker' (*Fall and Original Sin*, p. 98). Why, then, should God judge it as He does ?

not remind you of Paul's description of the origin of heathenism through voluntary parting with an original knowledge of God—'knowing God, they glorified Him not as God, neither gave thanks; but became vain in their reasonings, and their senseless heart was darkened';[1] or of his demonstration of how both Jews and Gentiles have come short of God's glory, and are under condemnation.[2] The only reasonable presupposition of such a moral condition—if human beings were created as we should expect—is a voluntary declension of the race from an original state of uprightness. If a fall were not narrated in the opening chapters of Genesis, we should still have to postulate something of the kind to account for the Bible's own representations of the state of man.[3]

To this Scriptural doctrine of the origin of human sin through man's voluntary renunciation

[1] Rom. i. 21.   [2] Rom. iii.
[3] Whether is it more reasonable to regard the story of the fall as a private speculation of a prophetic narrator, which there is nothing in the narrative to suggest it was (it plainly gives itself out in its whole character and Babylonian colouring as old); or as a genuine world-old reminiscence of the most tragic event in the history of the race?

of his allegiance to his Creator, it has already been shown that the modern evolutionary philosophy stands in strongest opposition.[1] It is an axiom of the modern view that man has not, as theology has taught, fallen, but has *risen*; that his history has been a slow ascent from an incredibly low state of animalism to his present high stage of attainment; that the forces through which this rise is effected are inherent in human nature, and operate through the law of selection and survival of the fittest. To speak of an Eden in the past which man has forfeited is held to be in contradiction with every principle of modern knowledge. I have already given my reasons for believing that this account of man's origin and primitive condition, and of his slow ascent from lowest savagery to noblest civilisation, cannot be sustained. There is no evidence, I have sought to show, that man was originally in this unspeakably degraded condition, and there is the strongest *a priori* presumption, derived from his moral constitution and relationship to God, that he was not. There is no proof that, if he ever was in the low state

---

[1] See above, pp. 14 ff., 157 ff.

described, he could by his unaided powers have raised himself out of it. There is no analogy to such spontaneous rise from lower to higher. It has been shown that the assumption that savage races — whether modern or prehistoric — stand nearer to primitive man, is unfounded.[1] Savage races, as experience proves, have all the moral and spiritual capabilities which we ourselves possess, and behind them often stand the evidences of higher civilisation. What explanation could be given of incalculable ages of immobile savagery, to be followed, within the last few thousand years, by a sudden leap into advanced civilisation? Much stronger is the probability that primeval man stood nearer in capacity to the races that evolved the mighty civilisations we are now disinterring from the mounds of Assyria and Babylonia, than to any feebler type.

Yet not only is this doctrine of man's primitive barbarism, and of his slow ascent through natural evolution to his present intellectual, moral, social, and religious eminence, an article of faith in the new science; but it is taken

[1] See, further, the valuable remarks on this subject in the Duke of Argyll's *Unity of Nature*, pp. 378, 386 ff., 522 ff.

over by Christian teachers, and is rapidly becoming an article of faith in the 'new theology,' which, it is claimed, is to displace the old. That through it the doctrine of sin, as hitherto understood, undergoes a vital alteration, is hardly denied. Sin, in truth, ceases to be sin, in the full Biblical sense of the term. It loses the tragic and catastrophic character it possesses on the Biblical view, and becomes a necessity of man's development—a stage it was inevitable man should pass through in the course of his moral ascent. That this is so in the coarser forms of naturalistic evolutionism is apparent at a glance. There is, as we saw, a positive gloating on the part of writers like Haeckel over man's alleged natural degradation, and subjection to determinism. It is in the image of the ape man is made, not in the image of God. But even in writers of a higher stamp — and it is important to notice this—there is no shrinking from the assertion of the necessity of sin, or what is called such. In Mr. Fiske, *e.g.*, by whom the story of Eden is made a pale reflection of Zoroastrianism, the necessity of sin is deduced from what he calls 'the element of antagonism' in the universe. It

ORIGIN AND NATURE OF SIN 205

is undeniable, he says, that we cannot know anything except as contrasted with something else.[1] 'If we had never felt physical pain, we could not recognise physical pleasure. . . . In just the same way it follows that, without knowing that which is morally evil, we could not possibly recognise that which is morally good. Of these antagonistic correlatives, the one is unthinkable in absence of the other. . . . In a happy world there must be sorrow and pain, and in a moral world the knowledge of evil is indispensable. The stern necessity for this has been proved to inhere in the innermost constitution of the human soul. It is part and parcel of the universe.'[2]

It is worth while following this out a little further. The existence of moral evil, it is said, is 'purely relative,' yet it is 'profoundly real, and in a process of perpetual spiritual evolution its presence in some hideous form throughout a long series of upward stages is indispensable. . . . In a process of spiritual evolution, therefore, evil must be present. But the nature of evolution also requires that it be evanescent.'[3]

---

[1] *Through Nature to God*, pp. 34-35.
[2] *Ibid.*, pp. 36-37.   [3] *Ibid.*, pp. 54-55.

If we inquire how this 'evanescence' of evil is to be brought about, we find ourselves quite able to dispense with any supernatural help, and with the agency of a Redeemer; this, too, it must be said, is the true logic of the theory. 'From the general analogies furnished in the process of evolution, we are entitled to hope that, as it approaches its goal, and man comes nearer to God, the fact of evil will lapse into a mere memory, in which the shadowed past shall serve as a background for the realised glory of the present.'[1] Professor A. Sabatier, also, in the Preface to his *Philosophy of Religion*, in replying to criticisms, boldly affirms sin to be a necessity for man by his creation, and explicitly accepts determinism. But, I ask, can this account of the nature of sin be admitted by any one who in his conscience has realised the awful and tragic significance of that dread reality? Does it not rather evacuate sin of all its real meaning? If sin lies in the constitution of things by creation—if it is a necessary outcome of the condition in which God made man, and of the nature He has given him—how can the creature be asked to assume

[1] *Ibid.*, p. 55.

responsibility—at least *serious* responsibility—for it? I do not think much time need be spent over Mr. Fiske's assumed law of antagonism—a sort of survival of the Zoroastrianism he condemns, with a touch of Hegelian dialectic thrown in. Evil, indeed, can only be known as the negation of good ;[1] but it does not follow that good —the positive conception—can only be known through experience of evil. This is precisely the serpent's doctrine in Eden over again. I do not know how Mr. Fiske would apply his doctrine to God Himself; but it is reasonably obvious that logic would require him to take up sin into the life of the Absolute—else how could God be good?—or to deny moral character to Deity altogether. Christian faith, at least, which knows of *one* absolutely sinless Personality in the history of mankind, will not be readily led away by these *a priori* sophisms.

It is now to be observed, however, that, even where the *word* 'necessity' is not used, the thing is still there in every evolutionary theory in which sin is viewed as an unavoidable result of man's nature and environment. I do not say that, in

[1] See below, p. 215.

some of these theories, there may not still be room for a measure of voluntary departure from such weak and wavering standards of right as man, even in his rudimentary stage, may be supposed to recognise. Grant everything that can be asked on this score; allow that from the beginning there stirs in man's nature the distinctively human element, that in some dim way ideas of right and wrong begin to shape themselves, that there are still possible certain elementary exercises of choice, which sometimes may be morally better, sometimes morally worse. Still this in no way yields us the Biblical idea of sin. This departure from rudimentary ideas of right in a being still rude and ignorant, wild and lawless in his passions, fierce and cruel in disposition, violent and sensual in his conduct, is so natural, so inevitable, so forced on him by his nature and circumstances—the palliation for even grosser violations of morality is so great—that nothing like *serious* responsibility can be held to attach to such a being for his 'falls'; the idea of guilt is weakened almost to the vanishing point; while the enormity of the wrong act as *sin*, i.e., as offence against God, practically disappears, for

ORIGIN AND NATURE OF SIN

there is hardly any idea of God, or of responsibility to Him, to produce the sense of sin, not to say to give depth and gravity to it. If it be considered that these theories, even the highest of them : (1) leave the greater part of what is ordinarily considered wrongdoing—*e.g.*, lust, cruelty, bloodshed, cannibalism—outside the category of sin, on the ground that the conscience of primitive man was not yet sufficiently developed to regard these things as wrong ; (2) attribute to man's first ideas of right and wrong so feeble and confused a character that disobedience to them is a transgression absolutely venial ; (3) deprive his acts, as just said, of the character of *sin*, through the absence of serious moral views of God ; (4) preclude the *possibility* of a sinless development of the race—it will be seen, I think, that the acceptance of such views, however earnestly held, must involve a subversion of the Biblical conception, which has for its presuppositions God's changeless holiness in His relations with man, moral law apprehended with sufficient clearness to show man his duty, the possibility of obedience, and sin as voluntary departure from rectitude.

It looks plausible, I know, to say that, however low we begin with man—however savage or semi-brutal his primitive condition—there is still *some* point at which the moral consciousness awakens, and man's 'fall' takes place whenever consciously he prefers something which, even by his poor standard, he counts wrong. This is the idea which lies behind most of those modern theories of the 'fall' to which reference was made in a former lecture.[1] But, apart from the objection just urged of the attenuation of the ideas of sin and guilt, it is a defect of these theories that they take no account of the fact that it is wrong for a moral being to be in this state of unredeemed brutality at all; that morality requires not only moral *acts*, but moral *state* and dispositions, right affections, harmony of the will with what is good; and that of all this the state supposed is the absolute negation. It does not rid us of this difficulty to talk of the moral ideal as in *process* of realisation. That ideal is not a

---

[1] See above, p. 158. It will be seen from the above argument that I am not fairly open to the charge of setting aside these theories, or the view of man's origin on which they depend, in the interest of a 'dogma,' or for the sake of what some may be pleased to call an old scrap of Hebrew literature—the early chapters of Genesis. I base my objections on the far deeper ground that *sin is actually sin*—one of the surest 'value-judgments' I know. (Cf. p. 300.)

thing which belongs to man's perfected condition only, but has its claims upon him from the first, and demands balanced, harmonious, dutiful character at *every* stage of the development.[1] May I not add that it is an unwarranted assumption in all these evolutionary theories that the highest type in a series is only to be looked for at its close. It is not clear that it has been so even in nature, for while on the whole, of course, there has been advance, it is likewise true that, in the different orders, the higher forms—in some cases, witness *e.g.*, the colossal reptiles of the mesozoic age, the very highest—appear early, to be followed by degradation or extinction.[2] It has not been so in philosophy, in literature, in art; there, as a rule, the master-spirits, the epoch-makers—the Homers, the Platos, the Shakespeares, the Handels, the Kants and Hegels—come first, and give the lead which others *longo intervallo* follow. It has certainly not been so in Christianity. In it the Archetype *precedes* the development which results from Him and is determined by Him, and which,

[1] Cf. Dorner, *System of Doctrine*, iii. pp. 36-37.

[2] 'Each new organic form, or each new variety of both, seems always to have been introduced with a wonderful energy of life' (Argyll, *Unity of Nature*, p. 425).

in Church and individual, is yet far from having attained its 'perfect measure.'[1] Why should it not have been so with man? Who can say that it was not?

In antithesis to these evolutionary conceptions, we have now to look at the Biblical conception of sin, and of its effects on human nature in the defacement of God's image. Sin, in the Biblical point of view, is, as I have already said, the tragedy of the universe. It is that which absolutely *ought not to be*: 'not something natural, normal, and necessary, but, both as actual and as hereditary, something which must find its explanation in a free act of the creature, annulling the original relation of the creature to God.'[2] Sin, therefore, it is first to be observed, is not merely an *ethical*, but, as Ritschl truly says, is a *religious* conception.[3] It does not denote simply wrong of man against man, but expresses a relation of the individual and his action to *God*. It does not regard the wrong act simply as violation or transgression of moral law, but as violation of duty towards God, or offence against

---

[1] Eph. iv. 13. [2] *Christian View of God,* p. 174.
[3] *Justification and Reconciliation,* pp. 350, 353; cf. p. 27 (E. T.).

Him. 'Against Thee, Thee only, have I sinned.'[1] Ordinarily we speak of sins against our fellow-men; in strictness we *wrong* our fellow-men—we *sin* against God. It is this reference to God, I think we may say, which chiefly differentiates *philosophical ethics* — the ethics of the moral philosophy class-room—from the *ethics of religion*, in their respective judgments upon conduct. Moral science, like religion, works with the ideas of law, duty, right, wrong; but its standard is the law in reason—in conscience; it does not bring deeds into the light of God's judgment, or regard them in their turpitude as offences against Him. Religion, on the other hand, views moral law itself as emanating from God, and having its ground in His essential Being; it brings conduct, and behind conduct the state of the heart, into the light of the divine holiness; it judges of the quality of the deed by its contrariety to the divine purity, and by its enormity as disobedience to the divine will. We cannot, therefore, speak properly of *sin* except in the sphere of religion; and only that religion can yield an adequate idea of sin which, like the Biblical, is based on a right conception of God as

[1] Ps. li 4

the all-holy and all-good.[1] There is, however, a *second* respect, arising from the same cause, in which philosophical ethics and the ethics of religion differ. The philosophical treatment, as a rule, takes cognisance of duty only as it relates to man himself and to his fellow-men; it does not take cognisance of any special class of duties which relate directly to God. Duty falls under the two main heads of duties to ourselves and to our neighbours; it is completed when we have discharged our obligations in these two directions. But religion goes far beyond this. If we stand in relations to our fellow-men, far more fundamentally do we stand in relation to God, and owe to Him our love, trust, reverence, obedience, with their appropriate manifestations in worship. Nay, our duties to our fellow-men will not be rightly performed, from the religious point of view, unless where this higher duty to God is fulfilled. To love the Lord our God with all our heart, and soul, and strength, and mind—this, Jesus says, is the *first* and great commandment; and the second is like to it, 'Thou shalt love thy neighbour as thyself.'[2]

[1] In philosophical ethics, as in Kant, you have *auto*nomy; in religion, as J. Müller points out, *theo*nomy.

[2] Matt. xxii. 36-40; Mark xii. 29-31.

Sin, therefore, is not simply wrongdoing as between man and man, but, far more radically, consists in a wrong state of heart and will towards God. It is not simply ἀνομία in the narrower sense, but ἀσέβεια—godlessness.

This fundamental judgment in regard to the nature of sin is now to be borne in mind in the attempt to discover the *true principle* of sin—that which underlies, and gives unity to, all its manifestations. The first thing to be distinctly held fast here is, that sin, as that which absolutely ought not to be, subsists only as the *negation* or *contradiction* of the good—has no meaning or quality as evil save as the antithesis of the good of which it is the contradiction. What, then, shall we say is the inner principle or essence of the good? Kant has finely said that there is nothing truly good on earth but a good will,[1] and he finds the principle of that good will in unconditional reverence for the moral law. Religion, however, goes yet deeper, and, in accordance with the distinction between philosophical and religious ethics just indicated, finds, with Augustine, the true principle of the good will in

[1] *Groundwork of Met. of Ethics*, ch. i.

love to God.[1] A will destitute of that principle—a neutral, indeterminate will, if such a thing were possible—still more a will enthralled and controlled by passion—would not be a good will in the religious sense. In contrast with this, how are we now to define the principle of the evil will? Shall we say with Martensen that the essence of sin is the choice of the world instead of God [2]—the loving and serving of the creature more than the Creator? [3] Or must we not go deeper, and, with Augustine again, say that the real essence of the evil act, when man chooses the world, is not his making the world his end, but the *self-will* which throws off God's authority, and arrogates to itself the right to choose its own end, and that another end than God's? Here, probing the matter to its core, we seem to get at the real principle of sin. The principle of the good is love to God, subjection of the whole will to God. Sin in its essence is the taking into the will of the principle *opposite* to this—that not God's will, but my own will, is to be the ultimate law of my life.

[1] On Augustine's views, cf. my *Progress of Dogma*, pp. 145 ff.; and see below, p. 123.
[2] Cf. Martensen's *Ethics*, i. pp. 96 ff.
[3] Cf. Rom. i. 25.

It is the exaltation of self against God: the setting up of self-will against God's will: at bottom *Egoism*.

While sin is the product of this baleful principle, it by no means follows that it discovers its full heinousness, or works out its whole deadly effect, in the first moment of transgression, or for long thereafter.[1] Still, it is in the nature of a principle to manifest itself, and, however veiled the real nature of the egoistic principle in sin may be from the subject himself, or in its first manifestations, it is certain, sooner or later, to reveal itself in its true and naked character. This, in truth, is the principle according to which, as we find, we can most naturally *grade* the manifestations of sin in history. (1) Lowest in the scale stand *fleshly* sins—lust, drunkenness, and the like—which often, through the social element involved, have the power of veiling for a time the naked selfishness of the principle in which they originate. It is, however, a poor disguise at the best; and closer observation soon discovers, in the callous heartlessness with which

[1] There are many checks to the working out of this principle in the action of conscience, the natural affections, the sense of shame, prudential considerations, and, at a more developed stage, in human law, education, social custom, public opinion, impressions of religion, etc.

the lustful man throws off his victim, and in the drunkard's cruel neglect of wife and home, how the Satanic side of fleshly sin leers through all the coverings by which sentiment or joviality may seek to mask its hideousness. (2) Mounting higher, we enter the sphere of *spiritual* sin— pride, vanity, envy, jealousy, love of power, covetousness, etc.; and how clearly here is the egoistic principle manifest—exaltation of self, grasping for self, isolation of self, resentment at the rivalry or success of others! (3) More hateful still—now merging in the *diabolical*— are those phases of sin in which evil is loved for its own sake—cruelty for cruelty's sake, wanton delight in the ruin or infliction of suffering on others; undisguised malevolence or malice. (4) The final stage is reached when, throwing off its last cloak, evil comes boldly out as God-hating, God-denying, God-blaspheming — the stage of *blasphemy*—as has happened in memorable periods of the world's history.[1] Evil which has reached this height of wilful sinning against

---

[1] On the development and forms of sin, cf. Müller, *Doctrine of Sin*, i. pp. 147-182; specially on this last stage, see Christlieb, *Modern Doubt*, pp. 138-140.

light puts the subject of it almost past redemption. It is the prelude to final obduracy: the blasphemy against the Holy Ghost[1]—the sin unto death[2]—for which, when consummated, there is no repentance.

Sin, therefore, in its essential nature, is a revolt of the creature will against the Creator—a voluntary departure from the good. This is precisely the idea embodied in the old-world story of the fall in Genesis, where sensuous allurement, and the desire for forbidden knowledge, have behind them the subtle infusion of doubt of God's Word into the mind—'Yea, hath God said.'[3] It is in the inward defection from God, not in the mere eating of the tree, that sin begins, that the real fall takes place.[4] This, however, is not the whole. It is a feature of the story which should not be neglected that temptation comes to the woman *from without*—from the serpent; which, whether taken literally or symbolically, represents here

[1] Matt. xii. 31. [2] 1 John v. 16. [3] Gen. iii. 1.

[4] Mr. Tennant, with Wellhausen, evacuates the story of nearly all moral content, by denying that the knowledge of 'good and evil' gained by eating of the tree was 'moral knowledge' . . . 'it is, on the contrary, general knowledge, or cleverness, which is here prohibited, and which man is represented as anxious to possess' (*The Fall and Original Sin*, pp. 13, 14).

a power of evil suggestion other than man's own thoughts. It is not enough to say that the serpent is simply one of the beasts of the field which the Lord had made: the 'subtilty' it displays rises above animal conditions into the region of the preternatural.[1] The serpent of the story not only *talks*—of itself a feature contrary to the tenor of the Bible representations, which carefully observe the limits between man and the animals—but it talks *evil*,[2] which, if nothing more than an animal is intended, conflicts with the idea of a good creation by Jehovah. Those, indeed, who treat the narrative as sym-

[1] Dr. Driver says: 'It appears soon, however, that it [the serpent] is more than an ordinary animal; it possesses the faculty of speech, which it exercises with supreme intelligence and skill. . . . The serpent had, moreover, in antiquity, the reputation of wisdom (cf. Matt. x. 16), especially in a bad sense; it was insidious, malevolent, "subtil." And so it appears here as the representative of the power of *temptation*; it puts forth with great artfulness suggestions which, when embraced, and carried into action, give rise to sinful desires and sinful acts. The serpent is not, however, identified in the narrative with the Evil·One' (*Genesis*, p. 44).

[2] Cf. Oehler, *Old Test. Theol.* i. p. 250. Mr. Tennant understates the case when he says that in the story 'the serpent is regarded as clever rather than evil' (*The Fall and Original Sin*, p. 28). Dr. Driver comments on Gen. iii. 4, 5: 'The serpent now goes on to deny flatly the truth of the [divine] threat, to suggest an unworthy motive for it, and to hold out the hope of a great boon to be secured by disobedience' (p. 45).

ORIGIN AND NATURE OF SIN

bolical—its elements borrowed from Babylonia —are least of all entitled to take the serpent as a simple animal, and few of them, perhaps, do.[1] It is, I take it, best interpreted as the personification of an evil principle outside man[2] —if not yet the 'Satan' or 'Devil' of later Scripture, yet in consonance with that idea, and a stage on the way towards it. It will not be denied that the idea that evil originated on our earth through an Evil One—through contact with a superhuman Evil—is one deeply embedded in the *New* Testament.[3]

A catastrophe, then, permitted by God in His

---

[1] Professor W. R. Smith (quoted by Tennant, p. 28) says: 'The demoniac character of the serpent in the garden of Eden is unmistakable; the serpent is not a mere temporary disguise of Satan,' etc. Mr. Tennant himself says: 'He was even more than the ordinary Jinn or demoniac animal. He is acquainted with the real nature and potency of the forbidden tree, and speaks as if he were on terms of intimacy with the divine circle. . . . This certainly seems to point to a more primitive story, in which the serpent was a superhuman being, higher than man,' etc. (p. 72).

[2] The serpent coiling up behind the woman has his place in the Babylonian 'temptation-seal,' which probably, though a good many scholars dispute it, has some relation to this narrative. Probably further discovery will yet throw clearer light upon the picture.

[3] John viii. 44; xvi. 11; 2 Cor. xi. 3; 1 Tim. ii. 14; Heb. ii. 14; Rev. xii. 9, etc.

mysterious Providence for ends on which only the future could throw light, took place in the entrance of sin, the disastrous effects of which reach down through all time. Some of these effects we are now to glance at. I shall briefly speak, with main respect to our leading thought of the defacement of the divine image in man: (1) of the *spiritual* consequence of sin in the depravation of the individual; (2) of the *racial* consequence in hereditary evil; and (3) of the *physical* consequence—which is also racial—in disease and death.

1. The real ruin of the soul, *spiritually*, is only seen when we keep true to our first principle, and regard sin in its religious aspect, *i.e.*, in its relation to God. So long as only moral law is regarded, it may be difficult to feel that sin is other than a comparatively venial offence—the transgression of some particular precept—which need not involve serious and irremediable injury to him committing it. We cannot but judge differently when we see in sin—what in reality it is—the revolt of the creature-will against the Creator, and the taking of an altogether new principle into the soul—the principle, viz., that

ORIGIN AND NATURE OF SIN 223

not God's will, but my own will, is to be my law. Sin means, as above shown, that henceforth my life is not to be, as it ought to be, from God to God—His will my law, His glory my end; but from self to self—egoistic in principle and aim. The gravity of such an act, rupturing the original bond between the soul and God, is further seen when we reflect that the *motive* of such an act is necessarily to obtain for some impulse an unlawful gratification, or, more generally, to give the creature a place in the affections which does not rightfully belong to it.[1]

It is obvious from this that sin, though spiritual in its origin, is, as I have elsewhere tried to explain,[2] anything but spiritual in its effects. Its first and immediate effect is to destroy the balance or harmony of principles in the soul, to dethrone love to God from its place of supremacy in the soul, and give the lower and sensuous side of the nature an undue and wrongful predominance. Not only are these lower principles now in the place of ascendency, but, the spiritual bond being cut which kept them in due relation and

---

[1] Rom. i. 21, 25.   [2] *Christian View of God*, pp. 172-173.

subordination, they are now turbulent, disorderly, warring among themselves, their motions are violent and irregular, sin reveals itself as a principle of anarchy (ἀνομία). This is on the manward side; but on the Godward side also there is necessarily a change, owing to the fact that the creature has now become guilty and impure, and has ceased from the relation of dependence. For even in the unfallen state it must be noted —and it was one of the merits of Augustine to emphasise this—man was not an independent, self-acting unit, but stood necessarily in a relation of dependence on God, and drew continually his supplies of strength from Him. His life was never intended to be one lived from himself, but was to be a life *in God*. Sin alters this in destroying that relation of dependence, and making it impossible for God to hold communion and friendship with one who has become guilty and impure, while awakening in man the sense of shame and distrust and fear towards God, through this consciousness of guilt. Thus, on the one hand, man falls into bondage to the sensuous and worldly principles for the sake of which he surrendered his allegiance to God; and, on the

ORIGIN AND NATURE OF SIN

other, he has lost his love to God, and is deprived of the spiritual aids which his dependence on God and his fellowship with God afforded him. While in the centre of his being he has enthroned a principle which in its essence is God-negating.

From these points of view we can readily understand most of the lights in which sin, in its effects on human nature, is presented to us in Scripture, with profoundest echo of the truth of its declarations in human experience. It is truly, as the terms used to describe it teach, a missing of the mark, or turning aside of man from his true end—the glory of God[1] ($\dot{a}\mu a\rho\tau\iota a$); transgression of a law ($\pi a\rho\acute{a}\beta a\sigma\iota s$); a falling away, or defection ($\pi a\rho\acute{a}\pi\tau\omega\mu a$); lawlessness ($\dot{a}\nu o\mu\iota a$). But more particularly—

(1) In this inversion of the lower and higher principles of man's nature—the predominance of the earthly and sensuous, and the enfeeblement and relative inoperativeness of the spiritual—we have the basis of the Pauline description of man as *flesh* ($\sigma\acute{a}\rho\xi$). It is not meant that the spiritual nature is altogether suppressed—the $\nu o\hat{\upsilon}s$ is there with its ineffectual protests[2]—nor is it meant

[1] Rom. iii. 23.   [2] Rom. vii. 23, 25.

that all sins are what we call 'fleshly'; but the whole nature has become one in which the natural, the sensuous, the carnal, have attained a sinful predominance, and give a character, a tinge, a bias to—infect with their disturbing influences—every part of the soul. Deepest of all, there is alienation of the heart from God, arising from the taking into the heart of a new principle opposed to God—the principle of *egoism*. The Scripture does not describe the effect of the introduction of this new principle too strongly when it says: 'The mind of the flesh is enmity ($\check{\epsilon}\chi\theta\rho\alpha$) against God.'[1] Ordinarily this $\check{\epsilon}\chi\theta\rho\alpha$ may be latent; may manifest itself as simple indifference; but wherever the claims of religion are brought more closely home to it, it speedily appears as open dislike, repugnance, impatience; as the opposition between God's will and the worldly, sinful way of life becomes manifest, it develops into open hatred. It is thus, accordingly, that the worldly life is described throughout Scripture— as *godless*. 'There is no fear of God before their eyes.'[2] Nothing is truer to experience. This is

---

[1] Rom. viii. 7.
[2] Ps. x. 4; Rom. iii. 18; cf. Eph. ii. 12; iv. 18, etc.

ORIGIN AND NATURE OF SIN

the root-sin of human life, and only familiarity can veil from us its awful heinousness; only thoughtlessness can hide from us the *marvel* involved in it, that beings made in God's image, and capable of knowing, loving, and obeying Him, should yet repel, shun, dislike, and flee from Him; should resent being reminded of Him; should *wish* to be without Him. Surely no one who thinks rightly will say that this is *natural*.[1] There is more than even unnaturalness in it; there is frightful guilt.

(2) In this ascendency of the lower over the higher elements in man's nature we can understand the descriptions that are given by Paul,[2] and in the Scriptures generally, of the sinful state, as one of enslavement—*bondage* (δουλεία). The individual, whether he realises it or not, is enslaved, held in thrall, by sin, and is unable to deliver himself out of that state and regain by his own efforts spiritual freedom and power.

(3) I would only add that, on the basis of what we have found to be true of man's aliena-

---

[1] On the 'unnaturalness' of man's moral condition, see the striking remarks of the Duke of Argyll in his *Unity of Nature*, pp. 370 ff.
[2] Cf. Rom. vii.

tion from God, and general spiritual insusceptibility, those Scriptures are justified which speak of the sinful state as one of spiritual *death*—of loss, that is, of the true life the soul should possess in God, with subjection to carnal principles, and absence of spiritual interests and aims.[1] I do not, however, at present dwell on this. Enough has been said to show in how true a sense we must speak of an obscuration or defacement of the image of God in man—a loss of that purity and harmony of nature in which he was created, with resultant weakening and depravation in all his faculties and powers.

2. I come now to the second and still more difficult aspect of the effects of sin in our nature —the *racial*. If sin is voluntary and individual in its origin, it does not follow that it is only individual in its results. Here open up the large and complicated problems of hereditary evil, or what is ordinarily called Original Sin, to which modern discussions on heredity lend new importance.

It seems hard to deny—though there are those in both ancient and modern times who have dis-

[1] Cf. Rom. viii. 6; Eph. ii. 1-3; v. 14, etc.

puted it¹—that evil has a racial side. It is one of the things which distinguish the human family from other conceivable orders of beings that it is a *race*, and that therefore any act performed by a progenitor in a representative capacity must have racial consequences. This is the real answer to the objection often raised to the *justice* of the arrangement which admits of such racial effects accruing from a primal transgression. That objection cannot be answered on a merely individualistic basis; what is really impugned is the organic constitution of the race, which we

---

¹ Pelagius taught that Adam's fall injured no one but himself, and leaves the power of human nature unimpaired for good. Ritschl, in modern times, it is well known, rejected the idea of original sin. Mr. Tennant thinks also that 'there is no hint' in Genesis iii. 'of Adam's moral condition being fundamentally altered by his act of disobedience. . . . The idea that his sin was the source of the sinfulness of succeeding generations, or in any way an explanation of it, is altogether absent from the narrative. . . . The history in Genesis iii. was not intended by its ultimate compiler to supply an explanation of the cause of universal sinfulness' (*The Fall and Original Sin*, pp. 9, 10, 11 ; cf. p. 89). If the narrative is not intended to furnish an explanation of the universal sin and death which is everywhere else assumed, it is difficult to see what it means, or why it stands where it does. Mr. Tennant's view is not that of most exegetes, nor does it seem quite consistent with some of his other statements. *E.g.*, on pp. 11, 72-73 he seems to see in the narrative an attempt to explain the existence of human ills, and to trace their cause to sin, etc.

know to be a fact, apart from all moral or theological difficulties arising out of it. As an aid to the removal of these difficulties, I may put the matter thus. There are, so far as we can see, two possible principles, and only two, on which a moral society could be constituted. The one is the principle of strict individualism—each individual created separately, and standing or falling by himself, with strictly individual responsibility.[1] Here there can be no talk of racial constitution, or hereditary vitiation of nature. The other is the principle on which our own race, like the whole of organic nature, is constituted. Here there is a race of beings evolved from a single source—generation born from generation—hereditary transmission of nature and qualities—intimate connection of the members with each other, and a necessary participation of each in the life—in the goods and evils—of the whole, with a consequent share of responsibility for the whole.[2] This idea of a corporate unity, or organic constitution, of the race enters deeply into modern scientific thought. On the question

---

[1] Such, we may suppose, is the constitution of the angelic world (Matt. xxii. 30).   [2] Cf. Rom. xiv. 7.

of the *justice* of such a constitution, considered in itself, there can, I think, be little difference of opinion. It is obvious that an organic constitution is one of enormous advantage to the race, provided the race develops normally, in harmony with its true idea and destination. It is in that case the *most beneficent* of all constitutions; an instrument adapted, through the operation of inheritance, for conferring the highest possible blessings upon those under it. Equally obvious is it, however, that where sin enters, the effect is as if an engine were reversed; and all the powers of this mighty constitution, intended to conserve and to hand down good, become as potent to accumulate and hand down evil. So it is that we are compelled to speak of racial as well as of individual effects of sin. If heredity is admitted in this sphere—on which I speak after —a fall from original integrity such as I have already described, with the profound disturbance and perversion in the life of the soul that accompanied and followed it, could not take place without producing the most powerful effects in the natures of those descending from the first transgressors. So violent a disturbance as sin creates must propagate itself in after generations. If it is the first man—the protoplast of the race, in whom all the potencies of humanity are germinally concentrated—who sins, its effects must be serious in the highest degree, and will reveal themselves in a universal defection of the race. The *how* of this propagation of a vitiated nature may be mysterious to us; but it is only part of that general mystery of transmission which every doctrine of heredity has to face.[1] Here theories of *traducianism* and *creationism* maintain their battles, with, as it appears to me, a side of truth in each;[2] here science brings in its startling suggestion of the immortality of the reproductive germ, and the absolute continuity of the life of the species.[3] But the fact of itself seems un-

[1] 'How can such hereditary transmission of the characters of the parent take place? How can a single reproductive cell reproduce the whole body in all its details?' (Weismann, *Essays on Heredity*, i. p. 73).

[2] The fact that life is propagated by life, organism by organism, and that the characteristics of the parent, not only the generic, but the particular, are handed down to the offspring, is undeniable (Traducianism); on the other hand, it is as obvious that in each human soul there is a principle which raises it to the rank of personality, which is original, distinctive, differentiated from every other, and therefore properly to be attributed to the Creative Source. Cf. Martensen, *Dogmatics*, pp. 141-2.

[3] On this theory of Weismann's see below, pp. 253 ff.

deniable that we do by birth inherit a nature which is impure and biassed to evil ; that personality awakens and evolves itself in a nature already fallen, perverted, and prone to sin—which, therefore, in the judgment alike of God and of the individual's own conscience, is itself evil.[1]

The theory of evolution also, it is now to be observed, has its doctrine of original sin—the 'ape and tiger' theory, we may call it, to distinguish it from the Biblical, with which, as a little reflection shows, it is in principle irreconcilable. We have, indeed, on this theory, the inheritance of baser tendencies, but they are simply our *natural* heritage from our brute ancestors, and have no moral cause in the history of the race, which stamps on them the character of sin. Mr. Fiske, again, may be taken to represent this theory. 'Thus,' he says in his book on *Man's Destiny*, 'we see what human progress means. It means throwing off the brute-inheritance—gradually throwing it off through ages of struggle that are by and by to make struggle needless . . . the ape and tiger in human nature will become

[1] Rom. vii. 18, 20, 23.

extinct. Theology has much to say about original sin. This original sin is neither more nor less than the brute-inheritance which every man carries about with him, and the progress of evolution is an advance towards true salvation.'[1] No doubt there are elements in human nature that resemble, and only too forcibly recall, the ape and tiger—the wolf, the fox, the serpent also, and many other animals—though it is not suggested that man has been evolved along the line of the tiger, the wolf, or any of these other creatures; which are not, therefore, exactly an 'inheritance' from the latter. It need only here, however, be remarked, that if original sin were simply our 'brute-inheritance,' it would in no proper sense be sin at all. The victim of it might groan under it as an all but unendurable cross, but he could never judge of it as the religious man does, when he looks down into his heart, and condemns himself for the self-seeking, impure, and God-resisting tendencies he finds in constant operation there.[2]

[1] P. 103.
[2] Matt. xv. 19. Cf. the Duke of Argyll, *Unity of Nature*, pp. 367 ff.

An objection, however, to this doctrine of an inherent sinful bias in our nature, due to a 'fall,' comes from the side of the newer school of evolution, which deserves more careful consideration. It is well known that disputes on heredity turn mainly at the present moment on the question of *the transmissibility of acquired characters.* Briefly, the question is: Are acquired characters inherited? Spencer and the older evolutionists said Yes; Weismann and an important school of younger biologists say No. Much depends on the answer given to this question for the theory of evolution itself. 'If these views be correct,' says Weismann, 'all our ideas upon the transformation of species require thorough modification, for the whole principle of evolution by means of exercise (use and disuse), as proposed by Lamarck, and accepted in some cases by Darwin, entirely collapses.'[1] The consequences, however, are hardly less serious for theology, since, if sin is voluntary in origin, as I have contended it must be, its effects on human nature take their place among those 'acquired' characters to which it is held that the law of heredity does not apply. The

[1] *Essays,* i. p. 69.

theory has, in fact, been applied in this way, with great acuteness, to disprove the doctrine of original sin by Mr. F. R. Tennant, in his recent Hulsean Lectures on *The Origin and Propagation of Sin*. 'The question,' says this writer, 'turns entirely on the possibility of the transmission of acquired modifications as distinguished from congenital variations,' and he declares, 'The conviction very largely prevails amongst the authorities that unequivocal instances of such transmission have never yet been supplied.' 'Heredity,' he thinks, 'in the strict sense of inheritance by birth or descent, and not in that of appropriation of environment, cannot take place "in the region of the spiritual personality."'[1]

The speculation is ingenious, though, as regards the question of original sin, experience will, I fear, prove too strong for it. The fact that the sub-

[1] Pp. 34, 36, 37. A chief reason which Mr. Tennant gives is that 'it is almost impossible to conceive the nature of the mechanism whereby a specific effect produced upon any organism could so modify its reproductive organs as to cause a *corresponding* modification in the offspring' (p. 37). But is a 'mechanical' explanation the right one, and should the fact wait on our ability to conceive such 'mechanism'? Mr. Tennant moves here too closely in the steps of Weismann, whose mechanical theories will not comport well with other parts of Mr. Tennant's doctrine. See Note XIII. on Weismann's Theory of Heredity.

ject of the transmissibility of acquired modifications is so keenly debated by opposing schools of biologists[1] is itself an evidence that the last word has not been spoken regarding it, and suggests the probability that the truth does not lie wholly on either side. This, if I mistake not, is really the state of the case. It seems to me that heredity in these discussions is treated too much *en bloc*, and that we are not necessarily shut up to the alternative—either *all* acquired characters are hereditary, or *none* are. It may be necessary, if admittedly difficult, to make a distinction. What occurs to me is, that there are some changes which go deeper into the nature than others, and produce profounder and more permanent effects on the organism, and that these may be transmissible, while others are not. *Physical* changes, *e.g.*, arising from external and accidental causes, as mutilations, go least deeply into the nature, and are ordinarily not inherited.[2] We are here, as

[1] Weismann himself says in the Preface to his new work: 'I only know of two prominent workers of our day who have given thorough-going adherence to my view: Emery in Bologna and J. Arthur Thomson in Aberdeen' (*The Evol. Theory*, I. p. viii). One of the most important criticisms is in Romanes, *Darwin and after Darwin*, ii.

[2] Even here there are facts adduced by the opponents of the theory

yet, at the periphery or circumference of the being. *Intellectual* acquisitions, again, are not inherited—*e.g.*, skill in languages or in music—though the talent which makes these acquisitions possible is. Here, however, it becomes more difficult to prove a negative, and high authorities maintain that to some extent acquired skill *is* inherited.[1] Darwin, *e.g.*, writes: 'A horse is trained to certain paces, and the colt inherits similar movements. Nothing in the whole circuit of physiology is more wonderful.'[2] Non-transmission, however, it must be allowed, is, in this sphere, the rule, and transmission is the exception. However it may be with horses and dogs, we know very well from experience that a parent's acquired skill and knowledge—his acquaintance, for instance, with Latin or French—do not

---

not easily explained away; account has to be taken also of the physical effects produced by emotion (see below), and of the results produced through long exposure to climatic influences (change of colour, thicker hairy covering, etc.). Ordinarily, however, it will be agreed that physical mutilations (*e.g.*, loss of a finger or leg), and artificial marks generally, are not inherited. Yet it is in this sphere chiefly that, so far as one can see, experiments have been attempted.

[1] Spencer's whole theory of mental and moral evolution is built on this possibility.

[2] *Animals and Plants under Domestication*, II. chap. x. p. 307 (American edition).

ORIGIN AND NATURE OF SIN

descend to his offspring.[1] We are still here in a region which lies outside the depths of the personal life. It seems different when, from the physical and mental, we enter the region of *emotional* life, and of the life of feeling generally. Deep impressions, as every one is aware, are often made on the organism by emotion—impressions which seem to go down to the very seat of life—and certain of the physical effects these entail are surely transmissible to offspring.[2] Their *general* effects, in debilitated and unstable nervous system, are admittedly transmissible.[3]

Even in the emotional region, however, we are still outside the properly *voluntary* life of man;

[1] It is a somewhat different question whether education and culture may not have some more general effect in developing capacity and heightening refinement.

[2] A strong mental shock—the witnessing of a murder, for example—may produce effects upon the body which descend to offspring. Dr. Carpenter gives striking instances of the physical effects of emotion. He narrates the case of a lady who saw the window-sash descend on the hand of her child, cutting off three of its fingers. Within twenty-four hours the three corresponding fingers of her own hand were inflamed and suppurating (*Mental Physiology*, p. 682).

[3] Cf. Romanes's criticism of Weismann's admissions on this score (*Darwin and After Darwin*, ii. p. 108). 'Even,' he says, discussing a case of artificially produced epilepsy, 'if it be but a "tendency," a "disposition," or a "diathesis" that is transmitted, it is not less a case of transmission,' etc.

but I would now remark that it is in the voluntary, and specially in the *moral* life, that the deepest effects of all seem to be produced upon his nature. Here influences proceed from the centre of the personality, which powerfully affect the whole being, and, as an accumulation of evidence seems to prove, transmit results, beneficial or baneful, to succeeding generations. The moral forces of life, if good, act as a lever to lift up; if evil, are as an axe to break down. In a recent life of the late Principal John Cairns the suggestive remark is made: 'The home at Dunglass, where religion was always the chief concern, was the nursery of a strong mind as well as of a strong soul, and both were fed from the same spring. In this case, as in so many others, spiritual strength became intellectual strength in the second generation.'[1] This is a not uncommon experience. Where the moral root is present, brain-power strengthens; where the moral root is wanting, brain-power deteriorates. This brings us directly to the cases of those who form, or are seduced into, vicious habits. All such cases Weismann would explain as the result of congenital predis-

[1] *Life of Cairns*, by his nephew, in 'Famous Scots Series,' p. 28.

position, with which will and conduct have nothing to do. But is this arguable ? Take the case, *e.g.*, of an individual who has no hereditary tendency to drunkenness—none at least which has ever appeared, or which would appear in his descendants, if he had continued to live in sobriety—but who is thrown into company, and induced to form habits which end in his becoming a confirmed drunkard. Is it really disputable that the effects of such lapse in deteriorated organism, depraved appetite, and weakened will, are handed down to offspring ? Dr. Carpenter, *e.g.*, in his *Mental Physiology*, writes : ' The drunkard not only injures and enfeebles his own nervous system, but entails mental disease upon his family. His daughters are nervous and hysterical ; his sons are weak, wayward, and eccentric, and sink under the pressure of excitement, or of some unforeseen emergency, or the ordinary calls of duty.' ' The children of drunkards are deficient in bodily and vital energy, and are predisposed by their very organisation to have cravings for alcoholic stimulants.'[1] Such testimony, agreeing, I sup-

[1] P. 370. The sentences are quoted. Another scientific writer, quoted by Elam in his *A Physician's Problem* (p. 30), says: 'The

pose, with the experience of most, could be indefinitely multiplied. Now, unless it is maintained that the same results would have followed from the parent's constitution though he had not personally fallen into vice, there would seem to be here clear evidence of heredity of acquired states.

The conclusion I arrive at, accordingly, is that there are moral changes which go into the depths of the nature as nothing else can do, and that the results of these changes are transmissible. I have used the familiar illustration of intemperance; but of course the same line of reasoning applies to all forms of vice. I take, therefore, precisely the opposite view to that of Mr. Tennant, in the Hulsean Lectures formerly quoted: 'Heredity in the strict sense . . . cannot take place in the region of the spiritual personality.' It is, to my mind, in the spiritual personality that we must seek the cause of the worst evils heredity entails upon us. But if this law holds good generally, it must surely hold good peculiarly with regard

most startling problem connected with intemperance is, that not only does it affect the health, morals, and intelligence, of the offspring of its votaries, but that they also inherit the fatal tendency, and feel a craving for the very beverages which have acted as poisons on their system from the commencement of their being.'

ORIGIN AND NATURE OF SIN

to the *first act* of sin in the progenitors of the race. This involved a shock to the moral and spiritual nature which we can now only faintly measure; it was the rupture of the original bond between the soul and God, and the dissolution of the harmony of the soul within itself; and its effect on the organism must have been proportionally great. In any case the fact is *there*, that the natural condition of man is one of moral depravation, and that this evil bias descends from generation to generation. Hereditary sin is a deep, dark strain in the history of our race, not to be explained away.

To discuss more particularly the character and degree of this hereditary deterioration of the nature through sin, and to investigate its bearings on responsibility,[1] would carry me further away from my immediate subject than I can venture at present to go. Roman Catholic theology, it is well known, distinguishes between man as a purely natural being, and the gift of supernatural righteousness bestowed on him at his creation. This latter is conceived of as something over and above his true nature—a *donum superadditum*; man would

[1] See Note XIV. on Heredity in Relation to Responsibility.

have been complete and faultless without it. The effect of the fall is that man comes into the world wanting this supernatural endowment, but otherwise not greatly impaired.[1] Baptism restores the lost grace. One consequence of this theory is, that, admitting concupiscence to remain even in the baptized person, it refuses to regard concupiscence as sin, while allowing that Paul in Romans does so characterise it.[2] The true element in this view is, that it recognises that man, even in the unfallen state, was dependent for his spiritual perfection on gracious communications from God;[3] but it errs in regarding this higher endowment as something separable from man's true nature, and its absence as not seriously impairing or corrupting his natural faculties. On the other hand, when Protestant theology speaks of 'total depravity,' 'the corruption of the whole nature,' and the like, we are not to read into these expressions the sense which is sometimes taken from them, but which they were never intended to bear, that every man, in his natural condition, is as bad as he

---

[1] Cf. Laidlaw, *Bible Doct. of Man*, pp. 153 ff. Hence Roman Catholic theologians can provide for unbaptized children in a place of 'natural' happiness.

[2] Rom. vii. 20. [3] See above, p. 224.

can be. It is not implied, *e.g.*, by these expressions, that man does not retain many traces of the divine image in intellect, in conscience, in will, in natural affections, in traits of character pleasing and praiseworthy in themselves. It is not meant that, in the moral sphere, man does not retain a measure of freedom, and is not capable of exhibiting many virtues; or that, even in the religious sphere, there is not still in his heart an inextinguishable longing after God—at least a consciousness of unrest in sin, and in all things earthly, testifying to the need of God. What they *do* signify is, that there is nevertheless no part of man's nature which has escaped the defiling and perverting influence of sin; that sin infects the *whole* man; that there is no faculty or member of his soul or body of which it can be said—this is perfectly pure.[1] The *virus* of sin is in the system, and subtly, or more manifestly, affects every part. Only, when everything is said in extenuation, it is difficult to exaggerate the awfulness of the change which sin has wrought in human nature, or the dire ruin that is certain to result, if grace does not mercifully interpose.

[1] See above, pp. 225-6.

3. I have now, lastly, to speak of the *physical* consequence of sin in death, or of the penal effect of sin in the dissolution of man's composite personality as a being consisting of body and soul. I shall discuss this in next lecture; then bring the subject to a close by considering the bearings of the whole on the system of Christian doctrine.

The Biblical Doctrine of Man and Sin in its Relation to the Christian Redemption —Restoration and Perfecting of the Divine Image

Still to be considered. 3. The *Physical* Consequence of Sin in Suffering and Death. Alleged Universality and Necessity of Death in the Organic World (Man included). Biblical View connected: (1) With its View of Man's Nature. Soul and Body not intended to be Separated. (2) With its View of Man's Primitive Condition. One of Moral Uprightness. Weismann's theory that Death is not a Necessity of Organisms. 'Immortality of the Protozoa.' Remarkable Longevity in Animal World. Man's case stands on separate footing. He founds a New Kingdom; is destined for Immortality. Death a Contradiction of the true Idea of Humanity. *Posse non mori* and *non posse mori*. Harmony of previous Discussions with the Scripture Doctrine of Redemption. The Doctrines of Man and Sin implied: 1. In the *Presuppositions* of Redemption. (1) The infinite Value of the Soul. (2) Man's Capacity for Divine Sonship. (3) Man's Need of Redemption as a Sinner. 2. In the *End* of Redemption. The Restoration and Perfecting of the Divine Image. 3. In the *Means* and *Method* of Redemption. (1) In the Doctrine of Incarnation. The Divine Image the Ground of the Possibility of Incarnation. Christ the Perfect Realisation of the Divine Image in Man. (2) In the Doctrine of Atonement. Guilt the Presupposition of Atonement. The Racial Aspect of Sin has its Counterpart in Redemption. The First and the Second Adams. The Penal Character of Death implied in Christ's Death for our Sins. (3) In the Doctrines of Regeneration and Renewal. Conformity to Christ's Image. (4) In the Doctrine of Resurrection and the Christian Hope of Immortality. Christ's Resurrection and ours. The Immortality of the Gospel, one in which the Body shares; an Immortality of the *whole* Person. Conclusion.

VI

THE BIBLICAL DOCTRINE OF MAN AND SIN IN ITS RELATION TO THE CHRISTIAN REDEMPTION—RESTORATION AND PERFECTING OF THE DIVINE IMAGE

I HAVE spoken of the *spiritual* consequences of sin in individual depravation, and of the *racial* consequence in hereditary evil, or, as it is commonly called, Original Sin. It remains to speak—

3. Of the *physical* consequence of sin in suffering and death.

There is nothing, perhaps, on which the 'modern' view of the world is clearer, or assertion is more confident, than on the universal reign of death over all creatures, man included. The idea that physical death is not a part of man's natural lot, but has entered the world through sin, is scouted as an absurdity. The Book of Genesis, it is generally allowed, represents death as the penalty of transgression,[1] and Paul expressly affirms that death entered the world through man's sin.[2] But the story in Genesis is dismissed as a myth; and Paul's opinion, based on that story, is held to be of no authority for us. Even Christian theologians, in deference to the evolutionary philosophy, very generally concede that physical death, as such, has no relation to sin, but must be viewed as the natural fate of man. But I would ask seriously: Is it so? I shall not base my demur on the simple statement in Genesis, or even on the dictum of the Apostle Paul. I take my stand on a much broader foundation—the whole Scripture doctrine on the nature and destiny of man, and on the character of his redemption. If the connection of physical death with sin is found to be an implicate of the total Christian view, we may be disposed to treat Paul's doctrine with more respect.

---

[1] Gen. ii. 17; iii. 19. Mr. Tennant, on the other hand, is 'more than doubtful' whether, within the limits of the Old Testament, 'death was as yet regarded as caused by Adam's sin.' 'It may be assumed, then, that there is no indication of the view that death is a consequence of our first parents' sin in Hebrew literature of earlier date than Ecclesiasticus' (*The Fall and Original Sin*, pp. 104, 117-119). Our view is that this idea was present as far back as the fall-story goes (see above, p. 199).

[2] Rom. v. 12.

CHRISTIAN REDEMPTION

Everything depends here, I grant: (1) on what we suppose man's nature to be; and (2) on what view we take of the original condition of man. On both points we have seen that the Christian view and the so-called 'modern' view go very widely apart; but I have sought to show also that there are the strongest grounds in both reason and science for holding the Christian view to be the true one.

(1) In respect of the nature of man, we have seen reason to regard man as a *compound being*, the denizen of two worlds, by his soul united to the spiritual world of rational and moral life, and by his body united to nature below him.[1] His complete personality consists of neither of these two elements in separation, but in the union of both. He is not pure spirit, like the angels, but incorporated spirit. Death, therefore, is not the same thing to him as it is to the lower animals—unless, indeed, we deny to him, as we do to them, immortality. Neither, as I said before, is the body to be regarded in his case, as the old philosophers thought of it, as a material prison-house, from which he should be glad to escape in death. It is *part of himself*:

[1] See above, p. 46.

an integral part of his total personality, and body and soul in separation are neither of them the complete man. It follows, if we deal firmly with this conception of man, that death is to him *not* a natural process, but something altogether *un*natural—the violent separation of two parts of his being which God never meant to be separated; a rupture, a rending asunder, a mutilation, of his personality.[1] The analogy of the animals is not in point here; for man is not a mere animal. He has what they lack, a personal life, and an immortal nature and destiny. It is quite arbitrary, therefore, to reason from the one to the other. If man's soul perished at death, the analogy would be complete. But it is an article of our faith that it does not perish. The Bible here is quite in harmony with natural feeling. We instinctively feel death, with its inroads of disease, and the long struggle which often leads up to it, to be something foreign to the true idea of man —something tragic, mournful, lamentable; and neither in heathen religions nor in the Bible is the life of a disembodied spirit viewed as either a complete or a desirable one.

[1] See above, p. 53.

CHRISTIAN REDEMPTION 253

(2) In respect of the original state of man I have tried to show reason for rejecting the conclusion of popular anthropology, which necessitates death as part of man's natural lot.[1] The standpoint of science itself, I ought here to remark, is itself changing in a remarkable way in regard to death and its necessity in the living organism. Formerly death was regarded as self-evidently a natural necessity—a law of all living beings that involved no mystery; the wonder was, not that organisms should wear out and die, but that they continued to live so long.[2] It is a startling change when we find a biologist like Weismann —so thoroughly naturalistic in his general views —speaking of 'the question of the origin of death' as 'one of the most difficult problems in the whole range of physiology,'[3] and declaring on grounds of pure science that there is no ascertainable reason why living organisms, apart, *i.e.*, from injury and violence, should ever die at all. In point of fact, he contends, in unicellular animals

[1] See above, Lect. IV.

[2] Prof. G. Henslow, *e.g.*, lays it down categorically in *The Liberal Churchman* (June 1905, p. 223): 'Physiology shows that a gradual decay and death of the body are as inevitable and necessary a part of man's terrestrial economy as are his growth and development.'

[3] *Essays on Heredity*, i. p. 20.

—not only in the Amœbæ and the low unicellular Algae, but also in 'the far more highly organised' Infusoria—they do not die. He has even coined a phrase, 'the immortality of the Protozoa.' Here are a few sentences illustrating his view. 'In the same manner,' he says, 'from a physiological point of view, we might admit that we can see no reason why the functions of the organism should ever cease.'[1] 'Death, *i.e.*, the end of life, is by no means, as is usually assumed, an attribute of all organisms. An immense number of low organisms do not die, although they are easily destroyed, being killed by heat, poisons, etc. As long, however, as the conditions which are necessary for their life are fulfilled, they continue to live, and they thus carry the potentiality of unending life in themselves.'[2] 'The low unicellular organisms are potentially immortal.'[3] 'Each individual of any such unicellular species living on the earth to-day is far older than mankind, and is almost as old as life itself.'[4] But even in higher organisms death, in his view, is no inherent necessity of the organism, but is only

[1] *Essays on Heredity*, i. p. 73.
[2] *Ibid.*, p. 33.
[3] *Ibid.*, p. 26.
[4] *Ibid.*, p. 73.

CHRISTIAN REDEMPTION 255

explicable through 'utility,' *i.e.*, the advantage to the individual or species of limited existence—an explanation which I do not discuss. As he says, 'Death is to be looked upon as an occurrence which is advantageous to the species as a concession to the outer conditions of life, and not as an absolute necessity, essentially inherent in life.'[1] 'The above-mentioned hypothesis upon the origin and necessity of death leads me to believe that the organism did not finally cease to renew the worn-out cell-material because the nature of the cells did not permit them to multiply indefinitely, but because the power of multiplying indefinitely was lost when it ceased to be of use.'[2] He shows that the necessity of death is not explained by such causes as the greater size and complexity of the animal, the rate at which the animal lives, etc. Facts demonstrate that no fixed relation exists between size or activity, and degree of longevity. The instances he adduces are very curious. 'Of all organisms in the world large trees have the longest lives. The Andansonias of the Cape Verd Islands are said to live for 6000 years. The largest animals also attain the greatest age.

[1] *Essays on Heredity*, i. p. 26.   [2] *Ibid.*, p. 25.

Thus there is no doubt that whales live for some hundreds of years. Elephants live 200 years.'[1] This great age is attained also by many of the smaller animals, such as the pike and carp. Eagles, vultures, falcons, ravens, parrots, wild geese, etc., are said to live upwards of 100 years. Eagles and vultures have lived in captivity 104 and 118 years.[2] One begins to see that there is no *inherent* impossibility in the great ages of the patriarchs, or even in ante-diluvian longevity, after all. It is interesting in this connection to recall that the skulls and skeletons of the palæolithic men of the mammoth period point to a race of remarkable height and strength—some seven feet high—and, apparently, of great longevity.[3] In Egypt, we are told, 110

---

[1] *Essays on Heredity*, i. p. 6.   [2] *Ibid.*, pp. 6, 12, 36-37.

[3] This at least is the view of Sir J. W. Dawson. See his *Meeting Place of Geology and History*, pp. 53, 58, 62, 66, etc. Speaking of the Mentone and related skeletons, he says: 'Another point which strikes us in reading the descriptions of these skeletons is the indication which they seem to present of an extreme longevity. The massive proportions of the body, the great development of the muscular processes, the extreme wearing of the teeth among a people who predominantly lived on flesh and not on grain, the obliteration of the sutures of the skull, along with indications of slow ossification of the ends of the long bones, point in this direction, and seem to indicate a slow maturity and great length of life in this most primitive race' (p. 63).

CHRISTIAN REDEMPTION 257

years was regarded as the number of a perfect life.[1]

These speculations of Weismann, it is obvious, however, apply to all animals, and can be pressed no further than to show that death is not an inherent necessity of the animal organism. Man's case still stands on its own peculiar footing. I do not question the prevalence of death in the animal world—there is not a word in Scripture to suggest that animals possessed immortality, or came under the law of death for man's sin. But man, as a rational, spiritual being, stands on a different footing entirely. He founds a new kingdom—the kingdom of rational and moral life; he bears the directly imprinted image of his Maker; he comes from his Creator's hand, as I have tried to show, in a condition of purity befitting his high vocation. The law of mere animal life has no necessary application to him. Both on the ground of the composite nature of man, and on the ground of his peculiar standing as a rational and moral

---

[1] Cf. Ebers (art. 'Joseph' in Smith's *Dictionary of Bible*, second ed. i. p. 1804) and other authorities. In the view of some, the venerable moralist Ptah-hotep, of the fifth dynasty (*c.* 3000 B.C.), claims to be already that age when he wrote his book (Birch, *Egypt*, p. 50, etc.). This was the age of Joseph at his death (Gen. l. 26).

agent, wearing the moral image of God, we are entitled to expect something wholly different.

On both of these grounds, therefore, as well as on others afterwards to be exhibited, connected with the Christian system, I resist the conclusion that death was the normal lot of man, and can only find a clear and consistent position on the hypothesis that it was not. We shall see that this idea of man's nature as above the law of death, and of the connection of death with sin, enters far more vitally into the organism of Christian truth than many people suppose. It affects the general view taken of death in Scripture ; the doctrine of Christ's death as an atonement for sin ; the doctrine of the resurrection, both Christ's and the believer's ; the Christian hope of immortality,[1] etc. We have but to ask the question : Would Christ, apart from His crucifixion, have been subject to bodily decay and death ? to see how closely the fact of death bears on the true idea of humanity. The only view that seems tenable, on grounds of Scripture, seems to be that man, in his original destiny, was not subject to mortality—that death was not an element in his original destiny, but

[1] See above, p. 53, and the further illustration below.

CHRISTIAN REDEMPTION

enters our race, as the Bible affirms, through sin. Man, we should perhaps rather say, was, as created, in strictness neither mortal nor immortal as regards his body. His condition was, as Augustine said, *posse non mori*. Had he continued obedient, continuance of life would have been assured to him : his state would have become *non posse mori*. The conditions under which life would have been lived had this possibility been realised—what changes the body, inhabited by a pure soul, growing continually in wisdom and goodness, would have undergone ; what transformation or 'translation' would finally have awaited it—analogous, perhaps, to that of Enoch or Elijah, or to the change which it is said will pass on living believers at the Lord's *Parousia*[1]—are matters which lie beyond our ken, and on which it is useless to speculate. Sin *did* enter the world, and with sin came that separation of soul and body we call *death*, the effect of which, so different from what lay in God's original design for humanity, we sorrowfully know.

I have now finished the consideration, in its

[1] 1 Cor. xv. 51.

main issues, of the Biblical doctrine of man and his sin in its relation to modern anthropological theories. My task, however, would still be incomplete if, in concluding the lectures, I did not seek to indicate, in however summary a way, some of the bearings of this important subject on the Christian system as a whole. The connection of Christian truth, which it is always interesting to trace, of itself makes this desirable; but there are two considerations which render it almost imperative that such a concluding glance at the correlations of doctrine should not be omitted. In the first place, the intimate connection of the doctrines we have been considering with the other parts of the Christian system is fitted to have a distinctly confirmatory effect upon our judgments, and *pro tanto* to serve as a test of the accuracy of the conclusions at which we have arrived. I do not think it can be sufficiently emphasised that Christian truth forms an *organism*—has a unity and coherence which cannot be arbitrarily disturbed in any of its parts without the whole undergoing injury. Conversely, the proof that any doctrine fits in essentially to that organism —is an integral part of it—is one of the strongest

CHRISTIAN REDEMPTION

evidences we can have of its correctness. And in the second place, the doctrine of the divine image in man cannot be regarded as fully exhibited till it has been shown how this image, lost or defaced by sin, has been graciously restored and perfected in Christ, Himself the perfect image of God in humanity, and the complete revelation of the divine idea of humanity. To this concluding indication of the relation of the Biblical doctrines of man and sin to the Christian redemption I now, accordingly, proceed.

1. That the Biblical doctrine of the image of God in man, and of sin as the voluntary departure from a condition of actual moral likeness to God, has much to do with the *presuppositions* of the Christian redemption, has already, I hope, been shown with sufficient clearness.

(1) On this doctrine rests, first of all, the idea of the *infinite value* of man in God's sight, and of his *capacity* for such a redemption as Christ brings. The infinite value of the soul is rightly specified by Professor Harnack in his recent lectures as an essential part of Christ's Gospel.[1] It is a mistake, however, to speak of this idea,

[1] See above, p. 27.

as is sometimes done, as one which Christ first brought into the world. It is, in truth, an idea which has its ultimate ground in the doctrine which stands on the first page of the Old Testament, and which underlies every part of the teaching of Scripture.

It is the fact that man is made in the rational and moral image of God which gives him, in a universe of selfless things, the value of an end in himself; which leads God to set value on him, and even in his sin to desire, and take infinite pains for, his recovery. Jesus but brings out into diviner clearness this great underlying truth of all revelation about man. It is sometimes very confidently asserted that, in the Old Testament, the individual as such counts for nothing in his relations to God; that only the tribe or the nation has value. Nothing, in my opinion, could be wider of the mark. To begin with, it is not a tribe or nation that is said to be created in the image of God, but *an individual pair*—man and woman ('male and female'); in the second narrative, Adam and Eve. Enoch and Noah are individual examples of piety, and with Noah, as a representative individual, God makes His covenant. Abraham, father of the Jewish nation, to whom every pious Israelite looked back as the type of the true religious relation to God, was eminently an individual—called of God, taken into covenant with Him, made the channel of blessing to the world. Even under the Law, not to multiply examples from history, from psalms, and from prophets, the individual transgressor was made responsible for his sin, and was required to bring his individual sacrifice in atonement. It is nothing to the point to speak of these early narratives as legendary. Assume for argument's sake that they are; they at least embody what men in the age when they were written believed about God and His relations with the individual, and furnish proof that *in their view* the individual had value in God's sight.

(2) What is true generally of the infinite value of man in God's sight is true particularly of man's capacity for a *divine sonship*.[1] Man, in the Christian Gospel, is called to a relation of sonship to God. But such a relation would be an impossibility for a being who was not already, in the essence of his nature, akin to God; who

[1] See above, pp. 190 ff.

was not, as the Bible says, made in the image of God. I grant—indeed would contend—that the sonship received in Christ is a gift of grace, a surpassing manifestation of love,[1] the result of a new life imparted to, and of a new relation bestowed on, those who are united by faith to *the* Son of God. Nevertheless I have sought to show above[2] that a relation properly described as filial was the goal of the divine dealings with man even in creation; and on any view a kinship with God in respect of rational and moral faculty —a spark of divinity in man's soul—must be allowed to be the necessary presupposition of such gracious sonship as God bestows on us in Christ.

(3) Most clearly of all are the doctrines we have been expounding the indispensable foundation of the representations which the Bible everywhere gives of man's *guilt*, and *moral and spiritual ruin*, rendering redemption necessary. Throughout Scripture, as we have seen,[3] there is but one picture given of man's moral state. He is a being who has missed his mark—who has turned aside from the end of his creation, and is in

---

[1] John iii. 1.   [2] P. 191.   [3] Lect. V.

CHRISTIAN REDEMPTION 265

revolt from, and active rebellion against, his Creator. For this reason he has come under condemnation. A judgment of God—a κατά-κριμα—rests upon him which he is powerless of himself to remove. His actual spiritual condition is described in the darkest colours. Forgetful of his Maker, he is unholy, prone to evil, the subject of sinful affections, following vanity, fulfilling the desires of the flesh and of the mind.[1] He is not only morally impure, but is in *bondage* to sin, and again is impotent to deliver himself from its rule. He is, as Paul says, 'in the flesh,'[2] or, as John puts it, is ruled by principles which exclude the love of the Father, as the lust of the flesh, the lust of the eyes, and the pride of life.[3] It is this view of man's condition which is the presupposition of the Gospel, and it is not denied that the picture is entirely altered, and loses its gravity, on the premises of the new evolutionary school.[4] The old doctrine faithfully reflects at least the teaching of Scripture on man's ruin, guilt, and disabilities; but the old doctrine emphatically needs the old view of man's essential

---

[1] Eph. ii. 1-3.　　[2] Rom. viii. 8.
[3] 1 John ii. 16.　　[4] See above, pp. 208-9; cf. Note VI.

nature as made in the image of God, and of his voluntary fall, to sustain it. A theology which thinks to do justice to the Scripture teaching on man's sin, condemnation, and need of renewal, while rejecting the Scripture presuppositions of man's fall, and subjection to death through sin, is bound, with whatever good intentions, to be a failure.

2. These are some of the presuppositions of the Christian doctrine of redemption. Let us now advance to look at the *principal ena* of the Christian redemption. The close connection of the Christian system with our subject is obvious when we reflect that, from one point of view, the whole of Christianity—perhaps I should rather say, so as to include all dispensations, the whole Scriptural scheme of redemption—is but a divine counsel and provision for repairing the ruin of man's sin, and carrying through the ends of man's creation, while exalting him in Christ to a dignity and privilege to which, on the mere creation basis, he could never have attained. It aims supremely at, in other words has for its end, the *restoration* and *perfecting* of the divine image in man, lost or defaced by sin. Many passages in Scripture

declare this in effect, notably Eph. iv. 23, 24—
'Be renewed in the spirit of your mind, and put on the new man, which after God hath been created in righteousness and holiness of truth'; and Col. iii. 10—'Seeing that ye . . . have put on the new man, which is being renewed unto knowledge after the image of Him that created him.' To the same effect are all the Scriptures which make conformity to Christ the goal of renewal. For Christ is pre-eminently the image of God in our humanity.

3. When, from the end contemplated in the Gospel, we look to the redeeming scheme itself, and consider the *means* or *method* by which this great end is to be accomplished, we find that the Gospel system gathers itself up into certain great doctrines, of which, in the present connection, we may look specially at *four*, viz., incarnation, atonement, regeneration, resurrection and immortal life. With all these the doctrines I have been expounding on the nature of man stand in inseparable connection; with their removal, not one of the other doctrines could logically be maintained.

(1) The great central mystery of the Christian

faith is undeniably the doctrine of the *incarnation* —that God, in the Person of the Son, has become man for our salvation. Of that doctrine the Scripture affirmation of the divine image in man is, beyond a doubt, the indispensable presupposition. It would be so if, with certain theologians, we consented to recognise Jesus simply as the most perfect revelation of God in humanity — the incarnation of the *principle* of the absolute religion—the archetype and model of the perfect religious relation of man to God. Such theories err, not in what they affirm, but in what they *fail* to affirm, or, more, deny. Jesus is all that these theories represent—the perfect revelation of God in humanity; only, if faith is to rise to the full height of the Christian testimony, and safeguard itself from sinking back into humanitarianism—which is the modern tendency [1] —it must affirm a great deal more. It must recognise that here is one who, in the root of His Personality, is divine, as no other is divine —who had a subsistence in and with God prior to His manifestation in time [2]—who, as

---

[1] See my *Christian View of God*, Lect. II.
[2] John i. 1; xvii. 5, 24; Col. i. 15, etc.

CHRISTIAN REDEMPTION 269

God's eternal Image to Himself, was before all worlds, and was the Creator of the worlds: the Everlasting Son. But in whatever degree the Person of Christ is worthily conceived, the affirmation of man made in the image of God is the foundation of it.

(*a*) First, if the subject is taken at its deepest, we perhaps gain a point of view that carries us further than we have yet been able to go in the apprehension of *the nature of the divine image* itself. It lies in the doctrine of the Trinity that the Son of God is the Father's eternal image; but more, that He is the principle of revelation in the divine Being; more still, that the revelation in the creation of the world and of man takes place through the Son, and that, in a profound sense, He is the abiding ground, connecting point, and sustaining power in creation—nay, is Himself the end of it. All things were created in Him and for Him, and in Him all things consist, or hold together.[1] He is the Creator, and the life and light, of man.[2] Must we not say, then, that if man bears the divine image in his soul, it is because his being is grounded in, and derives

[1] Col. i. 16, 17.　　[2] John i. 14.

its godlike attributes and powers from, the Son or Word, who is Himself the essential and eternal image of God? In this sense it is not erroneous to say that man was created in the image of the Son, and that it is the same image in which he was created which was afterwards realised in humanity in the incarnation.

(*b*) Waiving such transcendental speculations, it is at least certain that it is the fact that humanity is created in the image of God which made such an event as the incarnation possible. The simple fact that God, in the person of the Son, has entered into our humanity—has assumed our humanity to Himself—has made it the organ of the perfect revelation of the Godhead, is proof that in humanity there is a receptiveness for the divine—an affinity to the divine—which could not belong to it save as it bore by creation the image of the Eternal. On the other hand, if we concede this dignity to belong to humanity, then a point of view is gained which makes incarnation —even a personal incarnation—not only possible, but even reasonable and natural. That God should enter into closer and ever closer relations with this humanity He has made—should in-

CHRISTIAN REDEMPTION 271

creasingly identify Himself with it—should make it the organ of His perfect revelation of Himself —is no more than might have been anticipated.[1] Two things at least are certain : (1) that *without* this doctrine of the divine image in man the incarnation is an impossibility; and (2) *with* this doctrine the chief *a priori* objections to the incarnation disappear.

(*c*) The last point I shall mention in which our doctrine connects itself with the incarnation is, that in Jesus Christ there is historically presented to us *the actual realisation of the divine image* in man. So far as the assumption of our nature—true body and true soul—involves the manifestation of the general attributes of humanity (reason, conscience, will, etc.), I need not dwell upon it. The resplendently glorious fact about Christ as man is that in Him we have the perfect realisation of the moral image of the Father. Alone of all who have ever lived on earth, Jesus was absolutely and stainlessly holy. No flaw of imperfection marred His character; every moral and spiritual excellence existed in Him in the highest conceivable degree: His will was through-

[1] Cf. *Christian View of God*, pp. 120-121.

out in complete unison with the Father's. While of every other it has to be confessed that out of the heart proceed evil thoughts and desires, the thoughts and affections that issued from His heart were wholly pure. In His spirit shone the light of a perfect knowledge of the Father; His life was the model of perfect love, trust, obedience, submission to God's Fatherly will; the quality of everything He thought, said, and did, was what we call *filial*. He was the perfect realisation of the spirit of sonship. In Him therefore, as the central personage of history—the archetypal man, second Adam of the race, its new and saving head —there was given the perfect realisation of the divine image in human nature, and in that the revelation of the capability of humanity to bear that image. Moreover, in His archetypal character Jesus is the realisation of the end or destiny of man. So far as the image of God embraced the idea of lordship over creation, that idea is now perfectly realised in Him. 'We see not yet all things put under him'—man—'but we see Jesus . . . crowned with glory and honour.'[1]

(2) I now pass to the second great doctrine

[1] Heb. ii. 9. See above, p. 57.

CHRISTIAN REDEMPTION 273

on our list—the doctrine of *atonement*—and here again the close correlation of Christ's work with the doctrines we have been considering is very apparent. As the incarnation connected itself specially with the doctrine of the image of God in man, so the atonement connects itself specially with the doctrine of sin and death. In various well-known passages in the Gospels Jesus expressly attributes to His sufferings and death a redeeming efficacy, and connects them with the forgiveness of sins and life of the world.[1] More fully and clearly His death is uniformly represented in the Apostolic Gospel as a true propitiatory sacrifice for sin—the one means by which guilt is purged, sin put away, peace made with God, reconciliation effected. Paul sums up the Gospel he preached in the two articles, that Christ died for our sins according to the Scriptures, and that He rose from the dead on the third day, according to the Scriptures.[2] Christ's Cross is thus the meeting-place between God and a sinful humanity. From the standpoint of the New Testament, I cannot allow that the reality of

---

[1] Matt. xx. 28; xxvi. 28; Luke xxiv. 46-47; John iii. 14-17; vi. 51, etc. [2] 1 Cor. xv. 3, 4.

Christ's atoning work, on which our whole salvation rests, can be lawfully made so much as an open question in the Christian Church. But nothing can be plainer than that this doctrine of Christ's atonement stands vitally in connection with the body of Scripture teaching on man's sin, and of God's relation to that sin.

(a) The first presupposition of the doctrine of atonement is that the world is in a state of *sin* and *guilt* from which it *needs* redemption. This has been largely dwelt on in previous lectures,[1] but, as the hinge of the whole discussion, cannot have too much prominence given to it. If sin is not, indeed, that infinitely evil and condemnable thing which the Bible represents it to be—something against which the holiness of God must eternally declare itself in judgment and penalty; if the world is not really in a state of estrangement from God, and lying under the doom of death, with eternal judgment to follow; if sin is truly nothing more than an imperfect stage in man's ascent from the brute condition to true moral life—then the foundations are self-evidently taken away from every doctrine of atonement,

[1] See above, pp. 19, 28, 197 ff.

CHRISTIAN REDEMPTION 275

for there is, in truth, no real guilt left to atone for. The world is not perishing, but improving. Evolution has power within itself to accomplish the perfection of the race, and a Saviour is rendered superfluous.[1] It is for this very reason, as I showed at the beginning, that so many, under the influence of the new conceptions, have become estranged from the New Testament doctrine of the Cross. The remedy will only be found in a return to more Scriptural views of God's holiness, of man's nature as made in the image of God, and of the voluntary origin and deadly effects of man's sin.

(*b*) It is important to notice, however, that the same doctrine of sin which shows the need of atonement, furnishes also a helpful light on the *possibility* of atonement. We saw, in speaking of sin, that, through the organic constitution of our race, sin has not only an individual, but a racial aspect. No man lives to himself, and no man dies to himself.[2] We are compelled, whether we will it or no, to assume responsibilities for one another, to be the means of blessing or of curse to others, to lift others up, or drag them

[1] See above, pp. 17, 23, 206.   [2] Rom. xv. 7.

down, by our well-doing or ill-doing. It is as the result of this organic constitution of the race that the innocent are continually called upon to suffer for the guilty. Through it we are involved in ruin by the transgression of our first head. But it is clearly most equitable that if, under the government of God, this principle has wrought for our undoing as a race, there should be admissible a counter-application of it in grace for our salvation. If in Adam all die, why should it be objected to that in Christ all—all in actual relation with Him—should be made alive? If by the trespass of the one (or one trespass) judgment came upon all men to condemnation, why should it not be that by the righteousness of the one (or one act of righteousness) the free gift should come unto all men unto justification of life? If by the one man's disobedience many were made sinners, why cavil at it that by the obedience of the one many are made righteous? So Paul argues in Romans v.,[1] and his reasoning seems irrefutable. The organic constitution of our race, most beneficent, as we saw, in itself, but which tells so heavily against us where sin is concerned,

[1] Ver. 12-21.

again proves its beneficence by becoming, through the Second Adam, the instrument of our salvation. The representative principle brought us under condemnation; the same representative principle works deliverance.

(*c*) Look finally in this connection at the place of *death* in Christ's work. 'Christ died for our sins.' Everywhere in the New Testament the very kernel of His reconciling work is placed in that submission to death. Why was this? There is but one answer—death was that in which was expressed the judgment of God upon the sin of our race. It appears in the context of New Testament doctrine as a penal evil to which Christ voluntarily submitted for the abolition of our curse. He was made sin for us; He redeemed us from the curse of the law, having become a curse for us: as it is appointed unto men once to die, and after this the judgment; so Christ was once offered to bear the sins of many.[1] Even Dr. M'Leod Campbell says — in this, I think, coming very near the heart of the matter —'Further, as our Lord alone truly tasted death, so to Him alone had death its perfect meaning as

[1] 2 Cor. v. 21; Gal. iii. 13.; Heb. ix. 27, 28.

the wages of sin. . . . For thus, in Christ's honouring of the righteous law of God, *the sentence of the law* was included, as well as *the mind of God* which that sentence expressed. . . . Man being by the constitution of humanity capable of death, and death having come as the wages of sin, it was not simply sin that had to be dealt with, but an existing law with its penalty of death, and that death as already incurred.'[1] But if this is all wrong—if death has no such meaning, but is simply the natural fate of all living beings—what becomes of this New Testament interpretation of the death of Christ? It is subverted. On the other hand, the fact that this view of death is implied in the New Testament doctrine of atonement confirms our previous conclusions, and shows the intimate coherence and firm consistency of the Biblical system of ideas.

(3) The third New Testament doctrine to which reference was made was the doctrine of *regeneration* by the divine Spirit. It is not only forgiveness of sins that man needs, but renewal unto holiness; a radical change of heart, the impartation of a new principle of life, progressive

[1] *The Nature of the Atonement*, pp. 259-262 (4th edit.).

transformation in sanctification into the image of Him who created him. But it need hardly be said that this whole doctrine of the work of the divine Spirit, of which the New Testament is so full, rests again on just those conceptions of man's nature, and of the origin, character, and effects of his sin, which have already been unfolded. In the doctrine of the divine image in man lies the ground of that *receptiveness* of man for the new divine life which the Spirit imparts—a life which, once imparted, becomes the individual's own life. In the doctrine of man's fall, and of the effects of the fall in depravation, hereditary sin, and spiritual inability, we have the explanation of his *need* of regeneration. In the positive realisation of the divine image in Christ, we have the *model* or *pattern* to which his redeemed nature is now to be conformed. To put on the new man is but to put on the image of God in Christ. To this we are predestinated that we should be conformed to the image of His Son.[1]

(4) Finally, the doctrine of man has a most direct bearing on the Christian doctrine of *immortality*, and, as included in this, on the Christian

[1] Rom. viii. 29.

hope of *resurrection*. It has already been noted as a feature of the Biblical religion that it puts a marked honour on the body. The body is never despised, as it is in some other religions, and as it came to be afterwards in the Christian Church itself: it is honoured, magnified, spoken of as the temple of the Holy Ghost; a great destiny is prepared for it. Therefore God is to be glorified in it; it is to be kept pure for His service during life.[1] Accordingly, as was to be anticipated in the religion of the incarnation, Christianity never loses sight of the body in its hopes for the future. The Christian religion knows nothing of the abstract immortality of the soul of the philosophic schools. It affirms the survival of the soul; but the disembodied state, as we saw before, is always regarded as a mutilated, imperfect, temporary one. The immortality of which it holds out the hope is an immortality of *the whole man* —body and soul together. It is the whole man in his complex nature that Christ has redeemed, not a part of man simply.[2] It will be seen how

---

[1] Rom. xii. 1; 1 Cor. vii. 19-20.
[2] Cf. Laidlaw, *Bible Doctrine of Man*, pp. 341 ff. · Salmond, *Immortality*, p. 469 (4th Ed.).

entirely this accords with the views to which we were led of the composite nature of man, and of death as a violent and non-natural rupture of the parts of that nature.

An immediate corollary of this view is the doctrine of *resurrection* ; and it is most instructive, and confirmatory of our previous reasonings, to note how deeply this doctrine enters into the substance of the Christian system. It is usual with many to trace this doctrine of resurrection to late Parsee or other external influences. To my mind it has its roots in the essential Biblical ideas of God, man, sin, death, and redemption, and in more or less pronounced form can be traced through the whole of Scripture. The Old Testament saint shuddered at the thought of Sheol, and when he rose to the hope of immortality through his faith in God, it was to the hope of *deliverance from Sheol*, and of restored life in God's presence and fellowship.[1] I do not think we read too much into the Old Testament expressions on these subjects; I think we often read too little. But it is nevertheless in the New Testament, and through Jesus Christ, that life

[1] See in *Christian View of God*, App. to Lect. v.

and incorruption have been brought clearly to light.[1] And here the doctrine of resurrection assumes at once a leading place in the Christian hope. Jesus Himself did not remain in the grave. He rose in the body. His was no mere immortality of the soul; He claimed the body as part of *Himself*. In the body He ascended; in the body, now glorified, He lives and rules; in the body He will appear again, the second time, unto salvation. Not only, however, has He himself risen in the body, but His resurrection is set forth as the pledge of ours.[2] The hope of the believer is not simply that his *soul* shall live hereafter, but he looks for the adoption, to wit, the redemption of the body.[3] The body of his humiliation shall yet be changed into the image of Christ's glorious body.[4] The problems and difficulties of the doctrine of the resurrection I cannot even touch on here—they arise in part from misconceptions which do not properly belong to the doctrine;[5] but there is surely no mistaking the bearings of these remarkable lines

[1] 2 Tim. i. 10.
[2] 1 Cor. xv. 20 ff.
[3] Rom. viii. 23.
[4] Phil. iii. 21.
[5] Even Romanes seemed prepared latterly to accept the bodily resurrection (*Thoughts on Religion*, pp. 145, 162).

CHRISTIAN REDEMPTION 283

of truth on such questions as whether death is a natural fate for man, and on the view which Scripture takes of human nature generally.

Here I close this imperfect survey of an interesting section of divine truth. The conclusion I draw for myself, and which I would fain have others draw, is that 'the firm foundation of God standeth,'[1] and that, as time rolls on, and the full bearings of scientific discoveries become apparent, there will be felt to be less need than ever for being 'carried about with every wind of doctrine.'[2] 'Now unto the King eternal, incorruptible, invisible, the only God' . . . 'the blessed and only Potentate, the King of kings, and Lord of lords; who only hath immortality, dwelling in light unapproachable; whom no man hath seen, nor can see.' . . . 'Unto Him be the glory in the Church and in Christ Jesus unto all generations for ever and ever. Amen.'[3]

[1] 2 Tim. ii. 19.
[2] Eph. iv. 14.
[3] 1 Tim. i. 17; vi. 15, 16; Eph. iii. 21.

NOTES TO LECTURES

NOTE I

MODERN NATURALISTIC VIEW OF THE WORLD (p. 4)

In general, what I mean by the 'modern' view of the world in these lectures is the type of theory which, sometimes in a more reasoned-out and aggressive, sometimes in a more diffused form, is found underlying a large part of the scientific thought of our time; which is characterised by a tendency to a materialistic and mechanical explanation of the phenomena of life and mind, by the rejection of 'teleological' considerations, and, of course, by an utter abandonment of the idea of the entrance of the supernatural into human history and experience, and therefore of the conception of divine revelation. It is the type of theory ably combated in such books as Ward's *Naturalism and Agnosticism*, and Balfour's *Foundations of Belief*. How deeply it has infected the thought of the age may be seen from current literature, or from the popularity of Haeckel's work referred to in the text. A suggestive light is afforded by the remarks on the prevalent scientific attitude in Professor W. James's Ingersoll Lectures on Immortality. Yet in the better circles of thought there is already a profound reaction from it, without, however, always the complete throwing off of its influences, or such return to a full Christian belief as happily was witnessed in the case of the late Professor Romanes (see below, Note III.). There is often a breaking with the modern view in parts— and these, as in the matter of teleology, very essential parts; while in other respects, by a curious inconsistency, the 'modern' theories are held to be unimpaired and irrefragable.

NOTE II

THE CREATION NARRATIVE AND SCIENCE (p. 40)

Haeckel's tribute to the creation narrative in Genesis, as coming from an unexpected quarter, is worth re-quoting. He says: 'The Mosaic history of creation, since, in the first chapter of Genesis, it forms the introduction to the Old Testament, has enjoyed, down to the present day, general recognition in the whole Jewish and Christian world of civilisation. Its extraordinary success is explained, not only by its close connection with Jewish and Christian doctrines, but also by the simple and natural chain of ideas which runs through it, and which contrasts favourably with the confused mythology of creation current among most of the ancient nations. First, God creates the earth as an inorganic body; then he separates light from darkness, then water from the dry land. Now the earth has become habitable for organisms, and plants are first created, animals later; and among the latter the inhabitants of the water and of the air first, afterwards the inhabitants of the dry land. Finally, God creates man, the last of all organisms, in His own image, and as ruler of the earth. Two great and fundamental ideas, common also to the non-miraculous theory of development, meet us in the Mosaic hypothesis of creation with surprising clearness and simplicity—the idea of separation or differentiation, and the idea of progressive development or perfecting. Although Moses looks upon the result of the great laws of organic development (which we shall later point out as the necessary conclusions of the doctrine of descent) as the direct actions of a constructing Creator, yet in his theory there lies hidden the ruling idea of a progressive development and a differentiation of the originally simple matter. We can therefore bestow our just and sincere admiration on the Jewish lawgiver's grand insight into nature, and his simple and natural hypothesis of creation, without discovering in it a so-called divine revelation' (*History of Creation*, i. pp. 37-38). The two grounds which lead Haeckel to conclude that it cannot be a divine revelation, viz. : (1) the geocentric error that the earth is the central point in the universe ; and (2) the anthropomorphic error that man is the premeditated end of the creation of the earth, are not of a kind likely to disturb many people's minds. The second (so-called) 'error' most will probably look on as an indubitable truth ; and, in light of the revelations of such a book as Dr. A. R. Wallace's *Man's Place in the Universe*, they may think twice before unconditionally condemning even the view that makes our world and man the centre of the physical universe.

NOTE III

MONISTIC METAPHYSICS—REACTION FROM HAECKEL
(p. 72)

Nothing could well be cruder or less defensible than the strange mixture of scientific, scholastic, and Spinozistic ideas which Haeckel dignifies with the name, 'our Monistic philosophy.' As H. Spencer works with the idea of 'Unknowable Power,' so Haeckel works with the idea of one sole eternal 'Substance'—an idea which he professes to derive from Spinoza and Goethe (*Riddle of Universe*, pp. 8, 70-77, etc.), but which he employs in a sense which is a travesty of the meaning of these thinkers. As hinted in the text, 'substance' is one of the obscurest categories in the region of philosophy, and, in the shape in which Haeckel uses it, is really a survival of scholasticism. Spinoza distinguishes 'Thought' and 'Extension' as attributes of a Reality identified with neither; but Haeckel, while in terms doing the same, in reality identifies 'substance' with 'matter,' and 'thought' with material 'force' or 'energy,' and so falls back into a view indistinguishable from crass materialism. A few sentences from his book will put this clearly. The basis of his system is the loudly-vaunted 'Law of Substance,' which 'fundamental cosmic law' 'establishes the eternal persistence of matter and force; their unvarying constancy throughout the entire universe' (p. 2; cf. more fully, p. 75). Again: 'Monism recognises one sole substance in the universe, which is at once "God and Nature"; body and spirit (or matter and energy) it holds to be inseparable.' . . . 'We adhere firmly to the pure, unequivocal monism of Spinoza: Matter, or infinitely extended substance, and Spirit (or Energy), or sensitive and thinking substance,' etc. (p. 8). The notion of substance (matter and spirit), accordingly, is resolved into 'the chemical law of the "conservation of matter," and the younger physical law of the "conservation of energy"' (p. 75). The 'soul' is a mode of material force. 'Our own naturalistic conception of the psychic activity sees in it a group of vital phenomena which are dependent on a definite material substratum [this he names 'psychoplasm'], like all other phenomena. . . . Our conception is in this sense materialistic' (p. 32). It need only be remarked: (1) that 'force' and 'energy' (notions which Haeckel wrongly identifies) are as mysterious and difficult of apprehension as 'substance'; (2) that the forces or energies connected with matter are something quite different from what Spinoza meant by 'thought'; and (3) that the law of 'conservation of energy,' which has to do only with motions, affords no clue whatever to the wholly disparate phenomena of consciousness. The energy of brain action is accounted for *wholly* in brain changes, and consciousness absorbs no share of it. It is, from the point of view of the physicist, an 'epiphenomenon,' to explain which theories of ' psycho-physical parallelism ' are invented—theories which Haeckel, with his thesis of unity, contemptuously sets aside (p. 76).

Popular as this crude philosophy may be in certain circles, it is well to recognise that it is really an inheritance from the materialistic tendencies of the middle of last century, and has long been on the wane among really influential thinkers. We do not need to go further for proof of this than Haeckel's own pages. Haeckel has not only to confess that, 'however natural the thought may be [that mind and matter are simply "two different aspects of one and the same object, the cosmos"], it is still very far from being generally accepted' (p. 76); but it is his constant lament in the course of his discussion that most of his own great lights have deserted him. If his theories were true, we should expect that scientific men who once upheld them would only grow the firmer in their conviction as time went on. Unfortunately, as his pages show, the opposite has been the case. One of his chief authorities, *e.g.*, from whom much was hoped, was Virchow. Virchow, in the days of his early activity, was a monist of Haeckel's own type—'a *pure monist* in the best days of his scientific activity . . . one of the most distinguished representatives of the newly-awakened materialism' (p. 33). But Haeckel has to bemoan his defection. 'Twenty-eight years afterwards Virchow represented the diametrically opposite view' in his famous speech on *The Liberty of Science* (1877), and monism has to throw him overboard (p. 34). Du Bois-Reymond is a second example. *His* loss has also to be mourned. 'The more completely the distinguished orator of the Berlin Academy had defended the principles of the monistic philosophy ... the more triumphant was the cry of our opponents when in 1872, in his famous *Ignorabimus* speech, he spoke of consciousness as an insoluble problem, and opposed it to the other functions of the brain as a supernatural phenomenon' (p. 34). A third illustrious example is Wundt. In Germany Wundt is considered to be the ablest living psychologist. Wundt, too, began as a monist after Haeckel's own heart. His work *On Animal and Human Psychology* in 1863 extended the law of the persistence of force to the psychic world, and made use of a series of facts of electro-physiology by way of demonstration. But, alas! thirty years afterwards (1892) Wundt published a second and much-modified edition of his work. 'The important principles of the first edition are entirely abandoned in the second': the monistic standpoint is exchanged for a dualistic one. Wundt tells us that 'he learned many years ago to consider the work a sin of his youth'; it 'weighed on him as a kind of crime, from which he longed to free himself as soon as possible.' As Haeckel says in sorrow, 'In the first edition he is purely monistic and materialistic; in the second edition purely dualistic and spiritualistic' (p. 36). There is yet, however, another example. Perhaps the one man on whose support, next to Darwin's, Haeckel leans in his book is George J. Romanes. His praise of Romanes is continual. 'I am completely at one with him and Darwin,' he declares, 'in almost all their views and convictions' (p. 38). Yet, as every one now knows, Romanes too deserted him, and died a devout believer. All the things that Haeckel had thrown overboard—the soul, free-will, immortality—became to Romanes again the profoundest verities. (See his *Thoughts on Religion*, edited by Gore; and *Life and Letters*, by his wife.) Yet Haeckel pleases himself with the belief that science has destroyed Christianity!

NOTE IV

R. OTTO ON PRESENT-DAY DARWINISM (p. 85)

The important series of articles in the *Theologische Rundschau*—a Review of sufficiently 'advanced' standpoint—by Rudolf Otto on *Darwinismus von Heute und Theologie* ('The Darwinism of To-day and Theology'), to which repeated reference is made in the footnotes, are five in number, and appear in the issues for December 1902, May and June 1903, and January and February 1904. They are exceedingly able and well-informed, full and candid in exposition, acute in criticism, and, altogether, highly significant as a sign of the times. They give a vivid impression of the extraordinary divergence of view which has manifested itself in evolutionary schools on the Continent; emphasise the distinction between a 'doctrine of descent' and the acceptance of the Darwinian hypothesis of evolution by natural selection; heap up evidence of what is termed (notwithstanding the advocacy of Weismann and other 'pure' Darwinians, who still depart considerably from Darwin) the 'Verfall' (Decay) of Darwinism in Germany; bring out the crucial point at which the Darwinian theory touches theology—the denial of 'teleology'; and make clear the points in which the newer evolutionism breaks with the old (inadequacy of 'natural selection' and of the principle of 'utility' to explain structures, denial of production of new forms by slow and insensible gradations, need of teleological principle, etc.—see below), and the multiplied difficulties attendant on the Darwinian view generally. The author shows how during the last forty years 'the differentiation and ramification of Darwinian theories has become the longer the wider,' and how 'the number and the manifold grouping and shading of

Darwin's scholars are well-nigh unbounded' (December 1902, p. 489). He points out that the characteristic thing in Darwinism—that which specially interests and constitutes a danger for theology—is its 'natural teleology,' *i.e.*, the explanation of the apparently purposeful and planned in nature by the operation of 'natural' causes, without intentional direction or striving to an end. 'In this sense his doctrine is an attempt at the abolition (*Aufhebung*) of 'teleology' (January 1904, p. 2; cf. December 1902, p. 486). We cannot enter into the detail of Otto's argument, supported by an exhaustive survey of the literature of the subject during the last ten years or more; but may give the *résumé* with which he closes of the chief contrasts between the newer and the older (*i.e.*, Darwinian) evolution. He places the points side by side in parallel columns, heading the one 'Darwin' and the other 'Korschinsky und die Neueren' ('Korschinsky and the Newer School'):—

DARWIN	THE NEWER
1. All organic being is capable of modification. Variation partly from inner, partly from external causes. Insignificant, imperceptible, individual differences.	1. All organic being capable of modification. This capability a fundamental, inner property of living beings generally, independent of external conditions. It is preserved, usually in a latent form, by inheritance. It breaks out here and there in sudden changes.
2. Struggle for existence. This accumulates, heightens, fixes useful properties, and causes those which are not useful to disappear. All marks and peculiarities of a formed species are results of a long-continued process of natural selection.	2. Sudden changes. These are under favourable conditions the starting-points for enduring races. The marks sometimes useful, sometimes quite indifferent to use or hurt. Sometimes not in accord with external relations.
3. The species is subjected to constant modification. Continuous object of natural selection and enhancement of properties. Through this again the origin of new species.	3. All species, once firmly built up, remain; still, through Heterogenesis there enters a splitting off (*Abspaltung*) of new forms, and shattering of the vital equilibrium. The new at first insecure and wavering. Gradually attains stability. Then new forms and races with a constitution gradually attaining fixity.

NOTES

4. The sharper and more painful the operation of external conditions of existence, the more intense the struggle for existence, and the more rapid and sure the development of new forms.	4. Only under exceptionally favourable conditions, only if the struggle for existence is weak or not present, can new forms originate or become fixed. Under hard conditions none originate. If they do originate, they forthwith perish.
5. The chief condition of development, therefore, struggle for existence and natural selection.	5. Struggle for existence only decimates the (in itself) much richer fulness of possible forms. It hinders, where it exists, the springing up of new variations, and is an obstacle in the way of new formation. In itself it is a factor hostile and not favourable to evolution.
6. If there were no struggle for existence, there would be no evolution, no adaptation, no perfecting.	6. If there were no struggle for existence, there would be no perishing of forms which had originated, or were in process of origination. The world of organisms would then be a genealogical tree (*Stammbaum*) of enormous height, and perfectly illimitable fulness of forms.
7. Advance in nature, the 'perfecting' of organisms, is only a more complicated, ever more complete adaptation to external conditions. It is attained in a purely mechanical way, through accumulation of marks at one time useful.	7. The adaptation wrought by natural selection has nothing to do with perfecting; for the organisms which physiologically and morphologically stand higher are not always better adapted to external relations than those which stand lower. Evolution is not explicable mechanically. The origin of higher forms out of lower is only possible through a tendency to advance which resides in the organisms. This tendency is nearly related to, or identical with, the tendency to change. It impels the organisms, so far as external conditions permit, towards perfection.

Otto concludes: 'This means now, certainly, the recognition of development and derivation, but sets Darwinism aside as a superseded hypothesis; partly establishes, partly renders possible, the striving to an end, inner causation, teleology; sets aside the accidental factors that stand in the foreground, and opens a glimpse into the metaphysical background of things' (February 1904, pp. 60-62). See further below, Note XI.

NOTE V

RECENT VIEWS ON THE DESCENT OF MAN (p. 136)

In the argument in the text, I have been content to go on the assumption of Haeckel, Huxley, Weismann, etc., that man is physically descended from some form of anthropoid ape (not of existing species). I have no interest in questioning the fact, if it should turn out to be established. It is right, however, to point out that, so far from being established, this line of descent for man through the anthropoid apes is very extensively challenged by recent evolutionists. Some go so far as to say that ' the prevailing view is that man cannot have come from the apes, nor from the lemurs, and that, beyond this, the case is perplexing.' However this may be, it cannot be disputed that the anthropoid descent is now widely contested. In his *Lessons from Nature*, Mr. Mivart already dwelt on the enormous difficulty of bringing man into relation with any known form of ape, his structure exhibiting affinities with many widely separated forms, lower and higher, among the primates (pp. 171 ff.). 'It is manifest,' he says, 'that man, the apes, and the half-apes cannot be arranged in a single ascending series, of which man is the term and conclusion. . . . On any conceivable hypothesis there are many similar structures, each of which must be deemed to have been independently evolved in more than one instance. . . . In fact, in the words of the illustrious Dutch naturalists, Messrs. Schroeder, Van der Kolk, and Vrolik, "the lines of affinity existing between different primates construct rather a network than a ladder"'(pp. 173, 174, 175). A 'fatal objection against deriving the human species directly from monkeys' has been 'found in the structure of the hind members. The human foot and the hind hand of all the monkeys are both excessively specialised and fixed, but in opposite directions, one for strength and erectness, the other for flexibility, prehension, and climbing. Hence neither can be derived from the other, nor can there be any intermediate form, except such as may continue the unspecialised limb of an ancestor from which both may have been descended' (Professor G. Macloskie, in article on 'Problems in Evolution').

The trend of recent investigation, in view of these difficulties, has been to seek the ancestry of man in some earlier form from which the various groups (anthropoid apes, man, etc.) may have descended. The anthropologist Topinard took a step in this direction in deriving the anthropoid apes and man alike from the *Pitheci*, or Old World Monkeys (*The Monist*, October 1895: I am indebted for this and other references to Dr. B. B. Warfield). Professor Cope, on the other hand, thinks a derivation through the monkeys impossible, and would substitute for it a descent of the *Anthropomorpha* (including man and the anthropoid apes) from the Lemurs (*Primary Factors of Organic Evolution*, 1896, p. 154). Finally, the learned Professor of Zoology in the University of Utrecht, A. A. W. Hubrecht, on the basis of extensive comparative studies on the Lemurs and the Tarsii (included by Cope among the Lemuridæ), contends that the placental characters of the Lemurs exclude them from consideration, and argues for a derivation from a Tarsiad form. But along with this goes the singular admission: 'Tarsius has taught us . . . to entertain a certain amount of healthy scepticism with respect to the traditional tables of mammalian descent. The genera known to us very rarely converge towards known predecessors as we go backwards in geological time; their respective genealogies run much more parallel to each other, the point of meeting being thus continually transported further backwards towards yet older geological strata' (*The*

Descent of the Primates, 1897, pp. 39, 40). To the unscientific mind this looks very much like the yielding up, not only of the descent of man from anthropoid apes, but of the proof of evolutionary descent *in toto*. For parallel lines, however far carried back, do *not* meet. And what of the unconscionable number of 'missing links' it is now necessary to suppose?

NOTE VI

MODERN THEORIES OF EVOLUTION AND THE FALL
(p. 158)

It is natural that Christian theologians who accept the doctrine of evolution should be concerned about its bearings on the doctrines of the Fall and of Sin, and should do their best to show how the two doctrines can be reconciled. There is, as I seek to show in the text, no contradiction, except on a particular view of evolution, viz., that man has slowly emerged from a state of animalism and barbarism, and did not start off with a pure and harmonious nature. This, however, is the view of man's origin currently accepted, with which it is sought to be shown that the doctrine of a real 'fall' can somehow be reconciled. The ablest attempt, probably, is that of Canon Gore (now Bishop of Worcester) in a lecture at Sheffield on 'The Theory of Evolution and the Christian Doctrine of the Fall,' of which a fairly full account is given in *The Expository Times* for April 1897. Dr. Driver represents the same point of view in a note on the subject in his *Genesis*, pp. 56-57. Other expositions on more or less similar lines may be seen in Illingworth's *Bampton Lectures*, pp. 143 ff., 154 ff.; in Bernard's article on 'Sin' in *Dictionary of Bible* (iv. p. 528); in Griffith-Jones's *Ascent through Christ*, pp. 138 ff.; in Abbott's *Theology of an Evolu-*

tionist, pp. 31 ff.; in Shepherd's *Three Bulwarks of the Faith*, pp. 29 ff., etc. Professor G. Henslow has a few remarks on the subject in his *Present-Day Rationalism*, pp. 318-319. For a sober discussion of the subject from an independent standpoint, see Principal Simon's *Bible Problems*, ch. vi.

The crucial point in all these theories is the compatibility of a fall and of the Biblical view of sin with an account of man's origin and nature which makes sin a necessity of his development. That difficulty, it seems to me, is nowhere satisfactorily dealt with, nor do I believe it can be got over on the original assumption. It is quite fair to say with Bishop Gore, Dr. Driver, and most of these writers, that the Bible does not represent man as created 'perfect,' *i.e.*, highly developed, civilised, etc. That is so, but 'perfect' in this sense is one thing, and pure, harmonious, capable of a life of obedience, is another; and it is the latter which the brute genesis of man denies. Bishop Gore is also justified in protesting against a science, or theory of evolution, which denies 'freedom' to man. 'If science persists in denying that sin is sin'—I quote from the summary in *Expository Times*—'persists, that is to say, in denying that man has any freedom of will, and, therefore, that he can have any responsibility for his actions—if science persists in denying that, then science and the Bible can never agree together.' But the real issue is not with a theory of determinism of this kind. Whatever limited measure of freedom we ascribe to man in the process of his ascent from the animal condition, no one who accepts the ordinary evolutionary theory can possibly hold that it amounted to power to live or develop in a sinless condition. With brute passions and propensities at their maximum, made fiercer and more lawless, probably, by the dawn of self-consciousness, while reason, conscience, power of self-control, are yet a feeble glimmer, there is no escape from the conclusion that sin is inevitable, and will be the dominant fact in man's development for an incalculable period. To the reply that may be given, that sin is not sin, or is not imputed, where there is no law, it must be answered that human sin, in that case, is emptied of nearly all its depth of significance in the Bible (see in text, pp. 208-9); and it is still not shown that a point *ever* comes at which sinless obedience is possible. It would be different if some other view of development were adopted, according to which man's immediate progenitors did not evince any such violence of passions and propensities as will could not from the first perfectly control; but that is not the view usually held by evolutionists. When, therefore, Dr. Driver says: 'It is sufficient for Christian theology, if we hold that, whatever the actual occasion may have been, and however immature, in intellect and culture, he may have been at the time, man failed in the trial to which he was exposed, that sin thus entered into the world, and that consequently the subsequent development of the race was not simply what God intended it to be: it has been attended through its whole course by an element of moral disorder, and thus in different ways it has been marred, perverted, impeded, or thrown back' (*Genesis*, pp. 56-57), he misses the essential point, which is that, in the condition in which evolutionary science starts man off, he had no alternative but to fail. No doctrine of abstract 'freedom' can be strained so far as to obviate that conclusion.

With some words of Bishop Gore in his lecture I am most heartily in accord. 'The doctrine of sin and of the fall in its true importance has a far securer basis than the supposition that Genesis iii. is literal history. The doctrine of the fall is not separable from the doctrine of sin, or the doctrine of sin from that of moral freedom. It rests on the broad basis of human experience, which is bound up with its reality. Most of all, it rests for Christians on the teaching of Christ, for Christ's teaching and action postulate throughout the doctrine of sin. But that doctrine, in its turn, goes back upon the Old Testament, which is full of the truth that the evils of human nature are due not to its essential constitution, but to man's wilfulness and its results; that the disordering force in human nature has been moral, the force of sin; that human history represents in one shape a fall from a divine purpose, a fall constantly repeated and renewed in acts of disobedience.' What I say is that such a view of sin and of the moral state of the world requires for its basis a different account of the origin of man and of his primeval constitution from that which ordinary evolutionary theories yield.

NOTE VII

RETROGRESSION AMONG SAVAGES (p. 161)

The following are some instances illustrating the statement that races ranked as savage have often behind them a much higher, and sometimes very advanced, civilisation.

Dr. Tylor observes: 'Degeneration probably operates even more actively in the lower than in the higher culture. Barbarous nations and savage hordes, with their less knowledge and scantier appliances, would seem peculiarly exposed to degrading influences.' He gives an instance from West Africa, and continues: 'In South-East Africa, also, a comparatively high barbaric culture, which we especially associate with the old descriptions of the Kingdom of Monomotapa, seems to have fallen away, and the remarkable ruins of buildings of hewn stone fitted without mortar indicate a former civilisation above that of the native population' (*Primitive Culture*, p. 39).

The same writer, in a paper in *Nature*, 1881, p. 29, says: 'Dr. Bastian has lately visited New Zealand and the Sandwich Islands, and gathered some interesting information as to native traditions. The documents strengthen the view which for years has been growing among anthropologists as to the civilisation of the Polynesians. It is true that they were found in Captain Cook's time living in a barbaric state, and their scanty clothing and want of metals led superior observers even to class them as savages; but their beliefs and customs show plain traces of descent from ancestors who in some way shared the higher culture of the Asiatic nations.'

A remarkable fund of information on the degradation of savages is contained in an address by Mr. Albert J. Mott on 'The Origin of Savage Life,' delivered before the Literary and Philosophical Society of Liverpool, October 6, 1873. Speaking of Easter Island in the Pacific, Mr. Mott says: 'Easter Island stands alone in the Pacific Ocean, 2000 miles from South America, and about 1000 from the nearest islands that are habitable. It is about twelve miles long by four in width; not so large as Jersey. The inhabitants, about 1000 in number, are savages. . . . This island is strewed with hundreds of carved stone images, many of them of extraordinary size. Some are nearly 40 feet long. Many of them are over 15 feet. Two of the smaller ones are in the British Museum. One of these is 8 feet high, and weighs 4 tons. Many of these images had separate stone crowns placed upon their heads, the crowns being from 2 to 10 feet across. Thirty of these crowns were found on the hill from the rock of which they were sculptured, waiting to be removed. The images were generally set on pedestals, upon raised terraces, of which there are many. . . .

'Similar terraces and images have been seen in other islands now uninhabited. The ruins of ancient stone buildings of great extent are found in the Philippine Islands, the

NOTES 303

Ladrones, the Marshall and Gilbert groups; the Society Islands, the Navigators and the Marquesas. They thus extend over 10,000 miles of ocean.'

The same authority says: 'The whole of North America, from the Gulf of Mexico to Canada, is full of ancient works of earth and stone, chiefly found in the form of mounds and embankments. They exist in countless thousands, and, I believe, in every State: but the most remarkable are in the great plain or valley between the Alleghanies and the Rocky Mountains, a district at least 1000 miles square. Some lines of embankment are 30 feet high. Many areas enclosed by them are from one to two hundred acres; some are double this size. . . . Many of the enclosures are in the form of circles and squares, and in many cases these figures are mathematically exact, notwithstanding their great size. . . . Neither a true circle, with a radius of 850 feet, nor a true square, with a side of 1080 feet, can be drawn upon open ground by any one without the help of exact measures and mathematical knowledge.'

He goes on to adduce evidence that the North American Indians, 'instead of springing from some lower state like that of the Australians,' are 'the successors of a people in every respect much higher than themselves.'

Reference only need be made to the exhumed cities of New Mexico, about which much has been written. The ruins are very extensive, covering hundreds of miles. The articles recovered include many thousands of clay vessels, implements of stone, utensils, articles of clothing and of ceremony, and also a vast number of prehistoric relics.

NOTE VIII

PROFESSOR BOYD DAWKINS ON TERTIARY MAN (p. 172)

The following quotations from Professor Boyd Dawkins's work, *Early Man in Britain*, summarise that writer's views on the question of Tertiary Man.

Eocene.—' It is obvious that man had no place in such an assemblage of animals as that described in this chapter. To seek for highly-specialised man in a fauna where no living genus of placental mammal was present would be an idle and hopeless quest' (p. 36).

Miocene.—' Man, the most highly specialised of all creatures, had no place in a fauna which is conspicuous by the absence of all the mammalia now associated with him' (p. 67). This on the ground of the fact that 'no living species of land mammal has been met with in the Miocene fauna.' He combats the views of those who think that traces of man are found in France belonging to this period. Either the flints relied on are not artificial; or, ' If they be artificial, then I would suggest that they were made by one of the higher apes then living in France rather than by man' (p. 68).

' When all this is taken into account, it will be seen how improbable, nay, how impossible it is that man, as we know him now, the highest and most specialised of all created forms, should have had a place in the Miocene world' (p. 69: Professor Dawkins spells throughout 'Meiocene,' 'Pleiocene ').

Pliocene.—' There is an argument against the probability of man having lived in Italy in Pliocene times that seems to me unanswerable. . . . It is to my mind to the last degree improbable that man, the most highly specialised of the animal kingdom, should have been present in such a fauna as

NOTES

this, composed of so many distinct species. They belong to one stage of evolution, and man to another and a later stage. . . . As the evidence stands at present, the geological record is silent as to man's appearance in Europe in the Pliocene age. It is very improbable that he will ever be proved to have lived in this quarter of the world at that remote time, since of all the European mammalia then alive only one has survived to our own day' (p. 93).

Pleistocene.—Traces of man in Early Pleistocene are doubtful; Dr. Dawkins thinks he finds evidences of man in Mid-Pleistocene; these Prestwich would relegate to *late* Pleistocene (p. 142).

NOTE IX

THE END OF THE ICE AGE (p. 175)

Mr. Warren Upham, a high American authority, writing on 'Primitive Man in the Ice-Age' in the *Bib. Sacra* for October 1902, apropos of the Lansing Skeleton (see Note XII.), says: 'According to the computations and estimates of Professor N. H. Winchell, Dr. Edmund Andrews, Professor G. F. Wright, and others, based on the rates of recession of waterfalls, of the accumulation of beach sands, and of erosion and deposition of sediments by streams and lakes, the time since the moraine hills were amassed, and since men lost their implements in the gravels and sands of the valleys flooded from the latest ice-melting, has been about 7000 years. Many independent estimates of the length of this post-glacial period have been made both in America and Europe, which agree together so well that this measure of the lapse of time since the Ice Age may be accepted with confidence' (p. 732).

I quote this because Mr. Upham, with his views of the length of the Ice Age, is himself an advocate of a very high antiquity of man in *Europe* (p. 741).

For the most recent calculations as to the end of the Ice Age in America—approximately in Europe—see article on 'The Revision of Geological Time,' by Professor Wright in *Bib. Sacra*, July 1903. Professor Winchell writes in September 1902: 'Post-glacial time has been computed in various ways, and it has been pretty nearly unanimously agreed that post-glacial time does not exceed 10,000 years, and probably amounts to about 8000 years.' Professor Salisbury, of the New Jersey State Geological Survey, writes in his Report in 1902: 'Many lines of calculation, all of them confessedly more or less uncertain, point to the retreat of the last ice-sheet from the northern part of the United States 6000 to 10,000 years ago. While these figures are to be looked on as estimates only, there are so many lines of evidence pointing in the same direction that the recency (geologically speaking) of the last glaciation must be looked upon as established' (p. 579). A valuable paper of older date by Mr. P. F. Kendal and Mr. Gray on 'The Cause of the Ice Age,' read to the British Association, August 4, 1892, should also be consulted.

NOTE X

THE 'NEW RACE' IN EGYPT (p. 179)

The state of opinion as to the character of early Egyptian civilisation has been materially affected by the remarkable discoveries made since 1894 of the tombs and relics of a race presenting peculiarities quite distinct from those of the dynastic Egyptians (cf. Budge, *History of Egypt*, i. pp. 5 ff.:

a good collection of the relics in Turin Museum). Professor Petrie, one of the most diligent explorers, holding its people to be, not pre-dynastic, but *intruders* into Egypt between the fifth and the eleventh dynasties, designates them 'The New Race'; others take them to be the aborigines inhabiting the country when the dynastic Egyptians invaded it. They represent a type of civilisation quite distinct from, and much ruder than, that of the dynastic Egyptians. Still they can in no way be spoken of as uncivilised. Their tombs abound in pottery—vases, jars, bowls, saucers, etc., some being of most unusual shapes, and others being ornamented with unusual designs (Budge, p. 7). Some of the tombs seem to have been stately affairs (p. 12); others were built of crude bricks, and were partially destroyed by fire (p. 13); others were mere pits, sometimes roofed over (p. 9). Professor Petrie says of them: 'They were great hunters, they were acquainted with the metals gold, silver, and copper, they were right-handed, they could spin and weave, they were masters in the art of working in stone and in the production of vases and vessels of beautiful shape and form' (p. 25). They had a peculiar system of sepulture—the knees being sharply bent and the thighs drawn up into a sitting posture; while often the skull was removed, and the body otherwise mutilated or dismembered—Professor Petrie thinks was sometimes partly eaten (pp. 10, 26).

The problems connected with this alleged 'New Race' are still far from being fully solved. If they were, as Dr. Budge and others think, the aboriginal inhabitants, it is singular that no representations of them should be found on the monuments: it is in favour of Professor Petrie's view, also, that the period between the fifth and the eleventh dynasties is a monumental hiatus, which requires to be filled up in some way (it is certain that the 'New Race' was in Egypt before the twelfth dynasty). On the other hand, the resemblance in burial customs (interment in sitting posture, mutilations, etc.) to those of later palæolithic man (Cro-Magnon, Mentone, etc.), may suggest a much earlier period, with distinct break from the Egyptians. No means at least of bridging the chasm between the two races seems yet to have been found. Probably the difficulty felt will be in crediting palæolithic man with a civilisation so high as already appears in this race; but, apart from *a priori* assumptions, that difficulty need not stagger us. More light, no doubt, will soon be obtained.

NOTE XI

OTTO ON THE SUDDEN ORIGIN OF MAN (p. 182)

In the third of his articles on 'Present-Day Darwinism and Theology' in the *Theologische Rundschau* (see above, Note IV.), R. Otto has some striking remarks on the bearings of evolution on the origin of man. 'But even on the theory of descent,' he says, '*e.g.*, in the way of development by a sudden leap (*sprungweise*), the difference in man might quite well be so great, that, in spite of his bodily derivation, he might, according to his spiritual capabilities, and emotional and moral endowments, belong to a perfectly new category, raising him far above all his predecessors. Nothing whatever hinders, and much speaks on behalf of, the supposition that the last leap (*sprung*) out of animality into humanity was one so great, that with it took place a free and rich development of the psychical (*seelischen*), incomparable to all that had gone before; through which, in truth, it [the psychical] first came to itself, and caused all that had preceded to rank as its prelude' (June 1903, p. 233).

I may perhaps add to this a sentence on sudden developments from Professor Cope's work, *The Origin of the Fittest*. He says: 'The results of such successful metamorphoses are expressed in geological history by more or less abrupt transitions, rather than by uniformly gradual successions' (p. 123).

NOTE XII

THE LANSING SKELETON (p. 184)

Full information regarding this discovery, which has been the subject of much interesting discussion, and has important bearings on the age of man in America, may be seen in a succession of papers in the *Bibliotheca Sacra* for 1902 (October) and 1903 (January and July). Lansing is a place in Kansas (about eighteen miles from Kansas City), and there, in February 1902, a human skeleton was found beneath a bed of loess, through which a tunnel was being excavated for the purposes of a farm. The skull is of a type not differing appreciably from that of modern Indian tribes. The decision of the age of the skeleton depends on the view taken of the nature of the deposit under which it is buried—whether 'true loess,' belonging to what is called the 'Iowan' stage of the glacial period; or post-glacial alluvium of much later date—a point on which opinions seem hopelessly divided. 'As yet, however, they [the experts] have not been able to agree, and the two interpretations offered by geologists are supported by leading advocates of the divergent views' (July 1903, p. 572).

It will be seen that on the determination of this question of the age of the skeleton it depends whether (so far as known) man appeared in America *during* or *after* the glacial period. Prior to this discovery, the only alleged trace of inter-glacial man (though of a late stage of the glacial period) was a slate implement found at Clayton, Delaware, and this was regarded as indecisive. Mr. Warren Upham, who reports on the new discovery, believes that the loess under which the skeleton was found 'was chiefly deposited in a late part of the Ice Age,' and he regards the Lansing skeleton as 'probably our oldest proof of man's presence on this Continent' (October 1902, pp. 734, 741). He assigns to it an antiquity of about 12,000 or 15,000 years. Professors G. F. Wright, N. H. Winchell, and others, agree with Mr. Upham in his general conclusions. On the other hand, a formidable body of authorities—Professor T. C. Chamberlin, Professor S. W. Williston, Professor E. Calvin, Professor R. D. Salisbury, and others—dispute entirely Mr. Upham's view of the deposit, and assign to the skeleton 'a very respectable antiquity, but much short of the close of the glacial invasion'—give 'the fossil man a considerable antiquity,' but deny 'him the age of glacial time' (July 1903, pp. 573, 576).

The interesting feature in this discussion is that the opposition to the age of the skeleton comes, curiously, not from those whose prepossessions are in favour of conservative views, but, as Professor Wright points out, from the 'anthropologists'—*i.e.*, the evolutionists, like Professors Chamberlin and Williston, who find in what they call the 'modern' character of the skull 'evidence which is convincing to some of them that it cannot be very ancient' (January 1903, pp. 29, 30). Hence they decline to admit it to be glacial. The more 'advanced' science here, accordingly, yields the more conservative result. It is not a very remote antiquity, comparatively, that Mr. Upham asks for the skull, yet it is refused to him. It will probably be felt that even the Lansing skeleton does not carry us much further in our search for indubitable evidence of inter-glacial man.

NOTE XIII

WEISMANN'S THEORY OF HEREDITY (p. 236)[1]

All theories of heredity have for their aim the explanation of how the characters of a parent are transmitted to his or her offspring. Weismann's theory may be looked at, first, as a theory of heredity generally; and, second, in its peculiarity as a denial of the transmissibility of 'acquired characters.' The two aspects are related, for Weismann's differs chiefly from other theories in the stringency with which it carries out the demand for a 'mechanical' explanation of the facts of inheritance. The case for the denial of the inheritance of acquired characters is based, partly, indeed, on the alleged insufficiency of the evidence for such inheritance; but partly also, and perhaps primarily, on the supposed necessity of finding a 'mechanical' explanation of the process. How this works out we shall see below.

The first condition of a 'modern theory of heredity, then —Weismann's included—is that the explanation is to be 'mechanical.' No talk of a living, organising principle in germ-cells, or in the structures that proceed from these, can be admitted. But here the curious fact emerges that, with all this desire to dispense with a vital principle, it yet seems impossible, when the actual construction of a theory is attempted, to get on without it. This will be seen by glancing at the relation of Weismann's theory to preceding theories. There is, *e.g.*, Mr. Darwin's theory, on which he set much

[1] This and the following Note consist of paragraphs from two lectures on 'Heredity and Sin,' delivered to the Summer School of Theology of Glasgow College, at its meeting in Edinburgh, 1904. They are here inserted as germane to the subjects under discussion.

store—the theory of 'Pangenesis.' The problem, it will be remembered, is, how parental traits can be transmitted to offspring? how a single reproductive cell can reproduce the whole body in all its parts? The essence of Darwin's theory is that every cell in the whole organism is continually, and at every stage in its development, throwing off minute portions of itself—granules, or 'gemmules,' as Darwin calls them—which, by a mysterious law, find their way to, and get stored up in, the *reproductive* cell, or in each such cell, whence, under suitable conditions, a new organism is produced, containing all the parts of the former. But, setting aside the thousand other difficulties which attend this theory, there is one which Darwin could not ignore, viz., how, even supposing the gemmules all safely stored up in the reproductive germ, they manage to arrange themselves in the precise positions and relations necessary to build up the new organism. The gemmules pour in, as it were, at random; the parts are infinitesimally small; they are numerous beyond computation: how is it that each gemmule is guided to the exact place it is meant to occupy in this mazy whirl, and manages afterwards to keep to it? Darwin's answer is in the phrase, 'elective affinities.' The gemmules have mutual 'affinities' which lead to their arranging themselves in precisely the proper order and relations. But this 'elective affinity'—what is it but our organising principle over again? As Weismann says: 'An unknown controlling force must be added to this mysterious arrangement, in order to marshal the molecules which enter the reproductive cell in such a manner that their arrangement corresponds with the order in which they must emerge as cells at a later period' (*Essays on Heredity*, i. p. 77).

Mr. Spencer also criticises Darwin, and has his own theory, but I cannot see that he is in much better case. He rejects 'elective affinity,' but only to substitute for it what he calls 'polarity.' There is, he tells us in his *Biology*, 'an innate tendency in living particles to arrange themselves into the shape of the organism to which they belong.' For this property there is no fit term; so he proposes this word 'polarity' (cf. his chapter on 'Waste and Repair'). Here also, it would seem, we might as well go back at once to our 'vital principle.'

Weismann, discarding these theories, takes another line, which opens the way into his peculiar doctrine. He falls back on what he calls the 'immortality' of the reproductive cell, or at least of the germ-plasm contained in it (*Essays*, i. p. 209). In contrast with the 'somatic' cells which compose the structure of the body (though these also originate in the reproductive cell), the reproductive cell, or germ-cell, or germ-plasm, is absolutely continuous. It divides and subdivides perpetually, but never dies. Each part, moreover, has in it all the properties and the peculiar molecular structure of the original cell; it therefore produces, when developed, precisely the same kind of body. Thus, he thinks, he solves the problem, 'How is it that a single cell of the body can contain within itself all the hereditary tendencies of the whole organism?' (p. 169). But it may be doubted whether, so far as the essential point, viz., *how* the germ-cell comes to possess this peculiar molecular structure, is concerned, we are not left as much in the dark as ever. To explain the rise and growing complexity of structure in the cell we are thrown back on the Darwinian hypothesis of unaided natural selection working on chance variations in forms of life originally unicellular, and therefore structureless. But even if it were granted, which it cannot be, that chance variations could ever produce the complex and finely adapted structures which we see, there remains the difficulty of how a single cell can give off its infinitely complex molecular constitution in its entirety to myriads of derivative cells, be it by fission or in any other way. It seems necessary that we supplement the process by a factor which Weismann refuses to recognise—an internal, directing, organising principle ; a principle which has in it the potency for building up a structure of a given type from the materials furnished to it. To what but this does Weismann himself come back in the admission that the unsolved mystery of cell-life is 'assimilation'—the power, as he explains it, which the organism possesses 'of taking up certain foreign substances, viz., food, and of converting them into the substance of its own body' (*Essays*, i. p. 73) ?

It can now, perhaps, easily be seen how, with logical stringency, Weismann arrives at his conclusion that acquired characters cannot be inherited. Given his theory that all changes that are inheritable take place in the reproductive germ, which, as 'immortal,' simply perpetuates itself, then the impossibility is seen of finding any 'mechanism' by which changes occurring in other parts of the organism—in the 'somatic' cells—can be transmitted to the reproductive cell, so as to become a permanent part of the structure of the latter. 'Use and disuse,' as he says in one place, 'cannot produce any effect in the transformation of species, simply because they can never reach the germ-cells from which the succeeding generation comes' (i. p. 400). The pillar of the theory, therefore, is that all changes that are reproducible are in the germ-cell, and in the germ-cell alone ; and that this is unreachable by influences from changes in other parts of the organism. The theory may be summed up, in closing, in one or two sentences of his own. 'The foundation of all the phenomena of heredity,' he says, 'can only be the substance of the germ-cells ; and the substance transfers its hereditary tendencies from generation to generation, at first unchanged, and always uninfluenced in any corresponding manner by that which happens during the life of the individual which bears it. . . . Heredity depends on the continuity of the molecular substance of the germ from generation to generation. . . . I believe that an explanation can in this case be reached by an appeal to known forces, if we suppose that characters acquired (in the true sense of the term) by the parent cannot appear in the course of the development of the offspring, but that all the characters of the latter are due to primary changes in the germ' (i. pp. 69, 70, 78).

It is, however, obvious that the problem is transformed if, discarding the attempt at a purely 'mechanical' explanation of vital phenomena, we fall back on the idea of the organism as animated by a single life pervading its multitudinous cells, in which, therefore, every part is in *rapport* with every other, so that no changes can take place in any part that are not attended by changes in other parts which defy all purely physical explanation.

NOTE XIV

HEREDITY AND RESPONSIBILITY (p. 243)

Heredity, in the naked, unqualified form in which it is often presented by science, would seem to destroy responsibility at its base. I do not quote Haeckel, but give one sentence from Maudsley, cited by Dr. Amory Bradford in his book on *Heredity* : 'There is a destiny made for man by his ancestors, and no one can elude, were he able to attempt it, the tyranny of his organisation' (pp. 81 ff.). At first sight it might seem as if the theory of Weismann, in denying the inheritance of contracted tendencies (as by vice), did something to relieve this pressure on posterity; and so Mr. Tennant, *e.g.*, is disposed to welcome its assistance. But it is a serious price we have to pay for any seeming help of this kind. It is not too much to say that no doctrine rivets fatality on man so completely as this doctrine of Weismann's. It does this by withdrawing the whole sphere of volitional life from the action of heredity, and, as a corollary of that, withdrawing heredity, which becomes a purely fatalistic process, completely from the control of will. The tendencies now hereditary were in their origin simply unfavourable variations; a rigid necessity has ruled the subsequent development; will has no influence at all in changing things from their preordained course. We have been accustomed to believe that a man's actions, good or evil, had some influence, not only on his own character, but on that of his offspring. This, if Weismann is to be credited, is a total mistake. So far, if the tendency was evil, this may seem a relief. But it is not a relief in reality, for evil tendencies are still inherited, only they are now withdrawn in their origin from the sphere of moral causation, and laid upon the nature as a blind result of accidental variation in the germ-cell. There is no gain there. Further, as human will had no share in inducing the deterioration which we see in so many broken specimens of our kind, so neither can will aid in remedying it. It can at least do nothing through the principle of heredity. That moves on its own splendidly isolated way, unaffected by accidents of external condition, by helping or hindering influences of environment, by good or evil volitions of progenitors. It is the deepest weakness of our so-called modern 'scientific' view that there is in it no room for personality, for will, for action outwards on the chain of 'mechanical' causation; therefore no room, properly, for responsibility or moral recovery. Even Spencer declares that our faith in the reality of freedom is 'an inveterate illusion'; that man is no more free than a leaf in a tornado, or a feather in Niagara (see the discussion in his *Psychology*, i. pp. 500 ff.). Happily for mankind, we are not shut up to these doleful theories, which would make work for the recovery of the lost a dismal mockery!

Taking heredity at its best, however, even freed from these exaggerations, we have to admit that the prospect for multitudes under its influence is sufficiently dark, and even, it might seem, hopeless. Heredity of nature is powerful enough for evil; but we have to add to it, in the case of myriads, 'social' heredity—that great complex of influences, education, example, custom, which we call 'environment,' which also in large measure is an outgrowth and product of heredity of nature. Leaving uncivilised races out of account, and looking only at our own doors—at the kind of surroundings into which multitudes of children are continually being born, at the foul and degrading influences which enswathe them from their infancy, at the sordidness and misery of their physical upbringing—what chance, we are compelled to ask, have they of ever becoming good and virtuous members of society, not to say heirs of the kingdom of heaven? Received, as Professor Seeley puts it in his *Ecce Homo*, from the first hour of their existence into the devil's church by a kind of infant baptism, have they a chance at all? Our hearts almost fail us in trying to answer that question. Yet they should not fail us; for there is no evil destiny binding human beings to ruin, and the success of our efforts in solving this dark problem will be in precise proportion to the loftiness of our motives, the wisdom of our methods, and the inflexibility of our determination to persevere until the work is done.

Certainly it is impossible to hope for large success with environment left precisely as it is. In these homes, amidst these surroundings, with these temptations, it is, humanly speaking, next to impossible to grow up good; though, through the marvellous grace of God, in seeming defiance of all laws of heredity, even this miracle does sometimes happen—

a wondrous encouragement and proof, if one were needed, that heredity is not the sole lord of human life!

Plainly, Christian duty, so far as this side of the matter is concerned, is to aim at breaking up this wrong environment, and securing, if need be compelling, decent conditions of existence for our fellow human beings—at giving them, especially the young, a *chance*. Still, this is only the beginning. To combat positively the influences of heredity and environment we must next call into play the latent forces of *personality*. Appeal must be made to every faculty that constitutes man a moral and responsible being—to reason, to conscience, to will, to affection, to the power which every soul in some degree has of appreciating what is praiseworthy and right when put before it. Above all, the individual we seek to save must be made to feel that he *has* personality—has a soul—is not the plaything of outside forces. For that in one sense is the supremely helping conviction!

I have to add that all this which has been said would fall short of the need of the situation if there were not yet diviner powers to be invoked. Deliverance from sin's power, in the last resort, can only come from God Himself, and it does come in the Christian Gospel. From the standpoint of heredity, Christ Himself is the supreme miracle in the history of our race. For here was One who was truly of ourselves, yet in Whom this power of heredity for evil—though He felt the pressure of temptation—was absolutely broken, over Whom it had no influence whatever, Who was pure in the midst of the world's defilement, in Whom the law of the Spirit of Life continually bore sway! Surely this, in any light in which we can regard it, is a proof that heredity is not everything: that One at least has walked our earth in absolute superiority to its influences; that He submitted, in mind and body, to the very worst the world could do to Him, yet proved Himself its Conqueror! But the kernel of the matter is only reached when we learn that His victory is intended to be ours also, and that through His life, and Cross, and Resurrection, there is opened to the world a divine deliverance from all its sin, peace with God, and the power of an endlessly holy and blessed life!

INDEX

ANIMAL and human intelligence, 9, 59 ff., 141, 144 ff. (See Man.)

Antiquity of man, 160; Ussher's chronology, 165; extreme claims for, 166, 168, 176, 180; revised views, 167; relation to glacial period, 169 ff., 173 ff.; physical science on, 176 ff.; ancient civilisations, 178-9, 203; bearings of evolution on, 180 ff.

Argyll, Duke of, on creation and evolution, 87; on sudden origins, 114; on man's mind, 141; on primitive man, 186, 203; on flood, 173; on high character of early types, 211; on unnaturalness of man's moral condition, 227, 234.

Atonement, modern repugnance to, 11, 275; a Scriptural doctrine, 258, 273, 275-6; coherence with Christian view, 274; meaning of death in, 277-8; M'Leod Campbell on, 277.

Augustine, on unfallen man, 224; on death, 259.

BABYLONIA, early civilisation in, 165, 178-9, 186.

Brain, in man and apes, 128 ff.; dependence of mind on, 69, 73, 75 ff. (See Mind.)

Budge, E. A. W., on 'New Race' in Egypt, 179, 306 ff.

CAIRNS, J., 28.

Calderwood, H., 141, 144, 145, 151.

Calvin, on image of God, 55.

Campbell, J. M'Leod, on atonement, 277.

Carpenter, W. B., 108; on heredity, 241.

Christ, Person of, 23; eternal Image of God, 269; realises image of God in humanity, 55, 57, 271; atoning work, 28, 273 ff.

Christianity, conflict with modern view, 4, 17 ff., 29; demand for re-interpretation of, 6; of Christ and Apostles, 25-6; Harnack on, 27, 261; positive essence of, 26-8; an organism of truth, 7, 260.

Creation narratives, 35 ff., 43 ff.; relation to Babylonia, 38; relation to science, 39, 288.

DANA, J. D., 111; on man and ape, 130, 133; on geological periods, 177.
Darwin, Charles, his theory of origin of species, 89 ff.; rejection of teleology, 90-1; inadequacy of theory, 95 ff.; scientific objections and difficulties, 99 ff.; concessions of, 104, 113; modern changes on theory, 104 ff., 293 ff.; on antiquity of man, 176; on descent of man, 121-2; on primitive man, 159; on evolution of intelligence, 141, 143-4; on inheritance of habits, 238.
Darwinian theory, not identical with evolution, 89 ff.; sketch of, 92 ff.; modern admissions of inadequacy, 99 ff.; more recent views, 104 ff., 293 ff. (See Darwin, above.)
Dawkins, W. B., on *Pithecanthropus*, 135; on early man, 141; on antiquity of man, 170-1; on Tertiary man, 172, 304 ff.
Dawson, J. W., on ice-age, 169, 173-4; on appearance of new species, 117; on flood, 173; on primitive man, 183-4, 256.
Death, in relation to man, 53, 249 ff., 280-1; Weismann on, 253 ff.; relation to hope of resurrection, 280-1; in Christ's work, 277.
Delitzsch, F., 37-8, 46.
De Vries, his production of new species, 114.
Driver, S. R., on man's creation, 36, 40; on image of God in man, 54, 56, 61; on reason in man, 62; on antiquity of man, 161, 166; on JE narrative, 199; on fall, 220, 298, 300.
Drummond, H., 163.
Dubois, E., his *Pithecanthropus Erectus*, 134-5.
Du Bois-Reymond, E., his seven riddles, 118, 124; Haeckel on, 291.

EGYPT, early civilisation in, 165, 178; the 'New Race' in, 179, 306 ff.
Ethics, philosophical and Christian, 213-4.
Evolution, ambiguity of term, 84 ff.; and creation, 87; not necessarily Darwinism, 89; distinction of *fact* and *how*, 97 ff.; naturalistic, 15, 82; idealistic, 20-2; bearings on religion, 87, 96; newer theories of, 110, 294-5; evolution of mind, 144 ff.; of moral ideas, 147 ff.; of body, 151 ff.; bearings on antiquity of man, 180 ff. (See Darwin, Darwinian theory, Otto, Man, Sin, etc.)

FACTORS in evolution, still under investigation, 97-8; Darwin's views on, 98; his later admissions, 104, 113; newer theories regarding, 110 ff., 293 ff.
Fall, of man, modern denials of, 14, 19, 21-2, 29, 204 ff., 208-9;

evolution and, 21, 157 ff., 219-20, 298 ff.; reality of, 29, 197 ff., 219 ff., 221. (See Man, Sin, etc.)
Fiske, J., on rational nature of man, 41, 60, 127, 154; on Darwinism, 89; on evolution of man, 15 ff., 141-3; on evolution of moral ideas, 148-50; on Sin, 204-5, 207, 233-4.

GEOLOGICAL time, 167, 175 ff.; periods, 177.
God, Biblical doctrine of, 7; importance of doctrine, 7 ff.; defective views of, 7, 8, 53.
Gray, Asa, 91, 108, 111.

HAECKEL, E., his monism, 5, 9, 20; his materialism, 69-70, 290; metaphysics of, 71 ff., 289 ff.; on evolution of man, 15, 16, 82 ff.; low view of man, 34; on reason in man, 62, 162; denial of free-will, 5, 9, 69, 147; of immortality, 6, 9; on antiquity of man, 176; on creation narrative, 288.
Harnack, A., 27, 261.
Henslow, G., on reason in man, 63; on life, 78; on Darwinism, 90, 100; on design (directivity), 90, 111; on factors in evolution, 97-8; on missing links, 135-6; on antiquity of man, 169; on death, 253; on fall, 299.
Huxley, T. H., on mind and brain, 67, 114; on evolution and creation, 87; on Darwinism, 89, 100, 120; on teleology, 90-1; on sterility of hybrids, 103; on transitional forms, 106-7, 131; on origin of life, 118; on persistence of types, 124; on 'jumps' in nature, 116, 126, 182; on man and ape, 127-8; on oldest skulls, 132, 183; on Lyell, 135; on ethical process, 148, 150; on antiquity of man, 168, 170.

IMAGE of God, in man, evolutionary denial of, 5, 17, 134, 204; in rational constitution, 53 ff.; in dominion, 57; in moral resemblance, 58, 156 ff., 187 ff., 197; grounded in Logos, 269; defaced by sin, 12, 58-9, 197, 222; realised in Christ, 271; restored in redemption, 261, 266 ff.
Immortality of man, 53; man's destiny, 257 ff.; Christian hope of, 279 ff.

KELVIN, LORD, on design, 112; on age of world, 176; on age of sun, 177.

LAIDLAW, J., on soul and spirit, 47-9, 52; on image of God, 54, 58-9; on superadded righteousness, 59, 244.
Laing, S., on antiquity of man, 172, 184.
Lansing Skeleton, 132, 171, 182, 184, 309 ff.

Lewes, G. H., 63 ; on new types, 117 ; on animal intelligence, 145.

Longevity, in animals and man, 255-6.

Lyell, Charles, on 'leaps' in nature, 115, 145 ; on origin of man, 134, 159-60 ; on antiquity of man, 166.

M'Cabe, J., 5, 145.

Mallock, W. H., concessions to Haeckel, 5, 66-7; on animal and human intelligence, 9, 162 ; on the 'hand,' 143.

Man, Biblical doctrine of, 9, 17, 34 ff. ; creation narratives regarding, 36 ff., 43 ff. ; head of creation, 40-1 ; link between two worlds, 41 ff. ; compound being, 46 ; soul and spirit in, 47 ff. ; image of God in, 54 ff. ; distinct in nature from animals, 60 ff., 139 ff. ; reason in man, 62 ff., 145-6 ; unity of man, 41, 154 ; theories of descent of man, 10, 15 ff., 18, 82 ff., 129, 136, 296 ff.; special origin of, 125, 133, 141 ff., 151 ff., 182, 308 ; primitive condition of man, 159 ff., 181 ff.; results of evolutionary view of, 17 ff., 208-9 ; skulls of early man, 132, 183 ff., 309 ff.; divine sonship of, 190 ff. ; immortality of, 190, 249 ff., 279 ff. ; redemption of, 266 ff. (See Image of God, Fall, Sin, etc.)

Martensen, M., on sin, 216, 232.

Materialism, in modern monism, 67, 70, 290.

Max Müller, on reason in man, 64 ; on savages, 161.

Mind and Brain, their relations, 73 ff., 125, 144, 152.

Mivart, St. George, on natural selection, 94 ; on Darwinism, 98, 100, 102, 108, 143 ; on reason in man, 63, 146 ; on special origin of man, 141 ; on rapid changes, 164 ; on man's descent, 296.

Monism, 5, 20 ; naturalistic, 67 ff.; metaphysics of, 7 ff., 289 ff.

Oehler, G. F., on man's nature, 45, 51 ; on image of God, 54 ; on fall, 220.

Organism of truth, in Christianity, 7, 260.

Otto, R., on Darwinism, 85, 89, 91-2, 101, 106, 110, 124, 131, 293 ff. ; on *Pithecanthropus*, 135 ; on sudden origins, 117, 182, 308-9.

Parallelism, psycho-physical, 69, 74 ff.

Pengelly, W., on Kent's Cavern, 168.

Petrie, W. M. Flinders, on 'New Race' in Egypt, 178, 307.

Prestwich, Jos., on glacial age, 169, 170, 172-3 ; on early man, 305.

Reason in man, 62 ff., 146. (See Man.)

INDEX

Regeneration, 267, 278-9.

Resurrection, 53, 280, 281-2.

Romanes, Geo. J., on Darwinism, 91, 94, 99, 101, 105, 111; on design, 91, 111-12; on animal intelligence, 141, 145; on evolution and fall, 157; on heredity, 237, 239; return to Christian belief, 287, 292.

SALMOND, S. D. F., on immortality, 280.

Sin, 8 ff., 197 ff.; subversion in modern view, 19 ff., 22, 158, 188, 202 ff., 204, 208-9, 265; Biblical doctrine of, 19, 198 ff., 212; Mr. Fiske on, 204 ff.; nature of, 212; principle of, 215 ff.; grades of, 217 ff.; result of temptation, 219-21; effect in depravation, 222 ff.; racial effects—original sin, 228 ff.; theory of brute inheritance, 233-4; sin and heredity, 235 ff., 315 ff.; meaning of total depravity, 245; physical consequences—death, 249 ff.

Skulls, oldest, 132, 183 ff., 309 ff.

Soul and Spirit, their relations, 47 ff.

Spencer, H., 120; on savages, 161; on Darwin, 101-2, 312; on mind and brain, 125; on heredity, 238.

Strong, C. A., on mind and body, 74.

TAIT, P. G., on age of world, 176-7.

Teleology and evolution, 90-92, 94 ff., 108-9, 110 ff., 295. (See Darwin, Huxley, Romanes, Otto, etc.)

Tennant, F. R., on primitive condition of man, 19, 157; on image of God, 57-8; on fall, 198, 200, 219-21; on original sin, 229, 236.

VARIATION, law of, 92 ff.; not indefinite, 120; not always slight, 100-1, 104; due to inner causes, 105, 111, 113; often sudden, 114 ff., 308. (See Darwin, Huxley, Otto, etc.)

Virchow, R., on man and ape, 133-4; Haeckel on, 70, 291.

WARD, J., on psycho-physical parallelism, 74; on origin of life, 119; on naturalism, 287.

Weismann, A., on evolution of man, 83, 297; on natural selection, 90-1-2-4; on factors in evolution, 97, 105; on correlated changes, 117; on spontaneous generation, 118; on mind and brain, 125; theory of heredity, 232, 335-6-7-9, 311 ff., 315-16; on death, 253 ff.

Wendt, H. H., on soul and spirit, 48-9.

Wright, G. F., on geological time, 167, 306; on glacial age, 169, 173-4; on flood, 173-4; on antiquity of man, 171, 173, 183, 185, 305-6; on Lansing Skeleton, 132, 167, 171, 182, 184, 310.

Zittel, Karl von, 97, 106, 131.

www.ingramcontent.com/pod-product-compliance
Lightning Source LLC
Chambersburg PA
CBHW051627230426
43669CB00013B/2212